The Fifth Corner of Four

The Fifth Corner of Four

An Essay on Buddhist Metaphysics and the Catuṣkoṭi

Graham Priest

OXFORD
UNIVERSITY PRESS

OXFORD
UNIVERSITY PRESS

Great Clarendon Street, Oxford, OX2 6DP,
United Kingdom

Oxford University Press is a department of the University of Oxford.
It furthers the University's objective of excellence in research, scholarship,
and education by publishing worldwide. Oxford is a registered trade mark of
Oxford University Press in the UK and in certain other countries

First Edition published in 2018
Impression: 1

Published in the United States of America by Oxford University Press
198 Madison Avenue, New York, NY 10016, United States of America

British Library Cataloguing in Publication Data
Data available

Library of Congress Control Number: 2018950876

ISBN 978–0–19–875871–6

Printed and bound by
CPI Group (UK) Ltd, Croydon, CR0 4YY

Contents

List of figures ix

Before the Beginning

Preface xv
- 0.1 Background xv
- 0.2 Overview xvi
- 0.3 Clarificatory Comments xvii
- 0.4 Thanks xix

Part I. Early India

1. General Background 3
   - 1.1 Introduction 3
   - 1.2 The History and Geography of Buddhism 3
     - 1.2.1 Buddhist philosophy I: India 4
     - 1.2.2 Buddhist philosophy II: China 6
   - 1.3 The Four Noble Truths 8
   - 1.4 The Metaphysics of Ignorance 9
     - 1.4.1 Impermanence 10
     - 1.4.2 The self 10
     - 1.4.3 Look for yourself 12
     - 1.4.4 Causation and unity 13
     - 1.4.5 The illusion of self 15
   - 1.5 Conclusion 15
2. *Quintum Non-Datur* 16
   - 2.1 Introduction 16
   - 2.2 The Catuṣkoṭi: The Early Sūtras 16
   - 2.3 The Origins of the Principle 17
   - 2.4 The Catuṣkoṭi: Some Dead Ends 18
   - 2.5 Interlude on Classical Propositional Logic 22
   - 2.6 First Degree Entailment 25
   - 2.7 The Buddha's Silence 26
   - 2.8 Presupposition Failure? 28
   - 2.9 Conclusion 29
   - 2.10 Technical Appendix 29
     - 2.10.1 Many-valued logics 30
     - 2.10.2 FDE 30
     - 2.10.3 Natural deduction 31

3. Well-Founded Metaphysics 32
3.1 Introduction 32
3.2 Abhidharma Mereology and the Dharmas 32
3.3 The Two Realities 33
3.4 Are There Dharmas? 35
3.5 The Reality of Partite Objects 39
3.6 The Dharmas: Conceptual Dependence 41
3.7 The Dharmas: Causation 43
3.8 Conclusion 44

Part II. Later India

4. Emptiness 49
4.1 Introduction 49
4.2 The *Heart Sūtra* 49
4.3 Emptiness 51
4.4 The Attack on Svabhāva 53
4.5 To be Empty 56
4.6 The Two Realities 57
4.7 Ultimate Reality and Ineffability 60
4.8 Enlightenment 62
4.9 Conclusion 62

5. The Fifth Corner 64
5.1 Introduction 64
5.2 Ineffability 64
5.3 The Fifth Koṭi 65
5.4 States of Affairs 67
5.5 Truth 68
5.6 Correspondence 70
5.7 Empty States of Affairs 71
5.8 Conclusion 73
5.9 Technical Appendix 73

6. Paradox and Ineffability 75
6.1 Introduction 75
6.2 The Paradox of Ineffability 75
6.3 Interlude: Western Connections 76
6.4 Having More than One Value 79
6.5 The *Vimalakīrti Nirdeśa Sūtra* 80
6.6 A Farewell to India 83
6.7 Conclusion 85
6.8 Coda: Jaina Logic 85
6.8.1 *Anekānta-Vāda* 86
6.8.2 The theory of sevenfold predication 87
6.8.3 The meaning of *i* 88

6.9 Technical Appendix 89
6.9.1 Plurivalent logic 89
6.9.2 Plurivalent FDEe 90
6.9.3 The Jaina version 90

Part III. East Asia

7. And So On 95
7.1 Introduction 95
7.2 From Daoism to Buddhism 95
7.3 The Two Truths: Stage 1 97
7.4 The Two Truths: Stages 2 and 3 98
7.5 The Problem 99
7.6 Pseudo Jizang 101
7.7 The Jizang Hierarchy 104
7.8 Conclusion 105
7.9 Technical Appendix 105

8. The Golden Lion 108
8.1 Introduction 108
8.2 *Ālaya-Vijñāna* 108
8.3 *Tathāgata-Garbha* 110
8.4 China and the Two Realities 111
8.5 *Li, Shi, Ji* 113
8.6 The Net of Indra 114
8.7 Identity 115
8.8 Emptiness 116
8.9 . . . and its Structure 117
8.10 Tying Everything Together 120
8.11 The Net Emerges 123
8.12 Interpenetration and Duality 124
8.13 Conclusion 124

9. Enlightenment 125
9.1 Introduction 125
9.2 Enlightenment 125
9.3 Chan 126
9.4 The Ox-Herding Pictures 128
9.5 Mountains Are Not Mountains 130
9.6 Dōgen and the *Shōbōgenzō* 133
9.7 Dōgen and Huayan 133
9.8 Dōgen on Saṃsāra and Nirvāṇa 134
9.9 Dōgen and Zazen 135
9.10 Dōgen and the Return to the Ordinary 136
9.11 Dōgen on Language 139

9.12 On Transcending Dualities 141
9.13 Conclusion 142

After the End

10. A Methodological Coda 147

Sino-Japanese Glossary 151
Bibliography 155
Index of names 163
General Index 166

List of figures

1. An image of the Buddha
   Anna Jurkovska/Shutterstock.com xxii
2. A representation of Nāgārjuna (fl. 2C CE)
   waikeat/© 123RF.com 46
3. A representation of Dōgen Kigen (fl. 13C CE)
   Scroll painted by Shamon Tekion Kinga and presented to Nishijima Roshi of Dōgen Sangha © Dōgen Sangha Buddhist Group 92
4. The ten Ox-Herding Pictures, by Gyokusei Jikihara
   Zen Mountain Monastery, zmm.mro.org 129
5. The Chinese symbol 'ensō'. This is not a Chinese character but a simple circle that represents enlightenment
   Elina Li/Shutterstock.com 144

It was the best of times, it was the worst of times, it was the age of wisdom, it was the age of foolishness, it was the epoch of belief, it was the epoch of incredulity, it was the season of Light, it was the season of Darkness, it was the spring of hope, it was the winter of despair, we had everything before us, we had nothing before us, we were all going direct to Heaven, we were all going direct the other way.

Charles Dickens, A Tale of Two Cities, opening lines

There is not the slightest difference
Between cyclical existence and nirvāṇa.
There is not the slightest difference
Between nirvāṇa and cyclical existence.

Nāgārjuna, *Mūlamadhyamakakārikā*, XXV: 19

Before the Beginning

Preface

0.1 Background

This is a book about certain aspects of Buddhist philosophy, notably its metaphysics and related matters. Buddhism, however, is no more one thing than is Christianity. Its thinking evolves over some two and a half thousand years in India, China, and other countries. In the process, several quite different metaphysical pictures emerge. This book tells a story of this evolution.

The evolution is seen through a certain lens, however: that of the *catuṣkoṭi*. At its simplest, this is a view to the effect that claims can be true, false, both, or neither. Of course, this makes little sense in logics which endorse the principle of non-contradiction or the principle of excluded middle—logics of the kind that the West (and some in the East) have tended to endorse.[1] It makes perfectly good sense, however, from the perspective of some kinds of contemporary non-classical logic, as the book shows.

The catuṣkoṭi itself evolves, however, much of this in tandem with the evolution of the metaphysical views with which it is intertwined. So the book tells the story of this evolution too. We will see how contemporary non-classical logic can make sense of these developments as well.

The book proceeds, then, by charting the evolution of Buddhist metaphysics through appropriate texts, and analysing the role of the catuṣkoṭi in the process, explaining and developing the appropriate techniques of formal logic along the way. The interaction is to the benefit of both the metaphysics and the logic. The Buddhist metaphysical ideas show how the logical ideas are no mere formalism. Perhaps more importantly: on the other side, the logic shows how the metaphysical ideas can be made precise and so shown to be coherent.[2]

Truth is, of course, another matter. The point of this book is not to argue for a particular view, but to tell a story of the engagement of certain views in metaphysics and logic. However, this does not imply that I will adopt a neutral attitude towards these views. I will often comment on how plausible they are, to

[1] As Tillemans (1999), p. 189, puts it: 'Within Buddhist thought, the structure of argumentation that seems most resistant to our attempts at a formalization is undoubtedly the catuṣkoṭi.'

[2] I might add that Western formal logic is also in a process of continuing evolution. The techniques of 'non-classical' logic deployed in the book are the product of the last fifty or so years, and their philosophical presuppositions are still rejected by many Western logicians.

what extent arguments used are sound, and so on. And as will be clear, I have more sympathy with some views than others.

0.2 Overview

I have divided the story up into three parts. The first part deals with matters as they pertain to the older form of Buddhism, which developed after the teachings of the historical Buddha until about the turn of the Common Era. After a general background to Buddhist philosophy and its historical and geographical development in Chapter 1, Chapter 2 presents the catuṣkoṭi in its earliest form. Chapter 3 then describes the metaphysical picture that developed in that period. Later Buddhist thought was a reaction against this, and cannot be understood without it.

The second part of the book concerns these later developments in Indian Buddhism; in particular, aspects of Mahāyāna Buddhism. Chapter 4 starts with the rise of this newer form of Buddhism in the *Prajñāpāramitā Sūtras*, a new class of sūtras that arose around the turn of the Common Era. It then shows how these ideas are developed in the metaphysical thought of Nāgārjuna—arguably the most important and influential Buddhist philosopher after the Buddha himself. The catuṣkoṭi is central to his thought; and in the process it evolves to take on a new form, as this chapter shows. By this time in the historical development, the notion of ineffability has become of central importance to Buddhist thought. This can be handed by a further development of the catuṣkoṭi. Chapter 5 shows how. But texts that talk of the ineffable obviously court paradox. Chapter 6 shows how this can be handled by yet another development of the catuṣkoṭi.

For the third part of the book, to witness further developments, we move to East Asia, and some of the Sino-Japanese forms of Buddhism. In Chapter 7, we see how, at the hands of Jizang and the Sanlun School, the catuṣkoṭi morphs into a dialectical progress of Hegelian proportion. Chapter 8 takes us into the metaphysics of the Huayan School, and further into the relationship between the conventional and the ultimate aspects of reality, a sticky talking-point of Buddhist philosophy ever since Nāgārjuna. Finally, Chapter 9 looks at the relation of all this to the Buddhist notion of enlightenment. We look, in particular, at the very distinctive form this takes in a third school of Chinese Buddhism, Chan (Zen). Much of this chapter deals with aspects of the thought of one of the most notable Zen philosophers, Dōgen.

In Chapter 4, we will meet the central philosophical notion of transcending duality. It will come fully into focus in Chapter 6. Much of the third part of the book deals with the notion in one way or another. The topic will allow many of the threads of the book to be tied together at its end.

A brief coda to the book takes the opportunity to reflect on the methodology employed in it, and some doubts one might have about this.

0.3 Clarificatory Comments

Let me now make some clarificatory comments on a few matters.

First, what the book is not. It is not a comprehensive history of the development of Buddhist metaphysics. There is much on that matter that does not feature significantly in the book, perhaps, most notably, the ideas of Indian Yogācāra Buddhism and Chinese Tiantai Buddhism.

More importantly, the book is not a scholarly work. I have neither the languages nor the patience to be a scholar. I am not trying to give an authoritative textual and historical interpretation of the texts we shall meet. The main aim of the book is to show how some ideas drawn from Buddhist texts and some ideas in contemporary non-classical logic can profitably inform each other. In the process, it is true, I do give interpretations of texts. (One cannot discuss texts without interpreting them; this is just Hermeneutics 100.) Many of the interpretations are not particularly contentious. Where this is not the case, I claim no more than that they hang together and make sense to me; and of course I hope that these are plausible—or at least interesting![3] And perhaps, where the interpretations are not standard, they may assume more plausibility when set within the framework I provide. I note that we are dealing with difficult historical texts, and there is much disagreement about how to interpret them, both in the Asian commentarial traditions themselves, and in the hands of Western scholars. So, let me emphasize again: I am happy to leave discussions of the correct interpretations of these texts (assuming such a notion to make sense) to those with the scholarly credentials to do so. That is *not* what I am engaged in here.[4]

Further on texts: the classical Indian texts are written in two languages, the vernacular Pāli and the more scholarly Sanskrit. Rather than mix these up, I have opted to use the Sanskrit version of the Indian words we will meet. All the classical Chinese texts are written in the same language, but there are two conventions

[3] I also note that my interpretations are not capricious. Every textual interpretation I give is, I believe, endorsed by some scholar; though maybe there is no one scholar who would endorse every textual interpretation.

[4] A reader from Oxford University Press advised me to reiterate this warning throughout the book, lest scholarly readers forget it, and take me to be doing what they would be doing if they were writing on the topic. Whilst I would hope that this is unnecessary, I will follow the advice.

about how to transliterate the characters: the older Wade-Giles convention, and the newer Pin Yin convention. Again, rather than mix these up, I have decided to use Pin Yin.[5] I have italicized the first occurrence of Sanskrit and Chinese words in the text, but not, generally, thereafter; and words that have become familiar English, like 'Mahāyāna', I have not italicized at all. A glossary of Chinese and Japanese characters is given before the Bibliography.

Which brings us to the texts themselves. Since I am in no position to translate them myself, I have used the translations of others. These texts are not at all easy to translate into English, and there can be significant differences between different translations. I hope that I have chosen ones that are reasonably authoritative. Translators' interpolations into the texts are marked by square brackets. On the rare occasions that I make an interpolation myself, I indicate that with my initials [GP: thus]. Italics, note, are always in the original quotations, unless I say otherwise.

Next, a word on dialetheism. A dialetheia is a true contradiction—that is, something of the form $A \wedge \neg A$ which is true; and dialetheism is the view that there are such things. This is a strongly unorthodox view in Western philosophy, though at least the coherence of the view is now coming to be accepted.[6] The truth of dialetheism is not at issue in this book. However, as will be clear, I will be interpreting many thinkers and texts as dialetheic. This, it seems to me, is the natural way to read them.[7] One of the virtues of the coherence of dialetheism is that when texts such as those we will be dealing with appear to endorse contradictions, we can, under appropriate conditions, take what is before our eyes literally, and so respect the integrity of the texts. We are not forced to misapply the principle of charity, and suppose their authors did not mean what they say.

In this context, it is worth quoting Tom Tillemans:[8]

> ...it's fair to say that, in Buddhist studies at least, attributing contradictions to Nāgārjuna has increasing fallen out of vogue, such an attribution being considered, by those of a philosophical bent, as tantamount to trivialisation of Madhyamaka's approach as exclusively mystical or even irrational. Some argue, more or less intuitively, that contradictions are rationally unthinkable. Others invoke a more sophisticated formal problem that anything and everything would follow from a contradiction, so that all reasoning

[5] I have adopted the policy of reproducing quotes as they appeared, however, preserving features such as capitalization, omission of diacritical marks, and the use of Pāli and Wade-Giles transliterations.

[6] For a general discussion of dialetheism, see Priest and Berto (2013).

[7] A defence of the matter can be found in Deguchi, Garfield, and Priest (2008), and the essays by Deguchi, Garfield, and Priest in *Philosophy East & West* 63 (2013), Issue 3. On Nāgārjuna, specifically, see Garfield and Priest (2003).

[8] Tillemans (2009), p. 67 of reprint.

would become indiscriminate; contradictions thus could supposedly never be tolerated by rational individuals on pain of "logical anarchy". In any case, the underlying idea is that, if the Madhyamaka in not to be trivialised—and I agree that it should not be so trivialised—it would have to rigorously respect the law of non-contradiction.

It should be noted that Tillemans himself is not against a dialetheic interpretation of early Mahāyāna texts, as his essay goes on to explain.[9] And it must be said that many of 'those of a philosophical bent' as Tillemans puts it—unlike Tillemans himself—knew nothing of developments in contemporary philosophical and formal logic (especially those concerning paraconsistency).[10]

Finally, logic. Given what I am engaged in here, I cannot but use the techniques and symbolism of modern logic at many places in the book. In the chapters of the book, I have explained the logical matters in as informal a way as possible. The exposition does presuppose a very basic knowledge of contemporary logic, though not much. A familiarity with truth tables will suffice. I am aware, however, that some readers of the book may not have the requisite background (particularly those coming from a background in Asian philosophy), so I have inserted an interlude in Chapter 2 (2.5) which briefly presents 'classical' propositional logic. For those who wish to see how the technical details developed in the book can be spelled out with rigour, I have put these into technical appendices and the occasional footnote, which can be omitted without loss by those with no taste for such matters.

0.4 Thanks

And finally, finally. It is always a pleasure to say thank you. First of all, to those philosophers who know the texts much better than I do, and from whom I have learned so much over recent years. Perhaps the most significant in this process have been (in alphabetical order!): Amber Carpenter, Yasuo Deguchi, Jay Garfield, Bob Sharf, Mark Siderits, and Tom Tillemans.

Next, thanks go to those who have heard me talk about the ideas in the book and provided helpful feedback. This includes those who attended the lectures I gave on these matters in Budapest and Kyoto in 2013. These are where the book started its life.

[9] For a discussion of Tillemans on this matter, see Deguchi, Garfield, and Priest (2013c).

[10] The relevant formal developments are explained in this book. The notion of rationality, which Tillemans raises, is not on the agenda here; but, contrary to superficial assumptions, it does not presuppose the Principle of Non-Contradiction. See Priest (2006), Part 3.

Drafts of the book have been presented in seminars at Lehigh University in April 2016, an honours course at the University of Melbourne in July 2016, and a graduate course at the CUNY Graduate Center in the Northern fall of 2016. Many thanks to all those present who made helpful comments and suggestions. There are too many people to thank individually, and I feel that it would be invidious to single out a few. However, a special thanks goes to Jong Jim Kim and Benjamin Weinberg for their pages of written comments.

Particular thanks go to Yasuo Deguchi and his students at Kyoto University, Jay Garfield, Bob Sharf, and Wang Wenfang for comments on drafts of the book. A special thanks goes to Bob Sharf for his help on matters to do with the Chinese and Japanese languages. Thanks for helpful comments are also due to two anonymous referees for Oxford University Press.

Last, but by no means least, thanks go to the always helpful and professional staff of Oxford University Press; and especially to Peter Momtchiloff, on whose thoughtful advice I knew that I could always rely.

Fig. 1. The Buddha

PART I

Early India

1

General Background

1.1 Introduction

In this book, we will be concerned with certain aspects of Buddhist philosophy. They are certainly central aspects, though there is much more to Buddhist philosophy than the topic of the book. The point of this chapter is to give enough detail of Buddhist philosophy in general to provide the context for what is to come (though I shall remind readers of some of it in subsequent chapters).[1] We will look at the history and geography of Buddhism and its development, the philosophical ideas encapsulated in the Four Noble Truths, and some of Buddhism's core metaphysical views.[2]

1.2 The History and Geography of Buddhism

Buddhism is no more a single view than is Christianity or Islam. In its two and a half thousand year history it has changed and developed considerably. Some things, for sure, have remained constant, but many other things, many other important things, have changed—both within India and as Buddhism spread through the whole of East and South East Asia. For what it is worth, it will morph yet again as it moves into 'Western' countries. It is already doing so. Future developments are, of course, unpredictable; but likely casualties are the doctrines of rebirth, and the patriarchal structure of the traditional Buddhist institutions. However, this is not the place to go into these matters. The major developments to date have been in India/Tibet, and China/Japan. Let us look at these in turn.[3]

[1] In this context, an attempt to be comprehensive would be forlorn. There are many books which can be consulted for a somewhat more general picture, such as Mitchell (2002).

[2] Of course, there is much more to Buddhism than philosophy; for example, matters concerning its sociology, art, religious practices, institutions, etc. These are not my concern in this book.

[3] Much of what follows in this section is from Priest (2014a), pp. xxiii to xxviii. I figured that I couldn't improve much on that.

1.2.1 Buddhist philosophy I: India

The earliest Indian texts of literature and religion are the *Vedas*. The earliest of these is probably the *Ṛg Veda* (pronounced *Rig Veyda*), which appears to have been in place by about 1200 BCE. The last installment of the *Vedas* are called the *Upaniṣads*, and are written between the eighth and sixth century BCE. The acceptance of these texts[4] defines orthodox Hindu philosophy and religion, central to which are the existence of a godhead, *Brahman*, and individual selves, *ātman*. Buddhism arose as a reaction against this (as did Jainism, about the same time). In particular, it rejected the existence of both Brahman and ātman. Of course, it retained a number of orthodox views (though these were reconceptualized). It retained the view of rebirth: people will repeatedly cycle through the realm of life and death (*saṃsāra*). It also retained the view that there is a way out of this: *nirvāṇa*.[5]

The foundations of Buddhist philosophy were laid by the historical Buddha, the Indian thinker Siddhārtha Gautama (Pali: Gotama).[6] (The word 'Buddha' itself is an honorific, like 'Christ', and simply means 'the enlightened (awakened) one'.) His exact dates are uncertain, but a traditional chronology gives them as 563 to 483 BCE. He enunciated principles often called the *Four Noble Truths*. These diagnose what one might call the human condition: an unhappiness-causing attachment to things in a world of impermanence (*anitya*) and interdependence (*pratītyasamutpāda*); they then give a recipe for what to do about it.

Buddhist thought developed for the next several hundred years, until a canon of writings emerged, the *Tripiṭaka* (Three Baskets).[7] One of these comprised the *sūtras* (Pāli: *suttas*), discourses featuring the historical Buddha and his teachings. Another was the *vinaya*, the rules for monastic living. The third was the *abhidharma* (higher teachings). A principal concern of this was to provide a taxonomy of things in the world and their parts. Thus, a person is just a collection of changing and interacting, mental and physical, parts (*skandhas*). Most objects of experience are of a similar kind, though this is not the way in which things appear. That is conventional reality (*saṃvṛti satya*), as opposed to the ultimate reality (*paramārtha satya*) of the way that things actually are. Naturally, a number of different schools of Buddhist thought developed in this period. Only one of these now survives, *Theravāda* (Doctrine of the Elders).

[4] Together with the somewhat later epic poems, such as the *Mahābhārata*.

[5] The term *mokṣa* (liberation) is also used for the enlightened state by Buddhists, Hindus, and Jains.

[6] He is also sometimes referred to as Śākyamuni—the sage of the Śākya (Siddhārtha's clan).

[7] The Pāli version of this is often called the *Pāli Canon*.

Around the turn of the common era, a new class of sūtras started to appear, the *Prajñāpāramitā* (Perfection of Wisdom) *Sūtras*. (These include the most famous, short and cryptic, *Heart Sūtra*.) They initiated a new kind of Buddhism, *Mahāyāna* (the Greater Vehicle). The new Buddhism differed from the old in ways both ethical and metaphysical. The older Buddhism was concerned with individuals liberating themselves from the human condition. Someone on this path was an *arhat* (worthy one). By contrast, according to Mahāyāna, the ethical path was to help *all* sentient creatures liberate themselves. People who had dedicated themselves to do this were said to be on the *Bodhisattva Path*.[8] In Mahāyāna, compassion (*karuṇā*)[9] therefore became the central virtue.

On the metaphysical front, the central concept became that of emptiness (*śūnyatā*). Not just the ordinary objects of our experience, but all things, are less substantial than they appear to be in conventional reality. Two different schools of Mahāyāna thought developed, which articulated this view in different ways. Historically the earlier was *Madhyamaka* (Middle Way). This was founded by Nāgārjuna. His dates are uncertain, but he flourished some time around 150–200 CE. His *Mūlamadhyamakakārikā* (Fundamental Verses on the Middle Way) was to exert a profound influence on all subsequent Buddhist thought. According to Madhyamaka, to be empty is to be empty of self-nature (*svabhāva*). All things lack this.

The historically later school was *Yogācāra* (Practice of Yoga), sometimes called by the more apt name *Cittamātra* (Consciousness-only). Traditionally, this is taken to have been founded by the half-brothers Vasubandhu and Asaṅga, the latter converting the former from the Abhidharma tradition. Again, the dates are uncertain, but their period was around the fourth century CE. According to Yogācāra, to be empty is not so much to be empty of svabhāva, but to be empty of subject/object duality; that is, to be free from the distinction between the object cognized and the consciousness cognizing.

Buddhist philosophy continued to develop in India until about the end of the millennium. Much of the development occurred in the great Buddhist university of Nālandā in northern India (427–1197 CE). The university produced some thinkers, such as Śāntarakṣita, who tried to fuse the two Mahāyāna schools, as well

[8] A *sattva* is a being. The traditional translation of *bodhi* is *enlightenment*—which of course has unfortunate overtones in the West. Slightly closer etymologically is *awakened*—not without its own share of overtones. A standard translation into Chinese is *wu* (Jap: *satōri*). In the texts we will be dealing with in the book, when applied to a person, the character means someone who has *apprehended* or *understood* (something)—'got it'. I decided, all things considered, to stick with the traditional translation.

[9] Again, *compassion* is the traditional translation, but *care* might be a better one.

as perhaps the greatest Mahāyāna ethicist, Śāntideva, who wrote the influential *Bodhicāryāvatāra* (Guide to the Bodhisattva's Way of Life). Both of these thinkers flourished in the eighth century CE. In this later period of Indian Buddhism, techniques of meditation were augmented with tantric practices.

Buddhism also spread outside the Indian subcontinent. Theravada Buddhism went south-east, into countries such as Sri Lanka, Myanmar, and Thailand. Mahāyāna went north into modern-day Afghanistan, China, and, relatively late in the piece, Tibet (Śāntarakṣita playing an important role in the Tibetan transmission). It was virtually wiped out in Central Asia and India by the waves of Moslem invasion late in the first millennium, Nālandā itself being sacked, and its library being burned, in 1197. A consequence of this is the fact that many Indian Buddhist texts are now lost, and exist only in back-translations from Tibetan or Chinese.

1.2.2 Buddhist philosophy II: China

Though the native Tibetan religion, Bön, did have some effect on Buddhism in Tibet, this was not enough for Buddhism to change its Indian heritage profoundly. Chinese Buddhism is a different matter.

Buddhist ideas began to enter China from Central Asia, across the Silk Route, around the turn of the common era. There they encountered the two indigenous Chinese philosophies: Confucianism and Daoism. Both of these originated at about the same time as Buddhism in India (and, for that matter, at about the same time that Greek philosophy was hitting its straps). The former derived from the thought of Confucius—Kongfuzi—(551–479 BCE), and his intellectual descendants.[10] His sayings are recorded in the *Lunyu* (Analects). The latter is derived principally from two texts, the *Daode jing* and the *Zhuangzi*. The former is traditionally attributed to Laozi, who is supposed to have flourished in the sixth century BCE; but it is almost certainly a compilation of sayings from different people, of a much later date. ('Laozi' can mean 'old masters'.) The second is an eponymously named text, Zhuangzi himself being dated at around 350–300 BCE (though much of this is a compilation of various writers as well). Of Confucianism and Daoism, it was the latter that was to be the more important for Buddhism. According to Daoism, there is a principle behind the flow of events, the Dao; and the Daoist sage is someone who does not cling, but 'goes with the flow' of the Dao.

Buddhism was not well understood when it entered China, and was taken to be an exotic form of Daoism. The Buddhist ultimate reality was (all too)

[10] 'Confucius' is, of course, a Latinization; 'zi', incidentally, is an honorific: a classy form of 'Mr'.

easily identified with the Dao, and the enlightened Buddhist person was, again, easily identified with the Daoist sage. A significant episode in Chinese Buddhism occurred with the translations of many Indian texts made by the Kuchean missionary Kumārajīva (344–413 CE) and his students. After this, Chinese versions of the two major Indian Mahāyāna schools developed, *Sanlun* (Madhyamaka) and *Weixin* (Yogācāra); but though they were influential, they soon disappeared in favour of the particularly distinctive Chinese forms of (Mahāyāna) Buddhism.

Four of the most important of these were: *Jingtu* (Jap: *Jōdo*), *Tientai* (Jap: *Tendai*), *Huayan* (Jap: *Kegon*), and *Chan* (Jap: *Zen*). The first of these is more notable for its devotionalism than for its philosophical developments.[11] The other three developed distinctive notions of ultimate reality (Buddha nature) and enlightenment, which bespeak not only Madhyamaka and Yogācāra influences, but also a Doaist influence. Perhaps the most sophisticated philosophically was Huayan (Skt: *Avataṃsaka*; Eng: Flower Garland), named after the sūtra which it took to be most important. The founder of the school is traditionally taken to be Dushun (557–640 CE), but philosophically more important is Fazang (643–712 CE), who parlayed the Indian notion of emptiness into a picture of the world in which all phenomenal objects interpenetrate and mutually encode each other.

The Huayan school gradually faded out, and had all but disappeared by the ninth century CE—though it still has a presence in Japan (*Kegon*) and Korea (*Hwaom*). But many of its ideas were incorporated into the Chan school. Legend has it that this school was founded by another missionary, Bodhidharma (Chin: Damo), who arrived in China some time in the fifth or sixth centuries CE. However, arguably the most important early document in the school's establishment was the later *Liuzu Tanjing* (Platform Sūtra), traditionally attributed to Huineng (638–713 CE). The emphasis of the Chan school was practical, rather than theoretical (as may be surmised from its name, a Sinification of the Sanskrit *dhyāna*, meaning meditation). A distinctive feature of the school—at least, the branch following Huineng—is that enlightenment can be sudden, and occurs with a conceptually unmediated, and therefore indescribable, encounter with ultimate reality (Buddha nature).

Buddhist ideas entered and took root in Japan around the sixth century CE, via the Korean peninsula. During the next centuries, nearly all the major Chinese Buddhisms were brought to Japan. Perhaps the most important period in Japanese Buddhism was the thirteenth century CE, when notable thinkers such as Dōgen

[11] In English this is called 'Pure Land Buddhism'. According to this, anyone who calls on the name of the Buddha Amitābha (Chin: Amituofo) will, at death, be reborn in a Pure Land which will provide a fast track to enlightenment.

Kigen (1200–1253) and Myōan Eisai (1141–1215) imported Chan, or Zen, as it is called there. When it entered Japan, Buddhism encountered the indigenous animistic view, Shintō. Shintō certainly coloured Japanese Buddhism, but it did not have a profound impact in the way in which the indigenous Chinese ideas had done, the general perception being that Shintō and Buddhism are quite compatible.

1.3 The Four Noble Truths

In this section we move to look at the Four Noble Truths.[12] These follow the form of a medical evaluation: illness, cause, prognosis, and cure.[13]

The First Noble Truth is that life is *duḥkha*. This is a Sanskrit word that is hard to translate. The most frequent translation is 'suffering'. This captures something of what is at issue, but is not adequate. The word's connotations standardly include: suffering, pain, discontent, unsatisfactoriness, unhappiness, sorrow, affliction, anxiety, dissatisfaction, discomfort, anguish, stress, misery, and frustration. The thought, whatever word one uses, is that all people get ill, suffer pain, age (if they are lucky to live long enough to do so), lose limbs, loved ones, jobs, treasured possessions—all of which gives rise to unhappiness, insecurity, mental dis-ease, and so on. This is not to say that there are not also times of happiness and joy. But like everything else in life, these are transient, and so prone to occasion the fear and unhappiness of loss. I must confess that the First Noble Truth strikes me as pretty ungainsayable: events of the kind I have mentioned are parts of anyone's life. There's not much to argue about here.

The Second Noble Truth says that there is a cause of duḥkha. This is *tṛṣṇā* (pronounced: *trishna*)—another word difficult to translate. The common translation is 'craving', which suggests the feeling one has for water when one has had no fluid for days. (Literally, 'tṛṣṇā' means *thirst*.) This really does give the wrong impression. Better, is something like 'attachment and aversion': mental attitudes connected with wanting something good to go on, or wanting something bad to go away. The thought is that when we experience duḥkha, it is caused by this attitude which we bring to affairs, the result of which is unpleasant, sometimes very unpleasant.

The truth of the Second Noble Truth is, I think, less obvious than that of the First. But if one reflects on the times when one has experienced duḥkha, I, at least,

[12] See, e.g., Harvey (2000), ch. 1, Siderits (2007), ch. 2, and Carpenter (2014), ch. 1. In this context, 'noble' means something like *ennobling* (someone who accepts and acts on their ideas).

[13] Again, much of what follows comes from Priest (2014a), 14.2.

find it hard to think of one when this kind of attitude did not play a role. This is not, of course, to say that the attitude is the only cause. Many causes have to conspire to bring about an effect. No doubt, unhappiness of this kind can be brought about by cars crashing, stock markets collapsing, earthquakes, wars, etc. But of all the causes that conspire, our mental attitude is the only one that is significantly under our control. It makes sense, therefore, to single that out.

The Third Noble Truth is but a corollary of the Second. If you can get rid of the cause, the attitude of tṛṣṇā, you can get rid of the effect, duḥkha.

The Fourth Noble Truth is a series of suggestions as to how to get rid of the attitude: the Eightfold Noble Path. The eight kinds of action of the path fall into three categories. *Wisdom*: right view, right intention. *Action*: right speech, right action, right livelihood. *Mental state*: right effort, right mindfulness, right concentration. When these suggestions are implemented in the appropriate way, they constitute what Foucault calls a technology of the self[14]—though as we shall see, this is not an entirely happy way of putting the matter: we might better say 'personal technology'. At any rate, whatever one calls them, these are practices which bring about dispositional changes in a person. Only the middle group would be thought of as ethical in traditional Western terms. But on the present picture, there is no real distinction. They all provide advice for attaining the same end. And, for the most part, when suitably spelled out, these strike me as pretty good advice; though I'm sure that there is much other good advice out there as well. Nothing more needs to be said about that matter here, however.

1.4 The Metaphysics of Ignorance

We turn now to some matters metaphysical. The first of the octet in the Eightfold Noble Path is *right view*; and there is good reason for this. The Second Noble Truth tells us that duḥkha is caused by tṛṣṇā, a dysfunctional affective state towards the world. But that state itself has a cause. We understand the world awrong. We mistakenly take ourselves to be living in a world where there are fixed things which can be grasped or circumvented; and indeed, take it that there is a self which can do these things. For whatever reason—our language, our need to get around the world, the demands of evolution—we have a natural disposition of ignorance (*avidyā*) towards the world in which we live. In this section we will look at two aspects of this false view.

[14] Foucault (1988).

1.4.1 *Impermanence*

The first is impermanence (*anitya*). We live in a world where everything that is conditioned comes into being and passes away. All things in the causal flux come to be, when causes and conditions are ripe, and cease to be when causes and conditions so conspire. They are in a constant state of pratītyasamutpāda, dependent arising and ceasing. An attitude of attachment is therefore foolish. Anything you want to possess or achieve in life is transient, and is sure to pass away in due course. Nor should you grieve when this happens. It was bound to happen sooner or later. I note that this does not mean that one should simply give up doing things for certain ends. Things that happen to ourselves and others are important; and we have some control over these. The point is that we need to see these things in the context of an ever-changing flux of events.

I presume that the early Buddhists held the view of impermanence on the basis of a simple inductive inference. However, contemporary science has certainly sided with them on this matter. Everything, from the stars and galaxies, at one end of the spectrum of size, to the subatomic particles at the other, comes into being in the evolution of the cosmos, and goes out of being in the same way. The cosmos itself came into being at the Big Bang. If it starts to contract, it will go out of existence in its mirror image. And if not, it will become a void: empty space/time, with matter of density as near zero as makes no difference. There's not much to argue about here.

1.4.2 *The self*

Let us turn to the second aspect of avidyā. There is nothing permanent to possess; but there is no self to possess it either. This is the doctrine of *anātman*. It is important to hear this view right. It is *not* a denial of the existence of persons. That is quite a different matter, to which we will come in due course. The point, rather, is this. Whatever else people are, they have parts. In traditional Buddhist thought, there are five kinds of such (*skandhas*). One kind is physical, *rūpa*. The other four are mental: *vedanā* (feelings), *samjñā* (perceptions), *samskāra* (mental formations), *vijñāna* (consciousness). What these all mean is not terribly relevant for us here.[15] It would not make make much difference for present purposes if we substituted some other taxonomy (psycho-physical, biological, subatomic). The

[15] A warning, though. The English translations do not mean exactly what Western philosophers tend to mean by the words. Consciousness, in particular, is a name for one sort of part; and these parts are just as impermanent as anything else. See, further, Siderits (2007), ch. 3.

important thing is that the self which is at issue in anātman is a part of a person which is constant, and present all the time that the person exists. Indeed, it is the part that makes the person the very person they are. There is no such part.

The truth of anātman is, I think, much more contentious than that of anitya, even in an Indian context. Indeed, anātman marked a significant break which the Buddhists made from Hindu orthodoxy. In the West, of course, it has been traditional amongst Christian philosophers to think of the soul as exactly such a self.

A standard Buddhist argument for anātman is one by analogy.[16] Take a car (well, the traditional example was a chariot). This is made of parts: the chassis, the engine block, the number plate, etc. These parts come together at a certain time, interact with each other and with the air, the road, and so on. Some of them wear out and are replaced. And in the end, they all fall apart. Crucially, there is no one part which makes the car that very car. There is no part that cannot be changed whilst the car remains numerically the same car. Even the registration details can be changed, for example if the owner moves state. Well, people are just like that.

Of course, someone who believes in a self will reject the analogy: there is something special about people. People, unlike cars, have a sense of self. Thus, when one wakes up in the morning after a deep sleep, it is as though a little voice says 'Hello, I'm back again'. Or as Kant put it in more Teutonic terms, every mental act is accompanied by an *I think*. This, according to him, is what it is that constitutes the *unity* of my mental life.[17]

So we do indeed have a *sense* of self. But do we really have a self? We know that the mind—or the brain whose functioning delivers it—plays tricks. At the back of the eyeball there is a place where the optic nerve joins it. There are no rods or cones there, so the joint produces a blindspot in the field of vision. Normally, though, we are quite unaware of this, since the brain 'fills in the visual gap'. In a similar way, there is a familiar illusion known as the *Phi Phenomenon* (made use of in the production of movies). Suppose there is a sequence of lights such that from left to right, say, each light flashes momentarily after the one before it. When one looks at this, one actually sees something moving from left to right. The brain 'fills in the gaps'. Maybe the self of which one has a sense is just the brain filling in the gaps between mental events, as it were, to create the illusion of something that does not really exist.

[16] E.g. in the dialogue between Nāgasena and King Milinda. See Rhys Davids (1890).

[17] *Critique of Pure Reason*, B131–B132.

This view receives support from current developments in cognitive science. Daniel Dennett summarizes the matter thus:[18]

There is no single, definitive "stream of consciousness," because there is no central Headquarters, no Cartesian Theater where "it all comes together" for the perusal of a Central Meaner. Instead of such a single stream (however wide), there are multiple channels in which specialised circuits try, in parallel pandemoniums, to do their various things, creating Multiple Drafts [GP: of a narrative of the self] as they go. Most of these fragmentary drafts of "narrative" play short-lived roles in the modulation of current activity but some get promoted to further functional roles, in swift succession, by the activity of a virtual machine in the brain. The seriality of this machine (its "von Neumannesque" character) is not a "hard-wired" design feature, but rather the upshot of a coalition of these specialists.

1.4.3 Look for yourself

The Buddhist view of the self, then, has good contemporary scientific credentials; but obviously the Buddhist thinkers of this period were in no position to avail themselves of these. How did they argue? Let us approach the matter via David Hume (who is often taken to have a similar view of the self). In the *Treatise on Human Nature* (I, IV, 6), he says:[19]

There are some philosophers who imagine that we are every moment intimately conscious of what we call our SELF; that we feel its existence and its continuance in existence; and are certain, beyond the evidence of a demonstration, both of its perfect identity and simplicity. The strongest sensation, the most violent passion, say they, instead of distracting us from this view, only fix it the more intensely, and make us consider their influence on *self* either by their pain or pleasure . . .

For my part, when I enter most intimately into what I call *myself*, I always stumble on some particular perception or other, of heat or cold, light or shade, love or hatred, pain or pleasure. I never can catch *myself* at any time without a perception, and never can observe anything but the perception . . . If anyone, upon serious and unprejudiced reflection, thinks he has a different notion of *himself*, I must confess, I can reason no longer with him. All I can allow him is, that he may be in the right as well as I, and that we are essentially different in this particular. He may, perhaps, perceive something simple and continued, which he calls *himself*; though I am certain there is no such principle in me.

But setting aside some metaphysician of this kind, I may venture to affirm of the rest of mankind, that they are nothing but a bundle or collection of different perceptions which succeed each other with an inconceivable rapidity and are in perpetual flux and movement . . .

[18] Dennett (1993), pp. 253–4. The book reviews the evidence and mounts the case for the view. See, especially, Part II of the book.

[19] Selby-Bigge (1978), pp. 251–2.

Buddhist thinkers would have endorsed Hume's words. Indeed, I'm told by people who practise a certain kind of Buddhist meditation that it is exactly an exercise in simply experiencing the constant arising and ceasing of mental states.

Given his empiricism, Hume inferred from the fact that we cannot perceive the self that there is no such thing—or at least, that we have no reason to suppose that there is. That's too fast. It is true that direct experience may give us no reason to believe in the self. But there are now many things which we take to exist, and which we cannot perceive, such as electrons and dark matter. What it *does* mean, is that the self has to be considered as a *theoretical posit*, like the scientific entities just mentioned. If there are grounds to believe in such a thing, then, these must be constituted by good theoretical reasons. The point is perfectly orthodox in Buddhist philosophy of mind. Thus, Vasubandhu, in his discussion of anātman, notes that if there is reason to believe in a self, it must either be perceived or appropriately inferred.[20]

1.4.4 Causation and unity

How, then, does such a thing earn its theoretical keep? There is a methodological principle termed *Ockham's Razor*—Buddhism calls this the Principle of Lightness:[21] one should not believe that something exists unless there is good reason to do so. And as in the case of all theoretical posits, this means that the posit must have explanatory value. If everything can be explained without it, one should not believe in it. So what might the existence of a self explain that cannot be explained by other things that we are already committed to?

The obvious thought is the Kantian one, that it is the self—whatever that is—which accounts for the unity of experience. Some mental events hang together in a way that others do not. It is precisely the self that is, supposedly, responsible for this.

Let us pass over the somewhat tricky question of how, exactly, the self might turn this trick; but look directly at the question of whether there are other possible explanations for this unity. The unity has both a synchronic aspect and a diachronic aspect. Let us consider each of these in turn. The standard Buddhist answer is that it is a certain kind of causality which turns the trick. Let us see how.[22]

[20] See Duerlinger (2003), pp. 73–4. [21] See Siderits (2007), pp. 44ff.

[22] The most sophisticated Buddhist discussion of the matter of which I know is by Vasubandhu in his 'Refutation of the Theory of Self', which is ch. 9 of his *Abhidharmakośa-Bhāṣya* (The Treasury of Abhidharma and Commentary). See Duerlinger (2003), pp. 71–110. For further discussion, see Carpenter (2014), ch. 6.

Synchronic. A motorbike drives past. I see it and hear it. Though one sensation is visual, and the other is auditory, they work together to produce a unitary experience. By contrast: you also see the bike go past, so we both have visual experiences of the bike, but there is no sense in which they are unified in the same way.

This distinction can, however, be explained in simple causal terms. There are causal relations between my auditory and visual sensations which do not hold between your visual sensations and mine. Specifically, the visual and auditory inputs of my brain are processed by different areas of my brain (the visual and auditory cortexes), but these two cortexes communicate with each other in a process of miltisensory integration to deliver the resulting mental experience. By contrast, there is no similar causal integration between your visual sensation and mine.[23]

Diachronic. This can be past-oriented or future-oriented. Past-orientated. Yesterday I saw a road accident. Today I have a visual memory of it. For me, the visual and memory events are integrated, in a way that any of your visual events are not related to my memory. But again, there is a perfectly natural causal explanation of this integration. When I saw the accident, the results from the visual cortex were encoded in the part of the brain which is responsible for episodic memory (the limbic system). These can be stimulated to generate the visual memory. Obviously there is no similar connection between your visual experience and my memory.

Future-orientated. Tonight I have a drink. Because of its pleasant effect, I drink too much. Tomorrow I have a hangover, with its painful mental symptoms. This evening's desire and tomorrow's headache go together. However, if you desire to drink, and drink too much, your hangover is not part of my experience. Again, however, there is a perfectly causal explanation of this. I desire to drink, so I drink. The alcohol enters my body, and the overdose gives me a mild case of alcohol poisoning, which my brain monitors the next day, giving rise to the headache. There is no similar causal chain between your drinking and any headache I might have the next day.

For similar reasons, it makes sense for me not to drink too much tonight if I don't want to have a hangover tomorrow—in a way that it makes no sense for me to try to stop *you* drinking so that *I* don't get a hangover. Thus, the causal relations also make sense of agency without a self.

[23] Of course there are also causal connections between your perception and mine; but they are just of the wrong *kind* to produce the unity in question. That's just a fact of neuro-anatomy. A similar point can be made with respect to the other examples in this section.

1.4.5 The illusion of self

Given all this, it would indeed appear that the experience of self is an illusion: there is no such thing. Of course, illusions can be useful. If you look in a mirror, what is behind you appears to be in front of you. This is an illusion; but it may be a useful one, since it lets you know what is behind you. And one can well imagine that an illusion of self is useful in evolutionary terms (which might, therefore, explain why certain kinds of biological organisms have it). Plausibly, a creature with the illusion of self is more likely to survive and pass on its genes.

However, at least in Buddhist terms, the illusion is pernicious. It generates a spurious duḥkha-generating attachment (tṛṣṇa) to this non-existent self. Once one comes to understand that the object of the attachment is non-existent, it makes no sense to maintain the attachment—any more than it makes any sense to be attached to, say, the plight of Mme Butterfly, if one knows her to be a purely fictional object.[24]

1.5 Conclusion

Of course, there is much more to be said about all the matters we have traversed in the chapter,[25] but the discussion here will at least provide sufficient stage-setting for what is to come. The next chapter will introduce us to one of the main characters in our drama: the *catuṣkoṭi*.

[24] For further discussion of the matter, see Carpenter (2014), chs. 1, 2.

[25] To find out more one can consult, as well as the references already cited, Siderits (2015).

2

Quintum Non-Datur

2.1 Introduction

In this chapter, we start in earnest. The topic is the catuṣkoṭi, in its earliest form. We will see what this is, its appearance in the early sūtras, and some of the background to these. We will then see how *not* to understand it, but how it may be understood in terms of the non-classical logic of First Degree Entailment. We will finish by looking at some early hints that there might be more to matters than this simple form.[1]

2.2 The Catuṣkoṭi: The Early Sūtras

In the West, the catuṣkoṭi is often called by its Greek equivalent, the *tetralemma*, 'four-corners'. The four corners are four options that one might take concerning some statement or other: that it is *true*, *false*, *both*, or *neither*. Thus, canonical Buddhist texts sometimes set up issues in terms of these four possibilities.

Take the following example. The aim of Buddhism is to achieve awakening (enlightenment). Concerning what, exactly, this is like, the early sūtras say little. It is quite unlike the Christian concept of going to heaven, however. It can be achieved in this life. (The Buddha, after all, was held to have achieved it.) But what after that? One thing is clear, the enlightened person is not reborn. So what does happen to them? Some people were naturally curious about the matter. Thus, we have in the *Agivacchagotta Sutta*:[2]

> "How is it, Master Gotama, does Master Gotama hold the view: 'After death a Tathāgata exists: only this is true, anything else is wrong'?"
>
> "Vaccha, I do not hold the view: 'After death a Tathāgata exists: only this is true, anything else is wrong.' "

[1] Some of the following is taken from Priest (2010a) and (2011).

[2] Ñāṇamoli and Bodhi (1995), p. 591. A *Tathāgata*—literally, (*one*) *thus gone*—is someone who has achieved enlightenment.

"How then, does Master Gotama hold the view: 'After death a Tathāgata does not exist: only this is true, anything else is wrong'?"

"Vaccha, I do not hold the view: 'After death a Tathāgata does not exist: only this is true, anything else is wrong.'"

If we were in Aristotle's Lyceum, the discussion would have to end there. All bases have been covered. But the dialogue continues:

"How is it, Master Gotama, does Master Gotama hold the view: 'After death a Tathāgata both exists and does not exist: only this is true, anything else is wrong'?"

"Vaccha, I do not hold the view: 'After death a Tathāgata both exists and does not exist: only this is true, anything else is wrong.'"

"How then, does Master Gotama hold the view: 'After death a Tathāgata neither exists nor does not exist: only this is true, anything else is wrong'?"

"Vaccha, I do not hold the view: 'After death a Tathāgata neither exists nor does not exist: only this is true, anything else is wrong.'"

It is clear from the dialogue that the Buddha's interlocutor, Vaccha, thinks of himself as offering an exclusive and exhaustive disjunction from which to choose. This framework is the catuṣkoṭi.

According to Aristotle, any statement must be either true or false, *tertium non datur*: there is no third possibility (and the *or* is exclusive). In a similar but more generous way, the catuṣkoṭi gives us an exhaustive and mutually exclusive set of four possibilities. It is something like a Principle of the Excluded Fifth.[3]

2.3 The Origins of the Principle

The origins of the catuṣkoṭi are lost in the mists of time. As the sūtras show, it was certainly in place as a general schema in the intellectual circles of Gautama, the historical Buddha. The philosopher Sañjaya (dates uncertain, but probably sixth or fifth century BCE) was also known for deploying the same four possibilities—indeed, for denying them all, as a way of rejecting all views.[4]

The roots of the catuṣkoṭi are clearly earlier than this, however, in Hindu literature. There is perhaps no need to wonder where the notions of truth and

[3] See Ruegg (1977), p. 1. The observant will note that the question actually put to the Buddha was of the form: is such and *only* such the case. It is therefore consistent with the Buddha's answers that he took *more* than one of the possibilities to be the case. Indeed, in due course, we will see that *something* like this later transpires in Buddhist philosophy. However, there are no canonical interpretations of these texts which interpret them in this way.

[4] See Raju (1956), p. 694.

falsity come from. So the first and second koṭis are unremarkable. The fourth koṭi can be found in the *Ṛg Veda*. For example, describing the origins of the cosmos, it says:[5]

> There was neither non-existence nor existence then; there was neither the realm of space nor the sky which is beyond. What stirred? Where? In whose protection? Was there water, bottomless deep?

It is also to be found in one of the most famous parts of Hindu philosophy: *neti, neti* (literally: *not, not*), meaning *not this, not this*, or *neither this nor that*. Thus, in the *Bṛhadāraṇyaka Upaniṣad*, we read:[6]

> This Self is simply described as "Not, not". It is ungraspable. For it is not grasped. It is indestructible, for it is not destroyed. It has no attachment and is unfastened; it is not attached, and yet it is not unsteady. For it, immortal, passes beyond both these two states (in which one thinks) "For this reason I have done evil," "For this reason I have done good." It is not disturbed by good or evil things that are done or left undone; its heaven is not lost by any deed.

The passage is most naturally read as saying that one must reject all claims about the self: it is neither this nor that. So we have the fourth koṭi. But at the same time, it *does* endorse claims about the self, for example, that it is immortal. So we are in the third, at least implicitly.

The third koṭi also appears to have been found explicitly in the writings of the Hindu Ājīvika sect. This was a sect that flourished for a while after about the fifth century BCE. Their texts are now lost, but in Abhayadeva's commentary on the *Samavayāṅga-Sūtra*, we find:[7]

> These Ājivikas are called Trairāṣikas. Why? The reason is that they entertain (*icchanti*) everything to be of a triple nature, viz. soul, non-soul, soul and non-soul; world, non-world, world and non-world; being, non-being, being and non-being, etc. Even in (*api*) considering standpoints they entertain a three-fold standpoint such as the substantial, the modal and the dual.

The ideas of the catuṣkoṭi were not, then, pulled from thin air.

2.4 The Catuṣkoṭi: Some Dead Ends

So much for the basic idea and its textual basis. How one can make sense of the catuṣkoṭi in terms of Western formal logic is not so obvious. It flies in the face

[5] Koller and Koller (1991), p. 6.
[6] Koller and Koller (1991), p. 22.
[7] Jayatilleke (1963), p. 155.

of the Principle of Excluded Middle (PEM: everything is either true or false) and the Principle of Non-Contradiction (PNC: nothing is both true and false)—which principles are orthodox in Aristotle-inspired logic.[8]

A simple-minded thought is that for any claim, A, there are four possible cases:[9]

(a) A
(b) $\neg A$
(c) $A \wedge \neg A$
(d) $\neg(A \vee \neg A)$

(c) will wave red flags to anyone wedded to the PNC—but the text of 2.2 seems pretty explicit that you might have to give this away. There are worse problems. Notably, assuming De Morgan's laws (that $\neg(A \vee B)$ is equivalent to $\neg A \wedge \neg B$), (d) is equivalent to (c), and so the two koṭis collapse. Possibly, one might reject the Principle of Double Negation (A is equivalent to $\neg\neg A$), so that (d) would give us only $\neg A \wedge \neg\neg A$. But there are worse problems. The four cases are supposed to be exclusive; yet case (c) entails both cases (a) and (b). So the corners again collapse.

The obvious thought here is that we must understand (a) as saying that A is true and not false. Similarly, one must understand (b) as saying that A is false and not true. Corners (a) and (b) then become: $A \wedge \neg\neg A$ and $\neg A \wedge \neg A$ (i.e. $\neg A$). Even leaving aside problems about double negation, case (c) still entails case (b). We are no better off.

Unsurprisingly, then, modern commentators have tried to find other ways of expressing the catuṣkoṭi. Robinson[10] suggests understanding the four corners as:

(a) $\forall x A$
(b) $\forall x \neg A$
(c) $\exists x A \wedge \exists x \neg A$
(d) $\neg\exists x A \wedge \neg\exists x \neg A$

The artifice of using a quantifier is manifest. Claims such as 'The Buddha exists after death' and 'The cosmos is infinite' (another case of a claim on which the

[8] On the other hand, simply assuming that Aristotle got logic right, and imposing this on interpretations of Buddhist texts, strikes me as an egregious act of cultural imperialism.

[9] For those unfamiliar with logical notation, here is what the symbols mean:

$\neg$	it is not the case that
$\vee$	or
$\wedge$	and
$\exists x$	for some x
$\forall x$	for every x

[10] Robinson (1957), pp. 102f.

Buddha refused to pronounce judgement, as we shall see in a moment) have no free variable (x). How, then, is a quantifier supposed to help? And why choose that particular combination of universal and particular quantifiers? Even supposing that one could smuggle a free variable into these claims somehow, case (d) entails case (b) (since $\neg\exists xA$ entails $\forall x\neg A$); and absent a misbehaviour of double negation, it entails (a) as well (since $\neg\exists x\neg A$ entails $\forall x\neg\neg A$).

Tillemans[11] enumerates the four corners slightly more plausibly, as:

(a) $\exists xA$
(b) $\exists x\neg A$
(c) $\exists x(A \wedge \neg A)$
(d) $\exists x(\neg A \wedge \neg\neg A)$

But we still have the problem of an apparently spurious quantifier. And unless double negation fails, corners (c) and (d) collapse into each other. Even if not, case (c) entails cases (a) and (b). Moreover, Tillemans's stated aim is to retain classical logic, in which case, cases (c) and (d) are empty. This hardly seems to do justice to matters.

Jayatilleke[12] suggests interpreting the four corners as:

(a) x is P in all respects
(b) x is $\neg P$ in all respects
(c) x is P in some respects and $\neg P$ in others
(d) x is not P in some respects and not $\neg P$ in others.

He illustrates this, not with respect to a tathāgata, but with respect to a text concerning the finitude of the world. He cites and translates the koṭis as follows:

I *Antavā ayaṃ loco (parivaṭumo)*, i.e. this world is finite and bounded all around.

II *Ananto ayaṃ loco (aparivaṭumo)*, i.e. this world is infinite and unbounded all around.

III *Antavā ca ayaṃ loco ananto ca*, i.e. this world is finite and infinite.

IV *N'evayām loco anantā no panānanto*, i.e. this world is neither finite nor infinite.

Now, there is nothing in the Sanskrit which says anything about some or all respects. Worse, under this interpretation, (c) and (d) collapse into each other again, since (assuming the PEM, which Jayatilleke does) being P in some respects

11 Tillemans (1999), p. 200.

12 Jayatilleke (1963), pp. 340ff.

and $\neg P$ in others is the same thing as not being P in some respects and not being $\neg P$ in others.[13]

Some commentators have suggested using a non-classical logic. Thus, Staal[14] suggests using intuitionist logic, so the corners become:

(a) A
(b) $\neg A$
(c) $A \wedge \neg A$
(d) $\neg A \wedge \neg\neg A$

Moving to intuitionist logic at least motivates the failure of double negation. But case (c) still entails cases (a) and (b), and case (d) entails case (b). To add insult to injury, cases (c) and (d) are empty.[15]

Westerhoff[16] suggests using two kinds of negation. Let us use $\times$ for a second kind of negation. The four corners are then formulated as:

(a) A
(b) $\neg A$
(c) $A \wedge \neg A$
(d) $\times (A \vee \neg A)$

We still have case (c) entailing cases (a) and (b). We can perhaps avoid this by formulating them as $A \wedge \times \neg A$ and $\neg A \wedge \times A$. So we have:

(a) $A \wedge \times \neg A$
(b) $\neg A \wedge \times A$
(c) $A \wedge \neg A$
(d) $\times (A \vee \neg A)$

[13] And he is quite clear that the four corners are supposed to be exclusive and exhaustive (1963), p. 339. A final comment on Jayatilleke. He argues that the Buddhists endorsed the PNC, on the ground that in some sūtras certain contradictions are rejected (1963), p. 339. This shows no such thing. From the fact that some contradictions were rejected it does not follow that all were. It merely shows that the particular claim at issue was not in the third koṭi. The enormity of the fallacy here is the same as that of claiming that someone thinks that nothing is true because they think that 'snow is green' is not true.

[14] Staal (1975), p. 47.

[15] This is not quite fair to Staal. His suggestion arises in connection with the possibility of rejecting all four koṭis. We then have:

(a) $\neg A$
(b) $\neg\neg A$
(c) $\neg(A \wedge \neg A)$
(d) $\neg(\neg A \wedge \neg\neg A)$

Cases (c) and (d) at least now have truth on their side, but vacuously: they subsume every other case.

[16] Westerhoff (2010), ch. 4.

What consequences this formulation has depends very much on how one thinks of $\times$ as working, and how, in particular, it interacts with $\neg$. Westerhoff points to the standard distinction in Indian logic between *paryudāsa* negation and *prasaja* negation, the former being, essentially, predicate negation; the latter, essentially, sentential negation. As he points out, the distinction will not be immediately applicable here, since both $\neg$ and $\times$ are obviously sentential. The important point, he takes it, is that *paryudāsa* negation preserves various presuppositions of the sentence negated. Thus, it may be held, 'the King of France is bald' and 'the King of France is not bald' both presuppose that there is a King of France, and so may both fail to be true. Call this an *internal* negation. Whereas, 'it is not the case that the King of France is bald' holds simply if 'the King of France is bald' *fails* to hold; and one reason why it may fail to do so is that a presupposition—namely, that the King of France exists—fails. Call this an *external* negation. The thought, then, is that $\neg$ is an internal negation and $\times$ is an external negation.

Be all that as it may, case (c) still cannot hold, since it is a flat contradiction (and would be if $\neg$ were replaced with $\times$). Moreover, Westerhoff's interpretation seems somewhat *ad hoc*, since there is no textual evidence that negation is functioning in two different ways in the catuṣkoṭi. And if it is, there would seem to be lots more cases to consider, since every negation in our original catuṣkoṭi is potentially ambiguous. Every way of disambiguating is going to be a separate case. (Though some of these may be logically interconnected.) Why choose just the ones Westerhoff lights on?[17]

Of course, there are probably more ways of trying to get out of some of these binds. In particular, if one does not want accept the third koṭi at face value, one must go in for some kind of disambiguation. However, as a moment's thought suffices to show, if there are ambiguities involved in this koṭi, then they will apply to all koṭis. Our four possibilities blow out, then, to many more. None of these cases obtained by disambiguations is discussed, raised, or even hinted at.

2.5 Interlude on Classical Propositional Logic

So much for attempts that do not work. To anyone familiar with contemporary non-classical logic, however, there is an obvious way to make sense of the catuṣkoṭi: the logic of First Degree Entailment (FDE). I will explain this in the

[17] Westerhoff suggests interpreting the external negation as an illocutory negation (p. 78); that is, as the speech act of denial. (See Priest (2006), ch. 6.) This, indeed, has a certain appeal. A problem with the approach, however, is that it makes no sense to put illocutory acts in propositional contexts. Thus, the first two of the four koṭis (at least as I reformulated them) make no sense. Worse: once the possibility of denying all four koṭis is on the table—as it is in due course, as we will see—the rejection of the fourth koṭi would have to be expressed as $\times \times (A \vee \neg A)$. This makes no sense, since $\times$ does not iterate.

next section. However, for those who are not familiar with 'classical' propositional logic, I insert this interlude explaining it briefly and informally. Those who are familiar with the subject can skim over this section, or omit it entirely.

An *inference* is an argument with a number of premises and a conclusion. An inference where the premises really do support the conclusion is called *valid*. Here is a valid inference:

Premise: All philosophers are happy.
Premise: Socrates was a philosopher.
Conclusion: So, Socrates was happy.

Note that the premises of a valid argument do not have to be true: many philosophers of my acquaintance are not particularly happy people! It just has to be the case that *had* the premises been true, the conclusion would have had to be true too.

Here is an example of an invalid inference:

Premise: The sun is shining in Brisbane.
Conclusion: The sun is shining in Melbourne.

Note that the premises and conclusion of a valid argument can both be true. (As a matter of fact, in this case, as I write, they are.) But the conclusion just doesn't follow from the premise. It is often the case that the sun is shining in Brisbane, but not Melbourne.[18]

Now, what logic is after is an account of what inferences are valid, and why. So how do we proceed?

The premises and conclusion of an argument are sentences of some language. Natural languages, such as English and Chinese, are notoriously irregular and idiomatic. Logicians prefer to deal with formal languages: languages with a well-defined syntax and semantics which approximate key aspects of natural languages.

The formal language of the propositional calculus has simple sentences with no relevant internal structure. These are called *propositional parameters*, and are usually written p, q, r. More complex sentences can be built up with connectives, such as $\neg$ (negation: *it is not the case that*), $\vee$ (disjunction: *or*), $\wedge$ (conjunction: *and*). So we can have complex sentences such as: $\neg p$, $p \vee q$, $q \wedge r$; and more complex things such as $\neg(p \vee \neg q)$, $(p \wedge q) \vee \neg\neg\, r$.[19]

[18] For those who do not know Australia, Brisbane is subtropical, and the sun shines there on most days. Melbourne, well, that's another matter.

[19] If it helps, think of propositional parameters as like numbers, 1, 2, 3, and $\neg$, $\vee$, and $\wedge$ as like the arithmetical operations $-$, $+$, and $\times$. Complex sentences are then the analogues of expressions such as $(1 \times 2) + - - 3$.

An inference is valid if there is no situation where all the premises are true, but the conclusion is not true. What, however, is a situation? A situation—which logicians usually call an *interpretation* or *evaluation*—is simply any division of the propositional parameters into two categories: the true and the false. Think of true sentences as being assigned the number 1, and false sentences as being assigned the number 0. Given an interpretation, we can then work out whether the more complex sentences are true or false in it, by applying some rules (called by logicians *truth conditions*). The rules for the three connectives we have met are as follows:[20]

- $\neg A$ has the value 0 just if A has the value 1
- $\neg A$ has the value 1 just if A has the value 0
- $A \wedge B$ has the value 1 just if A and B have the value 1
- $A \wedge B$ has the value 0 just if A or B has the value 0
- $A \vee B$ has the value 1 just if A or B has the value 1
- $A \vee B$ has the value 0 just if A and B have the value 0

So, for example, consider the sentence $(p \wedge q) \vee \neg\neg r$, and suppose that the values of p, q, and r are, respectively, 1, 1, and 0. r has the value 0, so $\neg r$ has the value 1; so $\neg\neg r$ has the value 0. But the value of $p \wedge q$ is 1. So the value of $(p \wedge q) \vee \neg\neg r$ is 1. We might depict the computation as follows, building complexity from top to bottom (the number in square brackets by the side of a formula is its value):

$$\begin{array}{ccc}
 & & r \quad [0] \\
p\ [1] \quad q\ [1] & & \neg r \quad [1] \\
p \wedge q \quad [1] & & \neg\neg r \quad [0] \\
 & (p \wedge q) \vee \neg\neg r \quad [1] &
\end{array}$$

An inference, as I said, is valid if every situation which gives all the premises the value 1 gives the conclusion the value 1—or alternatively expressed, there is no situation which gives all the premises the value 1, but does not give the conclusion the value 1.

There is an algorithm for determining which inferences are valid and which are not, but we need not go into this here. Here are a couple of examples. Consider the inference with premises p and $\neg p \vee q$, and conclusion q. (This is sometimes called the *Disjunctive Syllogism*.) This is valid. For suppose that p and $\neg p \vee q$ have the value 1. Since $\neg p$ has the value 0, q must have the value 1, as required. Or consider

[20] The conditions are often displayed in the form of tables:

A	$\neg A$
0	1
1	0

$A \vee B$	1	0
1	1	1
0	1	0

$A \wedge B$	1	0
1	1	0
0	0	0

the inference with premise $p \vee q$, and conclusion $p \wedge q$. This is invalid. To see this, consider the interpretation which gives p the value 1, and q the value 0. Then $p \vee q$ has the value 1, but $p \wedge q$ does not.

Finally, consider the inference with premises p and $\neg p$, and conclusion q. This is a principle sometimes called *Explosion*: contradictions entail everything. There is no interpretation in which both premises have the value 1. *A fortiori*, there is no interpretation where both premises take the value 1, *and* the conclusion does not. So Explosion is valid. (One might say, vacuously so.)

2.6 First Degree Entailment

Let us now turn to the logic of First Degree Entailment, FDE.[21] Again, I will explain this informally. In a technical appendix to the chapter I will give a more formal account, and further technical details.

Just to make matters clear: I am not suggesting the theory of validity delivered by FDE was endorsed by our Buddhist philosophers. Accounts of validity of this kind were just not on their agenda. The point is to show how the metaphysics of the catuṣkoṭi makes perfectly good and precise sense from the perspective of contemporary logic.

FDE can be set up in a number of different ways. Perhaps the simplest, given the previous section, is this. In classical logic, sentences are assigned exactly one of the values 1 and 0. We simply relax this assumption. Any sentence can take one of these values, both, or neither. Everything else works in exactly the same way!

So, suppose, for example, that A has the value 1, and B has the values 1 and 0. $A \wedge B$ has the value 1, since both A and B have the value 1; and it has the value 0 as well, since B has the value 0. Or suppose that A has the values 1 and 0. Then $\neg A$ has the values 0 and 1—exactly the same.

Return to the Disjunctive Syllogism: premises p and $\neg p \vee q$, and conclusion q. Consider an interpretation in which p has the values 1 and 0, and q has just the value 0. It is easy to see that $\neg p \vee q$ has the values 1 (since $\neg p$ has the value 1) and 0 (since both $\neg p$ and q have the value 0). Hence both premises have (at least) the value 1, and the conclusion does not. So the inference is invalid. For good measure, Explosion is also invalid in FDE. In the same interpretation both p and $\neg p$ have (at least) the value 1, and q doesn't.[22]

[21] The logic of FDE came out of work on relevant logic by Belnap, Dunn, and others. (A simple presentation can be found in Belnap (1977).) This work had absolutely nothing to do with the catuṣkoṭi.

[22] Logics in which Explosion fails are called *paraconsistent*. And if you are countenancing true contradictions, as the catuṣkoṭi does, you'd better use a paraconsistent logic, or it would follow that everything is true!

Another, and more perspicuous, way to formulate FDE, is as a many-valued (4-valued) logic. In a many-valued logic, sentences have exactly one value, but there are more than two. Now in the semantics with 1 and 0, we have four cases, and we can record each of these with a single value. Thus, a formula may be t (1, and 1 only), f (0, and 0 only), b (both 1 and 0), or n (neither 1 nor 0). These values can then be represented in the following Hasse diagram:

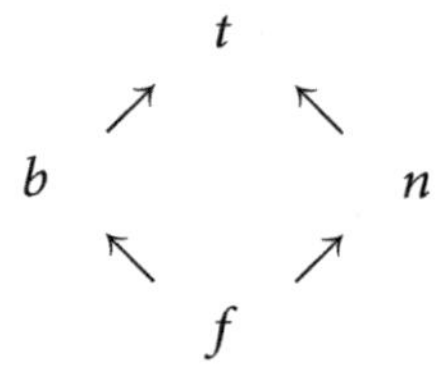

The four corners of the catuṣkoṭi literally appear before our eyes!

As may now be checked, the truth and falsity conditions given above amount to the following. Let us write the value of A as $|A|$. If $|A| = t$, $|\neg A| = f$, and vice versa; if $|A| = n$, $|\neg A| = n$; if $|A| = b$, $|\neg A| = b$. To conjoin two formulas, one just goes down the arrows till one gets to the greatest value less than or equal to both of their values. Thus, if $|A| = b$ and $|B| = f$, $|A \wedge B| = f$; and if $|A| = b$ and $|B| = n$, $|A \wedge B| = f$ as well. To disjoin two formulas, one does just the same, except that one goes up the arrows. Thus, if $|A| = b$ and $|B| = f$, $|A \vee B| = b$; and if $|A| = b$ and $|B| = n$, $|A \vee B| = t$.

What does validity come to in this framework? In a many-valued logic, such as this, some of the values are called *designated*, and a valid inference is one such that whenever all the premises are designated, so is the conclusion. In the 1/0 formulation of FDE, an inference is valid if whenever the premises have (at least) the value 1, so does the conclusion. In the 4-valued setting, having at least the value 1 corresponds to having either the value t or the value b. So those are the designated values. An inference is valid if whenever the premises take the value t or b, so does the conclusion.

2.7 The Buddha's Silence

The reader will have noticed that in the dialogue of 2.2 the Buddha refused to endorse any of the possibilities concerning the state of the enlightened person after death. There were, in fact, a number of issues on which the Buddha, famously, refused to pronounce: the unanswered/undeclared questions: *avyākṛta*. The *Agivacchagotta Sutta* and the *Cūḷamūllunkya Sutta* list essentially four such questions:

- Is the world eternal (in time)?
- Is the world infinite (in space)?
- Is the *jīva* (person, soul) identical with the body?
- Does the enlightened person exist after death?

Now, why did the Buddha refuse to pronounce on these questions?

A standard answer given in the sūtras is that these matters are of no soteriological importance; they are just a waste of time.[23] Thus, in the *Cūḷamūllunkya Sutta*, we read:[24]

"Suppose, Mālunkyāputta, a man were wounded by an arrow thickly smeared with poison, and his friends and companions, his kinsmen and relatives, brought a surgeon to treat him. The man would say: 'I will not let the surgeon pull out this arrow until I know whether the man who wounded me was a noble or a brahmin or a merchant or a worker.' And he would say: 'I will not let the surgeon pull out this arrow until I know the name and clan of the man who wounded me; . . . until I know whether the man who wounded me was dark or brown or golden-skinned; . . . "

"All this would still not be known to that man and meanwhile he would die. So too, Mālunkyāputta, if anyone should say thus: 'I will not lead the holy life under the Blessed One until the Blessed One declares to me: "the world is eternal" . . . or "after death a Tathāgata neither exists nor does not exist,"' that would still remain undeclared by the Tathāgata and meanwhile that person would die." . . .

"Therefore, Mālunkyāputta, remember what I have left undeclared as undeclared, and remember what I have declared as declared. And what have I left undeclared? 'The world is eternal'—I have left undeclared. 'The world is not eternal'—I have left undeclared. 'The world is finite'—I have left undeclared. 'The world is infinite'—I have left undeclared. 'The soul is the same as the body'—I have left undeclared. 'The soul is one thing and the body another'—I have left undeclared. 'After death a Tathāgata exists'—I have left undeclared. 'After death a Tathāgata does not exist'—I have left undeclared. 'After death a Tathāgata both exists and does not exist'—I have left undeclared. 'After death a Tathāgata neither exists nor does not exist'—I have left undeclared."

"Why have I left that undeclared? Because it is unbeneficial, it does not belong to the fundamentals of the holy life, it does not lead to disenchantment, to dispassion, to cessation, to peace, to direct knowledge, to enlightenment, to Nibbāna. That is why I have left it undeclared."

However, in some of the sūtras there is a hint that something else is going on—at least in some of the avyākṛta questions—in that the Buddha seems to explicitly reject all the options. Thus, in the *Agivacchagotta Sutta*, again, the Buddha says

[23] See Ruegg (1977), pp.1–2.

[24] Ñāṇamoli and Bodhi (1995), pp. 534ff. 'The Blessed One' is another honorific for the Buddha.

that none of the four koṭis 'applies'. When questioned how this is possible, he says:[25]

"What do you think, Vaccha? Suppose a fire were burning before you. Would you know: 'This fire is burning before me'?"

"I would, Master Gotama."

"If someone were to ask you, Vaccha: 'What does this fire burning before you burn in dependence on?'—being asked thus, what would you answer?"

"Being asked thus, Master Gotama, I would answer: 'This fire burning before me burns in dependence on grass and sticks.' "

"If that fire before you were to be extinguished, would you know: 'This fire before me has been extinguished'?"

"I would, Master Gotama."

"If someone were to ask you, Vaccha: 'When that fire before you was extinguished, to which direction did it go: to the east, the west, the north, or the south?'—being asked thus, what would you answer?"

"That does not apply, Master Gotama. The fire burned in dependence on its fuel of grass and sticks. When that is used up, if it does not get any more fuel, being without fuel, it is reckoned as extinguished."

What is going on here?

2.8 Presupposition Failure?

In the case of the fire, the question of the direction in which it has gone has no correct answer, because the fire has ceased to exist. To say, for example, that the fire has gone north would presuppose or entail that exists, which it does not.

If this is indeed analogous to the case of the enlightened person after death, the thought would be that anything one says about such a person presupposes or entails that they exist, which they do not. We have, then, a case of presupposition failure.[26] This way of looking at things might be thought to receive some support from the fact that the word for the enlightened state, *nirvāṇa*, can literally mean *extinction*. If one recalls that the enlightened state can occur before death, however, this seems less plausible. The extinction involved is not that of the person, but of their duḥkha.

In any case, this move would not seem to work in the present situation, where the catuṣkoṭi is in play. Let *a* be a name that refers, if it refers at all, to some *post*

[25] Ñāṇamoli and Bodhi (1995), p. 592.
[26] As suggested, e.g., by Siderits and Katsura (2013), p. 302.

mortem enlightened person. The question is how to understand the claim '*a* exists' if *a* does not refer to an existent object. Several answers are possible. The problem is that none of them takes us outside the catuṣkoṭi.

First, there is the noneist possibility. '*a*' refers to a non-existent object.[27] For a noneist, an object can have properties even though it does not exist. Existence is one that *a* does not have. So '*a* exists' is simply false. We are in the second koṭi.

The next possibility is that a sentence of the form *Pa* is simply false if '*a*' does not refer.[28] But in that case, we are again in the second koṭi.

In both of the previous approaches, '*a* does not exist' is simply true. And, note, that is essentially what Vaccha says at the end of the previous quotation: the fire 'is reckoned as extinguished'.

But there is also a third possibility. One might take it that if '*a*' fails to refer, *Pa* is neither true nor false.[29] But on this understanding, we are in the fourth koṭi.

Interpreting the Buddha's thoughts about not fitting the case in this way, does not, then, look very plausible—at least if one wishes to take them as true.

2.9 Conclusion

In this chapter, we have met the catuṣkoṭi in its earliest appearance in Buddhist thought. We have seen that it functions as a principle of excluded fifth. We have also seen how this makes perfectly good sense from the perspective of the logic of FDE. Finally, we have seen a hint there might be more to the matter than this. And indeed, the Buddha's silence does prefigure later developments concerning the catuṣkoṭi. We will come to these in Chapter 4. But before we get to these, another part of the story needs to be told. This concerns the notion of svabhāva, as it features in Abhidharma metaphysics. We turn to this in the next chapter.

2.10 Technical Appendix

In this technical appendix, I will give a more precise formulation of FDE, together with some more formal details.[30]

[27] See Priest (2005).

[28] This is what happens in 'negative free logics'. See Priest (2008a), 13.4. It would also be the case if we took '*a*' to be a covert definite description, and applied Russell's theory of descriptions.

[29] As in 'neutral free logics'. See Priest (2008a), 13.4. This is the line taken, e.g., by Frege concerning denotation failure.

[30] Further details can be found in Priest (2008a), chs. 8, 9.

2.10.1 Many-valued logics

Let us start with many-valued propositional logics, in general. Given some propositional language with a set of connectives, C, a logic is defined by a structure $\langle V, D, \{f_c : c \in C\}\rangle$. V is the set of truth values: it may have any number of members ($\geqslant 1$). D is a subset of V, and is the set of designated values. For every connective, c, f_c is the corresponding truth function. Thus, if c is an n-place connective, f_c is an n-place function with inputs and outputs in V.

An *interpretation* for the language is a map, ν, from the set of propositional parameters, P, into V. This is extended to a map from all formulas of the language to V by applying the appropriate truth functions recursively. Thus, if c is an n-place connective, $\nu(c(A_1, \ldots, A_n)) = f_c(\nu(A_1), \ldots, \nu(A_n))$. Finally, if Σ is a set of formulas, $\Sigma \models A$ iff there is no interpretation, ν, such that for all $B \in \Sigma$, $\nu(B) \in D$, but $\nu(A) \notin D$. A is a logical truth iff $\emptyset \models A$, i.e iff for every interpretation, ν, $\nu(A) \in D$.

2.10.2 FDE

The formal language with which we will be concerned here and in the rest of the book is as follows. The connectives of the language are $\neg$, $\wedge$, and $\vee$. $A \supset B$ may be defined as $\neg A \vee B$. The language may be augmented with quantifiers and additional non-extensional operators, such as modal operators, and a conditional operator. But these play no role in this book, so we may ignore them here.

In FDE, V is $\{t, f, b, n\}$, and $D = \{t, b\}$. $f_\neg$ is a function which maps: t to f, f to t, b to b, and n to n. $f_\wedge(x, y)$ is the greatest lower bound of x and y, and $f_\vee(x, y)$ is the least upper bound of x and y, in the lattice depicted in 2.6.

As indicated in 2.6, an equivalent way to set up FDE is, not as a many-valued logic, but as a relational logic. Specifically, an evaluation is now thought of as a relation, ρ, between the set of propositional parameters, P, and $\{1, 0\}$. We can define what it is for a formula to be true $\Vdash^+$ and false $\Vdash^-$, with respect to an evaluation, ρ, as follows. (A formula may be both or neither.)

- $\Vdash^+ p$ iff $p\rho 1$
- $\Vdash^- p$ iff $p\rho 0$
- $\Vdash^+ \neg A$ iff $\Vdash^- A$
- $\Vdash^- \neg A$ iff $\Vdash^+ A$
- $\Vdash^+ A \wedge B$ iff $\Vdash^+ A$ and $\Vdash^+ B$
- $\Vdash^- A \wedge B$ iff $\Vdash^- A$ or $\Vdash^- B$
- $\Vdash^+ A \vee B$ iff $\Vdash^+ A$ or $\Vdash^+ B$
- $\Vdash^- A \vee B$ iff $\Vdash^- A$ and $\Vdash^- B$

$\Sigma \models A$ iff for all ρ, if $\Vdash^+ B$ for all $B \in \Sigma$, $\Vdash^+ A$.

It is not difficult to show that these two formulations of FDE are equivalent.[31]

2.10.3 *Natural deduction*

A natural deduction system for FDE, in the style of Prawitz (1965), may be obtained as follows. The following is a (specially chosen) natural deduction rule system for classical logic. A double line indicates a two-way rule, and over-barring an assumption means that the rule discharges it.

$$\dfrac{A \quad B}{A \wedge B} \qquad \dfrac{A \wedge B}{A} \qquad \dfrac{A \wedge B}{B}$$

$$\dfrac{A}{A \vee B} \qquad \dfrac{B}{A \vee B} \qquad \dfrac{A \vee B \quad \begin{matrix}\overline{A}\\ \vdots \\ C\end{matrix} \quad \begin{matrix}\overline{B}\\ \vdots \\ C\end{matrix}}{C}$$

$$\dfrac{\underline{A}}{\neg\neg A} \qquad \dfrac{\underline{\neg(A \vee B)}}{\neg A \wedge \neg B} \qquad \dfrac{\underline{\neg(A \wedge B)}}{\neg A \vee \neg B}$$

$$\dfrac{}{B \vee \neg B} \qquad \dfrac{A \wedge \neg A}{B}$$

A rule system for FDE is obtained simply by dropping the last two rules—Excluded Middle and Explosion, respectively. For a proof of soundness and completeness, see Priest (2002b), 4.6, and Priest (2019).

I note that if one drops the value b from the many-valued semantics (or equivalently, does not allow a formula to be related to both 1 and 0 in the relational semantics), one obtains the 'Strong Kleene logic', K_3. And if one drops the value n from the many-valued semantics (or equivalently, requires a formula to relate to at least one of 1 and 0 in the relational semantics), one obtains the paraconsistent logic *LP*.[32] A rule system for K_3 is obtained by reinstating Explosion. A rule system of *LP* is obtained by reinstating Excluded Middle.

[31] See Priest (2008a), ch. 8.

[32] For both of these logics, see Priest (2008a), ch. 7.

3

Well-Founded Metaphysics

3.1 Introduction

The further developments of the catuṣkoṭi occurred as part of a reaction against the metaphysics that developed in the first five hundred years of Buddhism, and articulated in Abhidharma philosophy. Hence, to understand these developments, we need to understand the Abhidharma metaphysics. This chapter is devoted to providing the needed understanding.[1]

I will start by describing the Abhidharma view, and the concepts involved in it. We will then turn to look at arguments that may be used to support the views.

3.2 Abhidharma Mereology and the Dharmas

In 1.4.2 we saw that the view of the person articulated in connection with anātman took them to be a collection five kinds of parts: the skandhas.

In fact, it is not just people, but all the objects of our familiar experience which are composed of parts: natural objects such as trees, mountains, stars; and artifacts such as buildings, nations, music. In an obvious sense, these partite objects are wholes composed of their parts. So we arrive at the topic of mereology: the theory of parts and wholes.[2]

Suppose one takes any one of these partite objects, and considers its parts, their parts, *their* parts, and so on. Must we, in this process, come to partless parts, fundamental parts, out of which the object is ultimately composed? The Abhidharma philosophers said 'yes'. They called these *dharmas*. Dharmas are the ultimate building blocks of reality.[3] There was a debate about what sort

[1] A discussion of Abhidharma metaphysics can be found in Siderits (2007), ch. 6, and Ronkin (2014).

[2] For an account of contemporary views of mereology, see Varzi (2009).

[3] In Sanskrit, the word *dharma* means something like 'foundation'. The Abhidharma philosophers co-opted it as a metaphysical term of art. In Buddhist philosophy, *dharma* can also mean a doctrine or teaching, and especially the fundamental teachings of Buddhism (as in *Abhidharma*)—a quite different sense of foundation.

of thing dharmas are, but a common view was that they are tropes, particular instantiations of universals, of a certain kind.[4] Thus, the dharmas of an object might be its redness, its squareness, its hardness, etc. For our purposes, little will turn on what, exactly, the dharmas are.

Though they are metaphysical atoms, the dharmas are no more permanent than anything else. They, too, come into existence when causes and conditions are ripe, and go out of existence in the same way. Indeed, many Abhidharma philosophers took them to be very short-lived, even momentary.[5] An object, then, is composed of dharmas in a constant state of flux. The flux is not, of course, random; but is held together by causal processes. Indeed, it is these which make it natural to think of me as the same object over time. Thus, as we saw in 1.4.4, my drinking tonight and my having a hangover tomorrow morning (and similar causal connections) make it the case that the collection of my dharmas tonight and the different collection of my dharmas tomorrow morning hang together as *me*.

3.3 The Two Realities

What more is to be said of the dharmas? In all forms of Buddhism there is a distinction between two kinds of reality: ultimate reality, *paramārtha-satya*, and conventional reality, *saṃvṛti-satya* (pronounced 'samvriti satya'). I note that Sanskrit word *satya* might be translated into English as *truth* or as *reality*. In discussing the two *satyas* in the Buddhist traditions, the most usual translation is *truth*. In many cases, including the present one, I think that *reality* is a better.

How to understand the distinction between the two realities varies from school to school, as we shall see in due course. Here we are concerned with the Abhidharma understanding. And according to this, the distinction is extensionally equivalent to that between the dharmas (the ultimate), on the one hand, and the complex objects which have these as their parts (the conventional), on the other.

In a late Abhidharma text, *Abhhidharmakośa-Bhāṣya* (Commentary on the Treasury of Abhidharma), Vasubandhu puts the matter thus:[6]

> The Fortunate One has... declared two truths, (1) conventional or relative truth (*saṃvṛitisatya*) and (2) absolute truth (*paramārthasatya*). What are these two truths?...

[4] See, e.g., Ganeri (2001), ch. 4.

[5] It would be wrong, however, to equate this with the contemporary Western notion of being instantaneous. The ancient Indians had no conception of the real line. Momentary things could be experienced, and so had some minimal duration.

[6] De La Vallée Poussin and Sangpo (2012), Vol. 3, pp. 1891–2. I have removed many of the Sanskrit glosses. 'Fortunate One' is another honorific for the Buddha.

If the cognition of a thing disappears when this thing is broken into parts, this thing exists relatively or conventionally. An example is a pitcher, for when the pitcher is broken into shards, the cognition of a pitcher disappears, or does not arise.

If the cognition of a thing disappears when the [(constituent) factors of this thing] are mentally removed [*apoha*], this thing too should be regarded as existing relatively or conventionally. An example is water, for when—with respect to water—we [mentally] take and remove the factors, such as visible form or color [*rūpa*], etc., the cognition of the water disappears or does not arise.

To these things, e.g., pitcher, clothes, etc., water, fire, etc., different names or notions are given from the relative point of view or in accordance with conventional usage. Thus, if one says, from the relative or conventional point of view: "There is pitcher, there is water", one speaks truly, one does not speak falsely. Hence this is relative or conventional truth.

That which is other than this is absolute truth. Therein, even when a thing is being broken—or [likewise, even if its (constituent) factors] are mentally removed, and the cognition of this thing continues, then this exists absolutely. For example, visible form: for, therein, when a visible [thing] is broken into atoms or infinitesimal particles and when taste and the other factors have been mentally removed, the cognition of the intrinsic nature [*svabhāva*] of visible form persists. Sensation, etc., is also to be seen in the same way. As this exists absolutely, this is absolute truth.

Ultimate reality, then, is the reality of the dharmas. We do not, at least normally, have access to this; but it is what reality ultimately comprises. Moreover, each dharma is a metaphysical atom. It is what it is, completely independently of anything else. Its nature is intrinsic. In Sanskrit, it is described as having *svabhāva*, which may be translated as *self-being* or *self-nature* (sva-bhāva); I'll stick to the latter.[7]

Conventional reality, by contrast, is the reality with which we are familiar in everyday life: the world of people and stars, chairs, and rivers. This does not have the same kind of reality as the dharmas. The objects of this reality are conceptual constructions out of the dharmas. Think of the Equator. There is no actual line around the circumference of the Earth. But we have a word *Equator*, that applies to the points on the circumference, constituting it as an object of thought. In the same way, a partite object, such as Graham Priest, is simply an evolving bunch

[7] The notion of svabhāva has multiple resonances. (See, for example, the discussion in Westerhoff (2010), ch. 2.) In particular, it is sometimes translated into English as *essence*, namely, that without which something could not be the kind of thing it is. Furthermore, svabhāva cannot be 'analysed away', either mereologically or conceptually. (See the quote from Vasubandhu above.) However, having a certain intrinsic nature would seem to be the core of the matter. If the nature of something is intrinsic, it cannot depend on other things, such as parts and concepts. So it cannot be analysed in terms of these. Moreover, if something has an intrinsic nature, then that is its nature—that is, what makes it the kind of thing it is. Note that, in the Aristotelian tradition, the essence of something does not have to be intrinsic. Thus, Socrates is a snub-nosed man (that is, human). *Snub-nosed* is one of his accidents; *being human* is his essence. But being human depends on having certain physical and mental parts, and so is not intrinsic in the pertinent sense.

of dharmas, but we have a concept *Graham Priest*, which we apply to these, constituting them as a single object.

The concepts deployed in this process of construction are those which help us get around the world. Nor is this a fixed stock: the concepts of modern science and technology are novel by historical standards, but they help us get around in the contemporary world. The concepts, however, are conventional in a certain sense. Perhaps, had we been different creatures, say those with the sensory organs of a dog or a bat, we would have quite different concepts germane to our ends.

There is a standard question in mereology. Let Σ be a set of things. Which Σs are such that their members 'fuse' together to form one thing? Some, mereological nihilists, say *none*. Some, mereological universalists, say *all*.[8] Some, in-betweenists, say *some*: the parts of Σ fuse if they hang together in a certain sense. Thus, *my* parts hang together (at least on a good day); but there is no cohesion between the members of the set that contains just the Buddha's left earlobe, the Rings of Saturn, and the number π.

At the level of ultimate reality, the Abhidharma philosophers were nihilists. A fusion of parts can never be a dharma: it would be dependent on its parts, and so not have svabhāva. At the level of conventional reality, it is natural to see the Abhidharma philosophers as in-betweenists. We have a fusion just when there is an appropriate concept which applies to the dharmas constituting the parts.[9] Perhaps, in some sense, we have a concept 'x is an atom of the Buddha's left ear lobe, or the Rings of Saturn, or π'; but it is hardly one which we find helpful in getting round the world (at least at the moment!).

3.4 Are There Dharmas?

We now have the Abhidharma picture before us. It was attacked by Nāgārjuna, and we will come to his arguments against it in the next chapter. For the rest of this chapter, let us consider arguments which might be mounted in favour of it. For

[8] Though an exception is often made when Σ is the empty set.

[9] So, technically, let $x \prec y$ be 'x is a proper part of y' (i.e. a part that is not the whole). Let $\alpha(x)$ be 'x is an atom'. So if $\alpha(x)$ expresses the claim that there is no y such that $y \prec x$. Then we may define:

- $At(x) = \{y : \alpha(y) \wedge y \preceq x\}$

$At(x)$ is the set containing just x, if x is an atom, and the set containing all the atoms that are its parts otherwise.

- $At(\Sigma) = \bigcup_{x \in \Sigma} At(x)$

Given a set of objects, Σ, $At(\Sigma)$ is the set of atoms of all its members. Then if $\oplus\Sigma$ is the fusion of Σ:

- $\oplus\Sigma$ exists iff there is some C such that for any y, Cy iff $y \in At(\Sigma)$

The fusion of a set of objects exists iff there is some concept that applies exactly to its atoms.

the most part, the Abhidharma literature concerns itself mainly with articulating the view, rather than attempting to justify it. So let us see what can be done on its behalf. The Abhidharma picture contains a number of philosophical claims. Let us take these one by one.

First, and perhaps most fundamentally, there is the claim that objects are composed of partless parts—mereological simples. Why should one suppose that there are such things? Intuitively appealing as it may be, this is not at all obvious. Just consider the real line, and let its parts be all the open sub-intervals.[10] Take one to be a part of another if it is a proper subset. Then any part has parts, since any interval has left and right parts. The picture is perfectly coherent. So how might one argue that reality is *not* like that?[11]

One famous answer was given by Kant, in the Second Antinomy of his *Critique of Pure Reason*, and goes like this:[12]

> Let us assume that composite substances are not made up of simple parts. If all composition then be removed in thought, no composite part, and (since we admit no simple parts), also no simple parts, that is to say, nothing at all will remain, and accordingly, no substance will be given. Either, therefore, it is impossible to remove in thought all composition, or after its removal there must remain something which exists without composition, that is, the simple. In the former case the composite would not be made up of substances; composition, as applied to substances, is only an accidental relation in independence of which they must still persist as self-subsistent beings. Since this contradicts our supposition, there remains only the original supposition, that a composite substance is made up of simple parts.

Kant's argument is both dark and tangled—and, it should be remembered, he is going to argue that it does not work (since the simple is a noumenon, and so the categories cannot be applied to it). However, *in nuce*, it would appear to be this.[13] Given any substance, it is always possible to decompose any compound part, at least in thought. This is because the fact that something is arranged (composed) in a certain way is always a contingent one. Now, take any substance, and suppose that it is not composed of simples. Decompose it through and through. Nothing will be left, which is impossible since, in that case, the substance would have had no substance.

But the argument would not seem to work—even setting aside Kantian scruples about the noumenal. Take a substance, say the table on which I write. It is composed of cells of wood. These are composed of molecules, which are

[10] In other words, sets of the form $\{z : x < z < y\}$ for some $x \neq y$.

[11] In contemporary mereology, matter such that every part itself has parts is known as *gunk*. See Varzi (2009), 3.4.

[12] A434=B462ff. Translation from Kemp Smith (1933).

[13] See Priest (2002a), p. 90.

composed of atoms, which are composed of protons and electrons, which are composed of quarks, which . . . At each level, the behaviour of the parts explains the behaviour of the thing of which they are parts. Whether this regress does eventually terminate, we may never, in fact, know. But there is nothing logically absurd about supposing that physics will find indefinitely smaller and smaller particles—or maybe better, more and more fundamental kinds of thing—and so more and more fundamental explanations. The table is a substantial entity for all that.

But—it might be replied—there *is* something objectionable about such a regress: it is vicious.[14] Leibniz makes the point this way:[15]

> Were there only beings by aggregation [composite objects], there are no real beings. For every being by aggregation presupposes beings endowed with real unity [simples], because every being derives its reality only from the reality of those beings of which it is composed, so that it will not have any reality at all if each being of which it is composed is itself a being by aggregation, a being for which we must still seek a further ground for its reality, grounds which can never be found in this way, if we must always continue to seek for them.

Leibniz's words do not really get beyond a fairly bald and dogmatic assertion that the regress is vicious. What is needed is an *argument* that it is so. One might hope to find such an argument if one takes what is at issue here to be a matter of explanation. The parts of something explain its existence; so if the parts of something have parts, and so on all the way down, then the regress is vicious, since we have no explanation of why that something exists.

Now, when is a regress of explanations vicious? The essence of a vicious explanatory regress is demonstrated by the following example. Suppose that we have a chain made of links, and I want to join the links at the two ends, *a* and *b*. I ask you how to do so. You explain that I have to insert an intervening link, *c*. I ask you how you connect *a* to *c*. You explain that you have to insert an intervening link, *d*. I then ask how I connect *d* to *a*, and you reply . . . We have a regress, and it is clearly vicious. I never have an explanation of how to join *a* and *b*.

What has gone wrong? The infinity of the situation has, in fact, little to do with it. Something has gone wrong at the very first step. I wanted to know how to join two links, and your reply leaves me with exactly the *same* problem. The infinite regress is simply a consequence of this.[16]

[14] Regress arguments of this kind appear to have used by the Hindu Vaiśeṣika philosophers for the existence of atomic substances. (Koller (2002), p. 74.) Koller also claims (p. 185) that Sarvāstivāda (one group of Abhidharma philosophers) used regress arguments of this kind.

[15] Ariew and Garber (1989), p. 85.

[16] For further discussion of vicious infinite regresses, see Priest (2014a), 1.4 and 12.5.

The regress of physical parts is not, in fact, like this. The existence of an object, x, it explained by the existence of its parts, $y_1, y_2, y_3, \ldots$ The existence of each part, say y_1, is explained by the existence of *its* parts, $z_1, z_2, z_3, \ldots$ and so on. At each stage we are explaining something different: the existence of different objects. So the regress is not vicious.

But, it still might be objected, such a regress is problematic, simply because it leaves something to be explained: why there is a regress at all. Leibniz, again, makes the point as follows:[17]

> Let us suppose that a book of the elements of geometry existed from all eternity and that in succession one copy of it was made from another, it is evident that although we can account for the present book by the book from which it was copied, nevertheless, going back through as many books as we like, we could never reach a complete reason for it, because we can always ask why such books have at all times existed, that is to say, why books at all, and why written in this way. What is true of books is also true of the different states of the world; for, in spite of certain laws of change, the succeeding state is, in some sort, a copy of that which precedes it. Therefore, to whatever earlier state you go back, you never find in it the complete reason of things, that is to say, the reason why there exists any world and why this world rather than another.

Now, two points. That the regress fails to provide an explanation of why there is anything at all is a problem only if there *is* an explanation. There is only one possible reason that I am aware of for such existence, the Principle of Sufficient Reason: every event (or state of affairs) has an explanation. Quantum mechanics appears to have disposed of this, or at least shown that there is no reason to believe it to be true. (The decay of a radioactive atom is spontaneous.) In fact, Leibniz is invoking the principle in a very strong form. There must be a *complete* explanation; that is, an explanation where one cannot go on asking *why*. There is even less reason to believe this version of the principle.

Second point: even if there is an explanation for the whole regress, that the regress itself does not provide it is not a problem. It means only that something else must. Any number of things could do this: God, the laws of physics, etc. All that the regress of parts shows is that the explanation is not a mereological one.

One might attempt a final argument for the existence of dharmas as follows. For the Abhidharma, partite objects do not exist; only partless things do. So if all objects were partite, nothing would exist: we have collapsed into nihilism. Now, as put, this objection is unfair. For the Abhidharma, partite objects *do* exist conventionally. It follows, then, that if all objects are partite, all objects exist merely conventionally. This is not nihilism: indeed it was essentially the path

[17] Latta (1898), pp. 338f.

that Mahāyāna Buddhism was to take. But one might take the argument more provocatively as one to the effect that only dharmas *really* exist. Composite objects are of a different kind, and so cannot really exist. This brings us to the next subject for scrutiny.

3.5 The Reality of Partite Objects

Let us grant the existence of partless parts, atoms, at least for the sake of argument. Is it the case that partite objects do not have the same kind of existence as the atoms—that a table, for example, is nothing over and above its atoms? The table, one might think, is simply a bunch of atoms 'arranged table-wise'.[18] But why suppose this? In other words, suppose we have a set of atoms, Σ, and the fusion of Σ, $\oplus\Sigma$, exists, why should one suppose that it does not have the same kind of reality as the members of Σ?

Again, the view does comport with a certain intuition. Suppose I have a hydrogen atom composed of a proton and electron; how many objects do I have: two or three? *Three* seems to be over-counting. Once the subatomic particles are in place, the atom is perforce present. It would seem to be an 'ontological free lunch', in the words of David Armstrong.[19]

Still, this is too fast. For a start, when we count, we normally count by *kind* of object. In our example, we have two subatomic particles, and one atom. In a perfectly clear sense, there are three objects. Moreover, it is certainly the case that when the subatomic particles are present, so is the atom. But it is equally the case that when the atom is present, so are the subatomic particles. The situation is symmetric; and without some reason to privilege the parts, the parts and the whole would appear to be on the same ontological footing. In which case, three *is* the right count.[20]

At this point, to break the symmetry it is natural to appeal to the thought that the partite objects are conceptual constructions, and such constructions have existence only in the mind of the constructor.[21] Reality is something like a Seurat painting (or a bunch of computer pixels). In reality there is just a bunch of

[18] Some care is needed here. One cannot identify the table with (the fusion of) any particular bunch of atoms. For the atoms may change, and the table remain the same table. A more careful statement is to the effect that the table *at a time* is simply (the fusion of) its atoms *at that time*.

[19] Armstrong (1997), p. 12.

[20] One way to break the symmetry is to claim that the only things which are real are the things involved in the basic laws of nature. But even if there are such laws, there are plenty of laws of nature that involve partite things, creatures like people, substances like water, and objects like atoms. To rule out these laws of nature as reality-determining sounds like special pleading.

[21] What follows is heavily indebted to the elegant Varzi (2011).

pigmented dots; but, from a distance, our cognitive apparatus carves out people, rivers, and buildings.

Now, it is true that some conceptual constructions exist only in such a way. Take the Equator again. There is nothing in concrete reality which distinguishes its points. (They are not painted red.) Its existence is constituted simply by the fact that we apply the concept *Equator* to them. Or take the constellation Orion. The stars do not form a cluster in any natural sense (they are disparate in space and time). They are a constellation simply because we single them out and give them a collective name.

However, it is not at all obvious that many of the things one would be tempted to call conceptual constructions have no objective reality. As a natural object, the Mona Lisa is simply a bunch of brush strokes on a certain canvass, but it is a work of art because we conceptualize it in a certain way. The Mona Lisa is objectively there, nonetheless. Or consider the Pacific Ocean. This is just a bunch of water, continuous with all the other bits of non-inland water in the world. It gets to be the Pacific Ocean because we conceptualize it and name it such. Again, it is objectively there nonetheless.

It would seem, then, that, though we may pick out some bunch of atoms by a concept, their fusion is there, nonetheless, in objective reality. These things are not *mere* conceptual constructions. Some of our concepts carve nature at its joints, as Plato puts it (*Phaedrus* 265e).[22]

But on closer inspection, it is not clear that nature has any joints. Take the Pacific again. Its boundaries, both spatial and temporal, are indistinct. And there is nothing in reality, such as an underwater fence, that one crosses when one passes from the Pacific to the Atlantic. It starts to look as though the Pacific is just a bunch of water that we have arbitrarily singled out. And so, one might think, it is with all concrete objects. They are all vague in space and time. Take me for example. When did I start to exist? Presumably at some stage of gestation in my mother's womb; but there is no precise point (other than a purely arbitrary—say legal—one) at which *I* came into existence. And when will I cease to exist? Death happens by degrees.[23] Or when does my lunch become me: in my mouth, in my stomach, when it is absorbed through the walls of the intestines, when it is built into the cells of my body? There is no determinate answer.

The parts of the Pacific Ocean certainly interact causally with each other. But they interact with other things too: the atmosphere, coastlines, adjacent bodies of water. So there is nothing that naturally holds the Pacific together as one thing.

[22] See also his *Statesman* 287c.

[23] Even if I am blown apart in an explosion, it takes time for my parts to fragment.

And the same goes for me, as Buddhism insists. The Pacific Ocean, I, and all other partite objects, *are* merely conceptual carvings.

The problems here are essentially ones of vagueness, and most macroscopic objects are vague in space and time. But what of sub-macroscopic objects? Take a hydrogen atom—one proton and one electron. There seems to be no vagueness in this. True, there may be some epistemic uncertainty about the spatial and temporal extension of the atom, but there is no temptation to draw a boundary around anything other than these two things. Matters seem quite precise. We are back with nature having joints, and the reality of the mereological compound.

And while we are talking about precision, what of mathematical objects? (Not that these were on the agenda of Buddhist philosophers.) There is a whole menagerie of these: numbers, topological spaces, categories, etc. To keep things simple, let us suppose that the orthodox—but highly dubious—view that these are all sets of different kinds is correct. What is one to say about these? There is, of course, the question of what—if any—the parts of sets are. But a simple view is that the parts of a set include, at least, its members[24]—or if one is David Lewis, their singletons.[25] There would seem to be no vagueness here. The identity of a set is determined by the Axiom of Extensionality, as precise as one can get.[26] It seems, then, that at least once mathematical objects are part of our concern, considerations of vagueness cannot be appealed to.

What we have seen, then, is that there would appear to be at least some partite obects which have the same kind of reality as their parts, though many may well not do so.

3.6 The Dharmas: Conceptual Dependence

But whatever one makes of this question, one can at least agree that partite objects depend on their parts, and so have no svabhāva. The third Abhidharma claim that we should put under the microscope is that partless objects themselves have svabhāva. Are they, indeed, what they are, in and of themselves?

Well, what else could they depend on for being what they are? The one thing that they cannot depend on is their parts: they don't have any. Could the parts depend on the wholes of which they are parts? There are some philosophers who have held that parts depend for their identity on wholes, at least sometimes. Thus,

24 See Priest (2014a), 9.2. The universal of being a set is thrown in for good measure.

25 Lewis (1991).

26 I talk of standard sets here. Some hold that there are fuzzy sets, where membership comes by degrees. These are a different matter.

Aristotle held this for organic unities. A hand depends for its being a hand on the fact that it is part of a functioning person. Once it is cut off, it is no longer a hand.[27] But this seems implausible for most things. Thus, if I remove a tyre from my bike, it remains the very same tyre, whether or not I put it back on the bike. And without Aristotle's teleology, the view doesn't even seem very plausible for biological parts. Thus, if someone has their hand severed in some horrible accident, it is possible to take it, *that very hand*, and surgically reconnect it.[28]

Another possibility is that the atoms depend on our concepts. For the Abidharma, we know, the partite wholes depend on concepts, but why should the atoms themselves not depend on concepts? True, they are not conceptual constructions in the same way. But that does not show that they are independent of all concepts. Here we hit a major issue. If the parts depend on concepts, then everything does. So the view becomes one of conceptual idealism. (This, it should be noted, is exactly the way that Yogācāra Buddhism was to go.) Now, the debate between realism and idealism is a perennial one in philosophy East and West, and we are certainly not going to adjudicate it here.[29] But let me say a few general words.

Both realism and idealism are attractive in their different ways. Realism appeals to our common-sense and scientific thinking. The cosmos existed a long time before there was sentient—and so conceptual—life anywhere in it. Its history was driven by the laws of physics, and concerned quantum waves, subatomic particles, or whatever the current physics tells us to be our best understanding of the matter. These do not depend in any way on sentience. Indeed, sentience might never have evolved, and all this might have gone on, as it were, behind everyone's backs. But sentience did evolve, and a necessary condition for sentient beings to survive in the cosmos was that they have a certain grasp of their environment. This required a conceptual understanding of matters; and if this was to be effective, then the concepts had to be adequate, at least in a gross way, to the reality they were trying to grasp. A badly flawed understanding of one's environment leads to failure in action. In the human species, many of the concepts involved were generated in the process of pre-linguistic evolution, inadequate concepts delivering the literal extinction of their bearers. More sophisticated concepts started to become available when the production of concepts itself came under conceptual control. But even then, their adequacy had, again, to be filtered though practical success and failure.

[27] See *Parts of Animals* 1.1, esp. 640^b34–641^a10.

[28] There is one Buddhist tradition which holds that a part depends for what it is on the whole (as well as vice versa). This is the Chinese Huayen tradition. (See Jones (2009) and (2015).) But a lot of heavy-duty metaphysics has to go in to making this plausible. We will come to Huayan itself in Chapter 8.

[29] For some contextualization, see Priest (2013a).

Idealism appeals to a different way of looking at matters. We have no grasp of the world outwith our conceptual apparatus. To think of a world as it is, independently of deploying any concepts, is to reduce it to the realm of *dinge an sich*. If there are such things, we can know nothing of them. The reality we inhabit is thoroughly conceptually saturated. This is not to say that there was no world temporally prior to sentience; but only that any such world, like anything else is (and was) what it is (and was) only in virtue of our conceptualizing it in a certain way. The world, then, answers to our conceptualization.

Perhaps, realism, being the more common-sense view, is the natural default assumption; and it is up to idealism to dislodge it. This may give the realism of the Abhidharma tradition some advantage.[30] So the view that the dharmas are not conceptually dependent has the edge in the debate—at least unless some argument for idealism in general can overthrow it.

3.7 The Dharmas: Causation

Another thing that the nature of a partless part might be thought to depend on is the nature of other partless parts. The Abhidharma philosophers held, as we have seen, that there are causal relations between the dharmas. Such relationships did not, however, have anything to do with their nature. The view, at root, is similar to that of Hume. For him, reality is constituted by atomic existences. There is no objective causal glue which holds them together—at least as far as one can tell. Causation is a kind of constant conjunction. Hume's argument for his view on causation is, essentially, an empiricist one: we cannot perceive a causal connection as such. Now, it is not clear that this is right: at least arguably, I can not just feel the wind blowing and see the trees moving: I can perceive the wind *blowing* the trees. (Perception, as is now generally accepted, is theory-laden.)[31] But set this aside; such empiricism is now badly dated, due, if nothing else, to the developments of modern science, which tells us that there are lots of things we cannot see. So a defence of the Abhidharma view cannot go down that path.

The Abhidharma view is also similar to the atomism of Wittgenstein's *Tractatus*. States of affairs are completely independent of one another, and a world is constituted by a bunch of these, which can be mixed and matched at will. However, even Wittgenstein was forced to renege on this view. He recanted, in the only other thing he published in his lifetime,[32] due to the conceptual

[30] Note that a realist does not have to hold that *everything* is conceptually independent. Just that *some* things are.

[31] See, e.g., Chalmers (2013), ch. 3, and Hanson (1958).

[32] Wittgenstein (1929).

interdependence of colours. So there does not seem much joy for the Abhidharma tradition here either.[33]

So why might one suppose that the causal relations between things make their natures interconnected? (This was, indeed, exactly the direction in which Madhyamaka Buddhism was to go, as we shall see.) It is a fairly standard view, even in Western philosophy, that causation determines *when* something comes into existence, but not *what* it is.[34] But this is not at all obvious.

What makes me the very person I am? Answer (in part): the way my parents treated me, the education I received, my professional experiences, etc. These are causal factors. It might be thought that people are special in this way. Not so. What makes something an oak tree? The fact that it grows out of an acorn, delivers acorns, etc. If it grew out of an onion, and delivered, not acorns, but goldfish, it would not be an oak tree. So maybe it's just biological entities that are like this? Again, no. Take an electron. This is the kind of thing which repels particles of the same kind, which is annihilated by positrons, etc. If it were attracted by other particles of the same kind, and annihilated by neutrons, it would not be an electron. Causation, it would seem, *can* determine the natures of objects in the causal flux. Having seen this, much of the Abhidharma view that the dharmas do not relate to each other for their nature loses its appeal.

3.8 Conclusion

In the second half of this chapter, we have been looking at the sorts of grounds one might have for key elements of the Abhidharma view. Though the considerations can hardly claim to be conclusive, we have covered enough ground to see that there is plenty of room for doubt. And doubt to the point of rejection did develop in the Mahāyāna tradition. In the next chapter we will be concerned with how this played itself out in the Madhyamaka wing of Indian Mahāyāna.

[33] Some Abhidharma philosophers argued that a cause and its effect can never be simultaneous. In particular, when one exists, the other does not. Hence, there can never be a real relation between them. Such a relation is therefore a mere conceptual construction, and so cannot determine the nature of one of its relata. There are many ways one might object to this argument. For a start, one might contest the principle that there cannot be a real relationship involving something that does not exist. Thus, a giant meteor strike caused the extinction of the dinosaurs: it triggered a chain of events which led to their demise. The chain of events was real enough, even though at the time of the demise, the meteor strike had—let us agree—ceased to exist. Or one may contest the claim that cause and event cannot be simultaneous. Thus, a window starts to break the instant the baseball hits it; and depressing one end of a see-saw causes the other end to rise at the same time. For further discussion of Abhidharma and related views on causation, see Westerhoff (2009), ch. 5.

[34] See, e.g., the first few sentences of Tahko and Lowe (2015).

Fig. 2. Nāgārjuna

PART II

Later India

4

Emptiness

4.1 Introduction

In this chapter we turn to the reaction against the Abhidharma metaphysics of pre-Mahāyāna forms of Buddhism, and the role which the catuṣkoṭi plays in this. We will start by looking at the new sort of sūtra that appeared around the beginning of the common era, the *Prajñāpāramitā Sūtras*. We will then turn to the text that crystallized the philosophy of the new form of Buddhism, Nāgārjuna's *Mūlamadhyamakakārikā*. We will see, in all this, the central role of the notion of emptiness (*śūnyatā*), and the engagement of the catuṣkoṭi in the dialectic—a dialectic in which the catuṣkoṭi itself morphs into a new form.

4.2 The *Heart Sūtra*

The *Prajñāpāramitā Sūtras* (Perfection of Wisdom Sūtras) are a group of sūtras of uncertain origin, but which heralded the arrival of a new form of Buddhism, Mahāyāna (the Greater Vehicle).[1] There were central innovations of both an ethical and a metaphysical nature. On the ethical side, compassion (karuṇā) became of central importance. The older forms of Buddhism had always endorsed the importance of compassion. Compassion was an excellent technique for helping to get rid of the illusion of self. But in Mahāyāna Buddhism, it becomes the central virtue. Consequently, the Buddhist ideal becomes, not the arhat—someone who seeks to achieve enlightenment for themself—but the bodhisattva (awakening being), who is dedicated to achieving enlightenment for everyone. Indeed, enlightenment is now thought of as coming in stages, and the bodhisattva takes a vow not to take the final stage on the path, *parinirvāṇa*—though they could do so—until everyone can.

[1] See Williams (2009), ch. 2.

Our concern here is not with ethics, but with metaphysics, however.[2] The central concept here is that of emptiness (śūnyatā; Chin: *kong*; Jap: *kū*). The Abhidharma position, as we saw, held that nothing has svabhāva except the dharmas. Mahāyāna got rid of the exception. *Nothing* has svabhāva. That is, everything is empty (śūnya) of intrinsic nature: everything is what it is in virtue of its relation to other things.[3]

The matter is stated clearly in one of the shortest and most famous of the *Prajñāpāramitā Sūtras*, the *Heart Sūtra* (*Prajñāpāramitāhṛdaya*),[4] the central part of which starts as follows:[5]

> ... the venerable Śāriputra approached the noble Avalokiteśvara and asked him, "How should a son of noble lineage proceed when he wants to train in the profound discipline of the perfection of wisdom?" The noble Avalokiteśvara replied to the venerable Śāriputra: If any son or daughter of the noble lineage who wants to train in the profound discipline of the perfection of wisdom s/he should consider things in the following way: First, s/he should understand clearly and thoroughly that the five aggregates are empty of essence. Form is empty. Emptiness is form. Emptiness is not other than form. Form is not other than emptiness. In the same sense, feeling, perception, dispositions and consciousness are also empty. In the same sense, Śāriputra, all phenomena are empty. They have no defining characteristics. They are unarisen; they are unceasing. They are neither diminishing nor increasing.

Recall that the parts of a person are of five kinds: form (matter), feeling, discrimination, compositional factors, and consciousness. The text says that all these parts are empty of svabhāva; and then goes on to say that all phenomena are like that.[6]

[2] The connection, if there is one, between the ethical developments and the metaphysical developments is debatable. For my take on the matter, see Priest (2014a), ch. 15.

[3] That is, *some* other things. In the Huayan version of Mahāyāna, this becomes *all* other things, as we shall see in a later chapter.

[4] 'Heart' because it is held to contain the core of the Māhāyana views. Modern scholarship, however, suggests that the text is apocryphal, being of Chinese origin, somewhere between the second and fourth centuries CE. See Keown (2003), p. 106.

[5] The translation comes from Garfield (2016).

[6] The 'form is empty' passage is the heart of the *Heart Sūtra*. The apparent repetitiveness of this may puzzle. In his commentary, Garfield (2016) teases apart the quartet of claims involved as follows:

> "Form is empty" means that form lacks intrinsic identity, inherent existence, essence. It is empty of essence or of intrinsic nature. The reason for this is that all material phenomena are dependently arisen. Every material phenomenon is dependent in three important senses: dependent upon causes and conditions for its existence; dependence on its parts and on the wholes in which it figures for its existence and identity; and dependent on conceptual imputation for its identity. The details of each of these kinds of dependence are developed extensively in many Madhyamaka texts.
>
> "Emptiness is form" means that the fact that form is empty does not entail that emptiness is the *reality* lying behind an illusory material world. Emptiness is no more intrinsically existent or substantial than matter. Emptiness, that is, is only the

We are not done yet, though. The text goes on:

> Therefore, Śāriputra, in emptiness there is no form, no feeling, no perception, no dispositions, no consciousness; no eye, no ear, no nose, no tongue, no body, no mind; no visible object, no sound, no smell, no taste, no tactile sensation, no mental object; no sensory awareness; no cognitive awareness; no object of cognitive awareness. There is neither ignorance nor the end of ignorance; neither aging and death nor the end of aging and death. In the same sense, there is no suffering, no origin of suffering, no cessation and no path; no wisdom, and neither attainment nor lack of attainment. Therefore, Śāriputra, since bodhisattvas have no attainment, they depend upon and dwell in the perfection of wisdom; their minds are unobstructed and they are fearless. They transcend all error and finally reach their goal—nirvana.

Starting with the skandhas, the text runs through various bits of Abhidharma taxonomy whose details need not concern us here, and says that there are no such things. It then applies the same point to what are, in effect, the Four Noble Truths. There is no suffering, no cause of suffering, no cessation of suffering, no path to make this happen.

This sounds like Buddhist heresy. What is going on here? Recall the doctrine of two realities. What this passage is saying is that in ultimate reality there are none of these things: they are all merely conventional. We have, after all, got rid of all things with svabhāva. Everything that is left is empty.

4.3 Emptiness

Matters, however, are more complex than this. Note that the text talks not only about being empty, but empt*iness*, śūnyatā. (The Sanskrit -*tā* turns an adjective into an abstract noun.) The word *could* refer to the property of being empty; but that is clearly not how it is functioning here. When the text says 'Therefore, in

emptiness *of form*. No form, no emptiness of form (*mutatis mutandis* for the other aggregates). Emptiness is hence also dependently arisen, dependent upon that of which it is the emptiness.

"Emptiness is not other than form" means that if one spells out analytically what it is to be material form—a thing that comes into existence as a result of causes and conditions, that exists only dependently, only impermanently, that depends on its parts, etc. one has spelled out what it is to be empty. The relationship between emptiness—ultimate reality—and material form—standing in for conventional reality—is hence not accidental, but rather one of identity. To be conventionally real is to be empty.

"Form is not other than emptiness" makes the converse point. Emptiness is not a mysterious self-existent void. To spell out what emptiness is—dependency on causes and conditions, impermanence, dependence on conceptual imputation, etc., is to spell out the nature of conventional reality. To be empty is to be conventionally real.

emptiness, Śāriputra, there is no form . . .', it is not saying that the property of emptiness is not material. It is telling us something about some kind of reality, and it is obviously not conventional reality. 'Emptiness' is being used to refer to ultimate reality. But what is that? It is not the reality of the dharmas: they have gone. So what can it be? Here is a problem which was to exercise subsequent generations of Buddhist philosophers.

Some clues can be found from other things in the *Prajñāpāramitā Sūtras*. At one point in the *Aṣṭadaśasāhasrikā Prajñāpāramitā Sūtra* (*Prajñāpāramitā Sūtra* of 18,000 Verses) there is a discussion of how to grasp ultimate reality. The Buddha replies that one needs to give up making conceptual discriminations. When asked what that means, he says:[7]

> The non-duality of existence and non-existence, as well as the absence of intellectual multiplicity with regard to dharmas, such as form, etc. and also with regard to emptiness of form, etc. that should be viewed as the inherent mark of non-discrimination.

There is no duality in ultimate reality. Conceptual discriminations are, after all, a mark of conventional reality. One should give up all discriminations: even that between being empty and not being empty.

I note that we meet here for the first time the notion of duality and its transcendence. Questions about this were to assume an ever-increasing importance in Buddhist metaphysics, as we shall see in due course. All we need note for the moment is that if ultimate reality is free from all conceptual discriminations, it cannot be described: to describe is to employ concepts. The sūtras take the point to heart. In a discussion of how it is possible for the Mahāyāna view to 'go forth' (that is, be propagated), the same sūtra says:[8]

> When again Subhuti has said, "surpassing the world with its gods, men, and Asuras,[9] that vehicle [GP: Mahāyāna] will go forth," what then is the world with its gods, men and Asuras? The world of sense desire, the world of form, the formless world. If the world of sense desire, the world of form, or the formless world were Suchness, Non-falseness, unaltered Suchness, if they were the Unperverted, Truly Real, True Reality, That which is as reality is, the Permanent, Stable, Eternal, Not liable to reversal, existence and non-existence, then that great vehicle would not go forth, after having surpassed the world with its gods, men, and Asuras. But because the world of sense desire, the world of form, and the formless world have been constructed by thought, fabricated from fictions and feigned, because they are not as reality really is, but entirely impermanent, unstable, not eternal, liable to reversal, and non-existence, therefore the great vehicle will go forth, after having surpassed the world with its gods, men, and Asuras.

[7] Conze (1979), p. 651. [8] Conze (1979), p. 182.
[9] An Asura is something like an evil demon.

What is being said is that the conventional world is necessary for the propagation of Mahāyāna. If conventional reality were like ultimate reality (ineffable), this would be impossible. Note that ultimate reality is described in a number of different ways, and one of these is 'Suchness'. The Sanskrit is *tathātā*. 'Tathā' means *in that manner, so, thus* (as said when pointing). So a more accurate translation would be something like *thusness*. Ultimate reality is given that epithet precisely because it cannot be described: one can only point to it—or better, come face to face with in it. As the *Aṣṭasāhasrikā Prajñāpāramitā Sūtra* (*Prajñāpāramitā Sūtra* of 8,000 Verses) puts it:[10]

> With the thought that all these [GP: levels of awakening] are, through Suchness, not two, nor divided, not discriminated, undiscriminate, [a Buddha] enters on this Suchness, the nature of Dharma. After he has stood firmly in Suchness, he neither imagines nor discriminates it. In that sense, does he enter into it. When he has thus entered on it . . . he firmly believes that 'it is just this, just Suchness', and like that he plunges into it.

But don't these quotations describe thatness in a number of ways? Indeed they do. Here is a paradox which will concern us greatly in due course. But let us pass it over for the time being, and turn to Nāgārjuna.

4.4 The Attack on Svabhāva

It was the work of Nāgārjuna which put the metaphysical ideas to be found in the *Prajñāpāramitā Sūtras* on a more secure and systematic basis. He wrote several things, but by far the most important for our purposes is his *Mūlamadhyamakakārikā*, Fundamental Verses of the Middle Way (*madhyamaka*: middle way; *kārikā*: verses; *mūla*: fundamental). The text is often referred to (for obvious reasons!), simply as the MMK.[11]

This is a difficult and often elusive text; and this is so for a couple of reasons. First, as the name says, it is written in verse form. The tradition in which Nāgārjuna was working was a largely oral one. In this tradition, things were often written in poetry, so that the rhythm and rhyme made it easier for students to memorize. When teaching, recitations of the verses could be accompanied by a philosophical commentary by the teacher, explaining the points being made in detail. In some texts of this kind, the author's commentary (the *autocommentary*) is available. In the case of the MMK, nothing of this kind seems to have survived. Had it done so, this would surely have made many things clearer. Without it, a

[10] Conze (1973), p. 200.

[11] See Williams (2009), ch. 3, Siderits (2007), ch. 9. Much of what follows is taken from Priest (2013b).

good deal of philosophical reconstruction is required, and this is bound to be contentious. There are significant differences of interpretation within the Indian, Tibetan, and Chinese traditions, to say nothing of those in the West, where commentators often see the text though the eyes of Kantianism, Postmodernism, or some other Western *ism*.[12]

The second thing that makes the text difficult is that, like Wittgenstein's *Investigations*, many of the things said are in the mouths of interlocutors and opponents, but this is not flagged explicitly. If one is not reasonably clear about which words belong to envisaged interlocutors, one will be entirely confused. As in the case of Wittgenstein, one has to have a rough sense of what is going on before one can judge which words are those of interlocutors. Like Wittgenstein, too, Nāgārjuna does not identify his opponents. We are, then, thrown into Gadamer's hermeneutic circle—at the deep end.

So, to the content of the text. The first two thirds of this comprise a bunch of arguments against the view that things have svabhāva. This is agreed upon by virtually all commentators. The last third is an exploration of the consequences of this attack: both metaphysical and soteriological. This is where different commentators may well part company.

Let us start with the attack on svabhāva. The attack is largely piecemeal. Each chapter takes one of the things one might well take (or which had been taken) to have svabhāva, and argues against it. Thus, chapter 1 targets causation, chapter 2 targets motion, chapter 8 targets coming into being and passing away, and so on.

Typically, the text says that the thing in question does not exist. (Motion does not exist, causation does not exist, arising and ceasing do not exist.) One might therefore interpret the text as advocating some kind of nihilism: nothing of the form 'so and so exists' is true. Such an interpretation is indeed possible, but it sits ill with the only sūtra explicitly cited in the text, *Discourse to Kātyāyana* (MMK XV: 7), in which the Buddha says explicitly that one should take a middle way between reification and nihilism. It is better, then, to take the statements of non-existence to mean that the thing in question does not exist with self-nature; it exists, but dependently. (Of course, some things do not exist at all, such as the self.)

In each chapter, we start with an assumption that something or other has self-nature (though this is never made explicitly).[13] This is then shown to lead to unacceptable conclusions, and so rejected by *reductio*. Often the argument is by

[12] So let me, at this point, remind the reader of the warning of §0.3 of the Preface. The interpretation given here is close to that of Garfield (1995).

[13] See, e.g., Westerhoff (2010), p. 14.

cases. The cases, however, are those of the catuṣkoṭi, which Nāgārjuna takes for granted.[14] Each of the koṭis is shown to be unacceptable.[15]

Thus, in chapter 1 Nāgārjuna considers the possibility that something is (self-naturedly) caused by itself, by another, by both, or by neither, rejecting each. This is an important chapter, since part of the argument targets the Abhidharma view of causation. The notion of a causal connection between atoms is, he argues, incoherent. Since each is supposed to be entirely independent of the others, there can be no causal connection. Another example of the deployment of the catuṣkoṭi occurs in chapter 25, which is about nirvāṇa (the post-awakening state). Nāgārjuna considers the four possibilities, that it exists, does not exist, both, and neither, and rejects each. We will come back to this chapter of the MMK in more detail later.

Another form of argument that Nāgārjuna is fond of is a regress argument. He notes that on certain assumptions, an infinite regress of dependence arises (e.g. MMK VII: 3). This is not a problem for him. Since everything depends on something else, of course there is an infinite regress of dependence. However, it is a problem for his opponents; for someone who holds that there are dharmas with svabhāva, must hold such a regress to be impossible. The assumption of svabhāva, then, makes the regress unacceptable.

Nāgārjuna's arguments are often long and complex, and this is hardly the place to unpack all the details.[16] However, let us look at one in more detail. Often, the arguments Nāgārjuna deploys on each topic are specific to that topic. But Nāgārjuna does have one very general argument. The topic of MMK V is space. It has characteristics—concepts which apply to it; for example (not Nāgārjuna's), being infinite in all directions (or whatever your preferred geometry of space is); it is the locus of events (or objects); it exists through all time, etc. Moreover, it depends for being what it is on possessing those characteristics (or at least some of them). Thus, if it were grey, had a trunk, and roamed the plains of Africa (or an enclosure of some zoo), it would no longer be space. Hence, space depends

[14] It might be wondered how a *reductio* argument can work if the possibility of accepting a contradiction is explicitly on the table, given the third koṭi. The answer is that the *reductio* is reductio *ad absurdum*, not reductio *ad contradictionem*. And there are many non-contradictions that are more absurd than many contradictions. For example, it is more absurd that I am a poached egg than that the liar sentence is both true and false. Moreover, it should be remembered that Nāgārjuna is targeting many of his arguments against specific opponents. That is, they are *ad hominem* (in the non-pejorative sense). It is therefore necessary only that the *opponents targeted* find the consequence of the *reductio* unacceptable. And if the opponent does accept the Law of Non-Contradiction, a contradiction *is* an unacceptable consequence.

[15] Sometimes the third koṭi is dealt with summarily, as having been disposed of with the first. An argument against something being true is, after all, an argument against it being *both* true and false.

[16] A lot of unpacking is done in Westerhoff (2009).

for being what it is on possessing those characteristics—at least some of them, anyway. It does not, therefore, have self-nature. Though the particular topic is space, it is clear that this form of argument applies to anything with characteristics (that is, anything). We have here, then, a sort of 'master argument', in the sense that it is topic-neutral.

4.5 To be Empty

Let us now turn to the more vexed question of the picture that emerges in the last third of the text. One thing, at least, is clear. Nāgārjuna holds that everything that exists depends for being what it is on other things. That is, everything is empty of self-nature, just as the *Prajñāpāramitā Sūtras* say. The dependence in question may be of many different kinds. An object may depend on at least some or all of: its parts, its causes (and maybe effects), how it is conceptualized; and maybe even other things. But since everything depends on some things, there is no ultimate ground to reality.

As an aside, it is hard to think of a position that endorses such a view in Western philosophy.[17] Perhaps one reason why such a view does not register in the Western canon is that the regress of being is usually taken to be vicious (e.g. by Leibniz, Kant).[18] However, as we saw in 3.4, it is not.

But what, exactly, is it for something to have its being in an empty way? A perhaps helpful way of understanding this, especially for those coming from a background of Western philosophy, is by thinking of Leibniz's notion of time. What is it to be a particular time, say 1066? According to Newton, times are things existing in and of themselves. They would have been there, even had the universe been empty of all matter and events. By contrast, Leibniz gave a relational account of time. To be 1066 is to be before Britain's colonization of Australia, after Caesar's invasion of Britain, contemporary with the Norman invasion of Britain, and so on. 1066 is simply a locus in a set of temporal relations between events.[19] Does that mean that it does not exist? In a sense, yes: the time does not exist in the way that Newton took it to; it has no intrinsic being but it is, and is what it is, only as this locus in a bunch of relations.

[17] It might be thought that the structural realism of Ladyman et al. (2007) does this. But as I read this view, all things depend in the last instance on a structural relation-matrix, and the matrix itself does not depend on anything. Nāgārjuna might well be happy with the thought that objects depend on their structural matrix, but would insist that this matrix is as empty as anything else.

[18] See Bliss and Priest (2018).

[19] Of course, for Nāgārjuna, events themselves must be empty. I am not suggesting that Leibniz shares this view.

Similarly, what is it to be Graham Priest? My being is constituted by having been born in London in 1948, being the child of George and Laura, residing most of my adult life in Australia, being the father of Marcus and Annika, dying in ?, and so on. Anything that related to those things in those ways would be me; there is no *ding an sich*, Graham Priest. My being is essentially constituted by my place in that web of relations.[20]

This, then, is what it is to exist in an empty way. We will return to this matter in a later chapter.

4.6 The Two Realities

So far, so good. But now the complications start. Since nothing has svabhāva, everything has merely conventional existence, one might therefore have expected Nāgārjuna to jettison the notion of ultimate reality. And there are certainly places which suggest this. Thus MMK XXVII: 30 says:[21]

> I prostrate to Gautama
> Who through compassion
> Taught the true doctrine
> Which leads to the relinquishing of all views.

The views in question here are views about the nature of ultimate reality. All must be given up. This might suggest that there is nothing to be talked about.

Unfortunately, he does not so dispense. (And this verse can equally well be accounted for by supposing that the ultimate is ineffable. More of that anon.) MMK XXIV: 8–10 says:

> The Buddha's teaching of the Dharma
> Is based on two truths:
> A truth of worldly convention
> And an ultimate truth.
>
> Those who do not understand
> The distinction between these two truths
> Do not understand
> The Buddha's profound truth.

[20] How wide is the web of identity-constituting relations? Does it contain the relationship between me and a flower blossoming in the Central Australian Desert? The question, though interesting, is one which we do not need to resolve here. We need to note only one thing. If the location in a network of relations is to be uniquely individuating, then a relation cannot be merely any set of ordered pairs. For such sets are too ubiquitous to individuate.

[21] Translations from the MMK are from Garfield (1995).

> Without a foundation in conventional truth
> The significance of the ultimate cannot be taught.
> Without understanding the significance of the ultimate
> Liberation cannot be achieved.

Here, Nāgārjuna is just falling into line with the passages from the *Prajñāpāramitā Sūtras* which we noted above in 4.3.[22]

A natural thought at this point is that, though the Abhidharma dharmas have gone, there is something *else* with a different kind of reality—taking the lead from the *Prajñāpāramitā Sūtras*, emptiness itself. But this is not right. For Nāgārjuna, *everything* is empty; and this includes emptiness itself. MMK XXIV: 18 tells us that:[23]

> Whatever is dependently coarisen
> That is explained to be emptiness.
> That, being a dependent designation,
> Is itself the middle way.

Lines 3 and 4 tell us that emptiness ('That') is as ontologically dependent as anything else (and that the middle way consists in neither reifying it nor taking it to be non-existent). But on what does ultimate reality depend? The short answer is that it depends on conventional reality, these being two sides of the same thing. But this thought does not seem to have been greatly developed until Chinese Buddhism. We will return to this matter in Chapter 8.

For the moment, let us ask what sense can be made of the two realities, if there is only one sort of ontological status. A standard answer is that there is one reality with two aspects—a single bicameral reality. This answer was given by Candrakīrti (fl. in the first half of the seventh century), who is one of the most authoritative commentators on Nāgārjuna in the Tibetan tradition. He explains as follows:[24]

> The Buddhas, who have an unmistakable knowledge of the nature of the two truths, proclaim that all things, outer and inner, as they are perceived by two kinds of subject (deluded consciousness on the one hand and perfectly pure wisdom on the other), possess a twin identity . . . They say that the object perceived by authentic primordial wisdom is the ultimate reality, whereas the object of a deluded perception is the relative truth.

[22] Did he have any reason for retaining the notion of ultimate reality beyond faithfulness to the sūtras? Perhaps not.

[23] The passage occurs in a discussion of emptiness immediately following the one just quoted, where Nāgārjuna tables the distinction between conventional and ultimate reality. In this context, it is natural to read 'whatever is dependently coarisen' as a reference to conventional reality, and 'emptiness (śūnyatā)' as a reference to ultimate reality.

[24] Padmakara Translation Group (2004), p. 192.

That is, objects have only one kind of reality, but this has a dual nature—a double aspect, grounding two contradictory ways of perceiving it. When perceived correctly (without conceptual imposition), its ultimate aspect is seen. When perceived incorrectly—i.e. by ordinary benighted beings like you and me—only its conventional aspect is seen.

Does this mean that the reality itself is contradictory? Perhaps, but not necessarily. For example, we might interpret these aspects as dispositions to be perceived in certain ways. Having the disposition to appear such that A and the disposition to appear such that $\neg A$ are not contradictories.

At any rate, if these are both objective aspects of the one reality, what makes one of them ultimate—'more real'? It may be helpful to consider Kant here. According to his transcendental idealism, our perceptions ('intuitions')—say of a table—are the product of two things: a raw sensory input and a mental imposition: the forms of space and time, and the concepts of the understanding. The empirical object, then, has these dual aspects, and one of these involves conceptual imposition. What is imposed is not there *in re*.

Candrakīrti's account of reality might be thought of in the same way. (Though one should not push the analogy too far. There is no suggestion in Candrakīrti that the concepts are universal and *a priori*—quite the opposite. So much the better for Candrakīrti.) The difference between Candrakīrti and Kant concerns not the dual nature, or the conceptual overlay, but in our access to the conceptually naked. Seeing such a thing is an impossibility for Kant. Our perceptual apparatus just doesn't work that way. But it is what you *would* see if, *per impossible*, you were able to do this. For Candrakīrti there is no such impossibility. Difficult it may be; impossible it is not. It is exactly what training in certain meditative practices gives you.

More importantly—and to return to our question of the last paragraph but one—the one aspect of the reality of an object is more ultimate than the other, precisely because it dispenses with an extrinsic conceptual overlay.

Moreover, the conventional reality of something is misleading, in that it appears that the conceptual impositions are actually *in re*. Recall that the Sanskrit for conventional reality is *saṃvṛti-satya*. 'Saṃvṛti' is a somewhat ambiguous word. This can certainly mean conventional, true by agreement, dependent on the social and linguistic conventions, everyday; but it also carries the connotation of being deceptive.[25]

[25] There are passages in the MMK which might be taken to suggest that conventional reality is illusory. Thus, for example, MMK VII: 34 says: Like a dream, like an illusion,/ Like a city of Gandharvas,/ So have arising, abiding/ And ceasing been explained. (Gandharvas are mythical

4.7 Ultimate Reality and Ineffability

We are still not out of the woods yet, though. What is the conventional aspect of reality like? It is easy for Nāgārjuna to answer that question. It is the world of shoes and ships and sealing wax, and cabbages and kings—or the ancient Indian equivalents. It is simply our *Lebenswelt*. But what of the ultimate aspect of reality?

For Nāgārjuna's answer, come back to the status of the enlightened person after death, which we met in 2.2. Nāgārjuna picks up the Buddha's silence. MMK XXV: 17, 18 tell us:[26]

> Having passed into nirvāṇa, the Victorious Conqueror
> Is neither said to be existent
> Nor said to be non-existent.
> Neither both nor neither are said.
>
> So when the victorious one abides, he
> Is neither said to be existent
> Nor said to be non-existent.
> Neither both nor neither are said.

And why so? Nāgārjuna gives the answer in MMK XXII; he runs through the four cases of the catuṣkoṭi on the matter, rejecting each of them. He summarizes his conclusions as follows (MMK XXII: 11–12):

> 'Empty' should not be asserted.
> 'Nonempty' should not be asserted.
> Neither both nor neither should be asserted.
> They are used only nominally.
>
> How can the tetralemma of permanent and impermanent, etc.,
> Be true of the peaceful?
> How can the tetralemma of the finite, infinite, etc.,
> Be true of the peaceful?

Given that the tetralemma gives an exhaustive catalogue of things that can be said, it is clear that the state of the Buddha (Tathāgata) is ineffable.

But a few verses later, we are told that reality and a Tathāgata have the same nature, MMK XXII: 16ab:

> Whatever is the essence of the Tathāgata
> This is the essence of the world.

beings.) But a careful examination of the context of this verse (and others of a similar kind) shows that it is these states, taken to have self-nature, which are illusory—or perhaps a better way to put it, is that it is our (pre-enlightenment) view of the world which is deceptive.

[26] 'Victorious Conqueror' is one of the many honorifics for (a) Buddha.

Indeed, it is a common view in Buddhism that the Buddha has three distinct embodiments, one of which is just reality itself, the *Dharmakāya* (reality body, embodiment of truth). So we are being told that the ultimate reality of something is ineffable.[27] The distinctions of the catuṣkoṭi are, as the verse says, used only nominally, and cannot be applied to what cannot be named.

This does not mean that it cannot be experienced. It can (with appropriate training). But our knowledge of it can be only knowledge by acquaintance, not by description. All one can do, as it were, is point at it. It is a simple thusness.

That language (mental fabrication) does not apply to the ultimate is made quite explicit at MMK XVIII: 9, which says:[28]

> Not dependent on another, peaceful and
> Not fabricated by mental fabrication,
> Not thought, without distinction.
> That is the character of reality.

If reality is without distinctions (and the context makes it clear that it is the ultimate aspect of reality that is in question), one cannot say that it is thus or so, as opposed to thus and so. That is, it is ineffable. As the *Vajracchedikā Sūtra* (another of the *Prajñāparamita Sūtras*) says:[29]

> [The Buddha said]: Subhūti, words cannot explain the real nature of the cosmos. Only common people fettered with desire make use of this arbitrary method.

But doesn't Nāgārjua say quite a lot about it? He certainly does. For example, in the previous quote he says that it is peaceful and without distinction (non-dual). So we have a contradiction: we talk of the ineffable. We ran across this issue in 4.3 with respect to the *Prajñāpāramitā Sūtras*. Again, let us set the matter aside for a later chapter.

[27] It is worth noting that the founder of the Hindu school of Advaita Vedānta, Śankara (fl. early ninth century CE) also denied all four possibilities of the catuṣkoṣi when applied to ultimate reality, some of his followers going further and positing a fifth possibility, *none of the above* (according to Raju (1956), pp. 703ff).

[28] This verse might be thought to deliver an exegetical problem, since line 1 appears to say that reality is not dependent on anything else, and so is not empty. One way to restore consistency is suggested with Siderits and Katsura's (2013) translation of the verse: 'Not to be attained by means of another, free [from intrinsic nature], not populated by hypostatization, devoid of falsifying conceptualization, not having many separate meanings—this is the nature of reality.' This suggests, not that the reality is non-dependent, but that one's acquaintance with it cannot be mediated by anything.

[29] Price and Wong (1990), p. 51.

4.8 Enlightenment

Before we leave the MMK, and for reasons that will become relevant also in a later chapter, let us turn to one final section of the text, one concerning enlightenment.

Matters soteriological feature most prominently in MMK XXIV and XXV. XXIV starts by an interlocutor objecting that if everything is empty, the Four Noble Truths do not exist. Nāgārjuna replies that the objector has simply confused being empty with not existing. This triggers the discussion of the two realities, and the nature of emptiness, which we have already looked at. Nāgārjuna then turns the tables on the opponent by arguing that in a world in which things have self-nature, change is impossible, even the change of enlightenment. It is thus the opponent whose views make the Four Noble Truths false. Chapter XXV then takes up the discussion of nirvāṇa which we have already looked at. In the course of all this, however, we find a remarkable statement—perhaps one of the most striking in the whole of the *Kārikās*, MMK XXV: 19–20:

> There is not the slightest difference
> Between cyclical existence and nirvāṇa.
> There is not the slightest difference
> Between nirvāṇa and cyclical existence.
>
> Whatever is the limit of nirvāṇa
> That is the limit of cyclical existence.
> There is not even the slightest difference between them,
> Or even the subtlest thing.

Cyclical existence (*saṃsāra*) is our pre-enlightenment state (called 'cyclical' because of the Buddhist view of rebirth). So what these verses appear to be saying is that there is no difference between things pre- and post-enlightenment. This seems to make a complete nonsense of Buddhist teachings. Some of the sting is taken out of the words if one interprets them as saying that there is no ultimate difference between saṃsāra and nirvāṇa: there may yet be conventional differences. But even then, since you are certainly in saṃsāra now, it follows that you are ultimately in nirvāṇa now (and so already). What should one make of this thought? The text is of little help on this matter. Let us set the question aside until Chapter 9.

4.9 Conclusion

In this chapter we have examined the genesis of Mahāyāna Buddhism, from its origins in the *Prajñāpāramitā Sūtras* to its articulation and defence in the *Mūlamadhyamakakārikā*. In this, Nāgārjuna draws on the canonical Buddhist texts, together with the ideas of the *Prajñāpāramitā* literature, in an attempt to challenge and overthrow the older Abhidharma metaphysics. What emerges is a picture of reality which is bicameral, with a familiar conventional side, and an ineffable ultimate side.

The result is a master-stroke of synthesis. However, like all great works of philosophy, the pieces don't always fit together neatly. This left much work for succeeding generations of Buddhist philosophers. One way in which the pieces don't seem to fit together concerns the catuṣkoṭi. Nāgārjuna has put together the catuṣkoṭi of four corners with an apparently incommensurable fifth. How to juggle these, whilst keeping the other balls in the air, will be the topic of the next chapter.

5

The Fifth Corner

5.1 Introduction

In the last chapter, we saw the catuṣoṭi evolve at the hands of Nāgārjuna. What causes the evolution is taking ineffability on board. How to understand the resulting situation is not at all clear. This chapter investigates. We will do this by looking at a formal model of the new catuṣkoṭi, and exploring its ramifications.

5.2 Ineffability

Perhaps the most famous Buddhist story involving ineffability, sometimes called the *Flower Sūtra*, concerns how the Buddha chose his successor, Kāśyapa. One version of this goes as follows:[1]

> In ancient times, at the assembly on Spiritual Mountain, Buddha picked up a flower and showed it to the crowd.
>
> Everyone was silent, except for the saint Kasyapa, who broke out in a smile.
>
> Buddha said, "I have the treasury eye of truth, the ineffable mind of nirvana, the most subtle of teachings on the formlessness of reality. It is not defined in words, but is specially transmitted outside of doctrine. I entrust it to Kasyapa the Elder."

There is something that is ineffable, and by his actions the Buddha conveys this to Kāśyapa—or maybe better, because of the insight he has developed being with the Buddha, Kāśyapa grasps what cannot be said.

The sūtra is of Chinese origin, and the earliest known version is from the eleventh century. It is probably a Chan writing. Perhaps more than any other Mahāyāna school, Chan emphasizes the ineffability of ultimate reality, and developed practices in order to help people to grasp it. We will see more of Chan in Chapter 9.

[1] Cleary (1993b), p. 33. See also Dumoulin (1963), p. 68.

Though the sūtra is not canonical, the thought that ultimate reality cannot be grasped in words goes right back to the origins of Mahāyāna. The verse summary of the *Aṣṭasāhasrikā Prajñāpāramitā Sūtra* says:[2]

> All words for things in use in this world must be left behind,
> All things produced and made must be transcended—
> The deathless, the supreme, incomparable gnosis is then won.
> That is the sense in which we speak of perfect wisdom.

And Nāgārjuna is being faithful to this when he says (MMK: XIII: 8):[3]

> The victorious ones have said
> That emptiness is the elimination of all views.
> For whomever emptiness is a view
> That one will accomplish nothing.

Indeed, it is so important for him, that it is stated at the very beginning of the MMK in its dedicatory verses, which read:

> I prostrate to the Perfect Buddha
> The best of teachers, who taught that
> Whatever is dependently arisen is
> Unceasing, unborn,
> Unannihilated, not permanent,
> Not coming, not going,
> Without distinction, without identity,
> And free from conceptual construction.

There are no concepts in the ultimate.

The ineffable therefore has to be incorporated in Nāgārjuna's picture. There must be a fifth possibility beyond the four koṭis of the catuṣkoṭi. But a number of the *reductio* arguments in the MMK deploy the four-valued catuṣkoṭi. If there is a fifth possibility that is not also reduced to absurdity, the arguments are not valid. How are these two facts to be reconciled?

5.3 The Fifth Koṭi

To lay the ground for answering this question, let us first see how a fifth koṭi can be added to our current four. This is a very straightforward matter. (Further details can be found in the technical appendix to this chapter, 5.9.)

[2] Conze (1973), p. 12.
[3] Again, translations from the MMK are from Garfield (1995).

We will write the fifth value as *e*.[4] The five values are now *t*, *f*, *b*, *n*, and *e*, and can be depicted in the Hasse diagram:

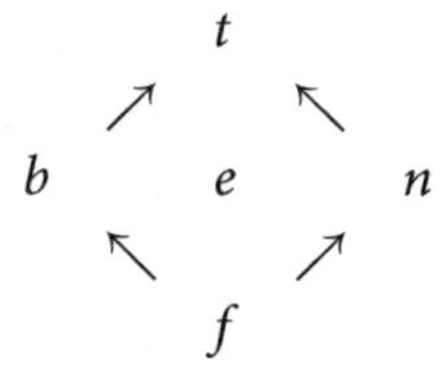

Since *e* is incomparable with the other four values (i.e. neither less than nor greater than any of them), its placing in the diagram is somewhat arbitrary. However, placing the *e* centrally maintains a pleasing symmetry, as well as suggesting that emptiness is at the heart of things.

Conjunction, disjunction, and negation work exactly as they do in FDE for the old values. For *e*, we simply add the condition that if a formula has the value *e*, so does its negation; any conjunction of which it is a conjunct, and any disjunction of which it is a disjunct, also have the value *e*. It follows that the only way a complex formula can get to take the value *e* is by its having a subformula (part) which has the value *e*.

That is exactly the way one would expect ineffability to work. If A is ineffable, so is $\neg A$; and if A or B is ineffable, so are $A \vee B$ and $A \wedge B$. Conversely, if A is effable, so is $\neg A$; and if A and B are effable, so are $A \vee B$ and $A \wedge B$.

The only thing that remains to be done to complete the specification is to say what the designated values are, i.e. those values that are preserved by valid inferences. From the old values, *t* and *b* are designated, since they are both species of truth. *e* is not designated: ineffability is not a species of truth. So the designated values are still just *t* and *b*.

I will call the logic just described FDEe.

I note that it would not be unnatural to think that the original catuṣkoṭi should have been formulated as the 4-valued logic whose values are *t*, *b*, *f*, and *e* (not *n*). In the origins of the fourth koṭi, which we looked at in 2.3, it might well be taken to be some notion of ineffability. And certainly being ineffable would seem to be one way of being neither true or false. Moreover, the logic we obtain if we simply delete *n* from the above machinations is a perfectly good 4-valued logic.

However, this possibility makes no sense, once we arrive at Nāgārjuna. As we saw, *e* behaves exactly as ineffability should be expected to behave; *n* does not. If

[4] Why *e*? (a) true, (b) false, (c) both true and false, (d) neither true nor false, (e) none of the above. Conveniently, it will also transpire that it is the value of the ultimate reality of things: emptiness.

A is e, so is $A \vee B$; but if A is n, $A \vee B$ may be t. And if e is to be the fifth possibility, it cannot have been the fourth.

5.4 States of Affairs

So far so good. But now a new issue needs to be faced. We have assumed so far, as in standard in contemporary logic, that the truth-bearers, that is, those things to which semantic values are assigned, are sentences. But we are understanding e as ineffability; and one thing that sentences cannot be is ineffable. They wear their effability on their face, as it were. So how are we to understand what sorts of things truth-bearers are in this new context?

Two possibilities come immediately to mind: propositions and states of affairs. Propositions are whatever it is that declarative sentences express; states of affairs are arrangements in reality—or if they are not *facts*, arrangements in some non-actual reality. The more robust choice here, it seems to me, is states of affairs. This is so for two reasons. First, if we suppose that there are ineffable propositions, we are in danger of losing our grip on the notion. Propositions are, on the above understanding, the sort of thing that can be expressed by declarative sentences. In the present context, they would have to go beyond this. What is this beyond? Secondly, what is a proposition anyway? There are a number of possible answers. One might take them to be abstract objects of some kind. But another answer is to see them as 'Russellian'.[5] Consider the state of affairs of Socrates being snub-nosed. This is a complex of Socrates himself, and snub-nosedness. Understood in this way, propositions just are complexes in reality, that is, states of affairs. In which case, we might as well just have opted for states of affairs in the first place.

So let us take the bearers of semantic value to be states of affairs.[6] There is still the question of what, exactly, these are. I will sketch a theory of states of affairs in a moment.[7] All we need to note for the present is that e may now be understood happily as ineffability: states of affairs are the *kind* of thing that can be ineffable. But our first four values now need to be reconceptualized ontologically, not semantically. Thus, to say that a state of affairs is true has to be understood as saying that it *obtains*; and to say that it is false has to be understood as saying

[5] The nomenclature is a reference to a theory of propositions developed by Russell in (1912).

[6] The presence of the value e in our machinery does nothing, therefore, to affect the T-schema, which concerns sentences.

[7] Other accounts can be found in Situation Semantics, as in Barwise and Etchemendy (1987), ch. 4. See also Taylor (1985) and Priest (2014a), 9.2, 9.3. The account given in the last of these concerns propositions; but it works just as well for states of affairs.

that its negation obtains. Our five semantic values may now, then, be thought of as follows (where *A* is a state of affairs):

- *A* has the value *t*: *A* is effable, *A* obtains and ¬*A* does not.
- *A* has the value *f*: *A* is effable, ¬*A* obtains and *A* does not.
- *A* has the value *b*: *A* is effable, both *A* and ¬*A* obtain.
- *A* has the value *n*: *A* is effable, neither *A* nor ¬*A* obtains.
- *A* has the value *e*: *A* is ineffable (as is ¬*A*).

Given this reinterpretation of the notions involved, the whole machinery now makes sense.

We are at last in a position to explain how it is that Nāgārjuna can use only four of the values in his *reductio* arguments, and maintain that there is a fifth. There are two catuṣkoṭis. The first one we can call *semantic*. This is where the bearers of semantic values are sentences, and there are only four such values. Nāgārjuna's *reductio* arguments are made of sentences, so it suffices to run through the four possibilities and show them all to be untenable.

The second catuṣkoṭi we may call *ontological*. The bearers here are not sentences, but states of affairs. And there are five classes of these: those that correspond to each of the four semantic values of the sentences which express them (if there are such); and the fifth, which is the value of something for which there is no such sentence: ineffability. To be faithful to the Sanskrit, it might be more accurate to call this structure the *pañcakoṭi* (five corners). However, I shall stick with the (more charming) oxymoron, '5-valued catuṣkoṭi'.

5.5 Truth

As I noted in 3.3, the Sanskrit word *satya* can be translated in two ways: as *truth* or *reality*. Drawing this distinction for Nāgārjuna's thought has just become crucial. The semantic catuṣkoṭi concerns truth; the ontological catuṣkoṭi concerns reality. In the previous section we had a closer look at reality. But what—as a somewhat notorious Roman governor of Palestine said a century or so before Nāgārjuna—is truth?[8]

In part, this is an easy question to answer. First, the doctrine of two satyas, as it is usually translated into English, is a doctrine of two truths: conventional and ultimate. Is the truth that is talked of in the semantic catuṣkoṭi conventional or ultimate? It's conventional. It applies to sentences, that is, things expressed in

[8] *John* 18:38.

words, that is, things that express concepts; and this is a mark of the conventional. Is there also a notion of ultimate truth (*not* reality)? No. Given the argument of 4.7, the ultimate is ineffable. It cannot be described in words. There is nothing, therefore, for a semantic notion of truth to apply to.[9]

Slightly harder: what is this semantic notion of truth? I don't know of any extended discussions of this in Buddhist philosophy; but of course it is a mainstream topic of debate in Western philosophy.[10] The obvious answer from Aristotle onwards[11] has been that truth and falsity are characterized by the T-schema and the F-schema. Let A be any declarative sentence, without context-dependent words, like 'I', and 'now'. I will use $\langle . \rangle$ as a name-forming device, so $\langle A \rangle$ is a name for the sentence A. Finally, let T and F be the predicates 'is true' and 'is false', respectively, then the schemata are:

- $T \langle A \rangle$ iff A
- $F \langle A \rangle$ iff $\neg A$

If we simply define $F \langle A \rangle$ as $T \langle \neg A \rangle$, as is natural, the F-schema is just a special case of the T-schema, and we do not need to consider it independently.

Now, of course, the T-schema is deeply involved in paradoxes of self-reference, such as the Liar Paradox. And in contemporary logic, many philosophers have rejected it as universally correct. Restrictions have to be put on it to avoid such paradoxes.[12] This is not the place to go into the matter. So I am simply going to set such concerns aside, and take truth to be characterized by the T-schema.[13]

Of more importance in the present context is what one should take the 'iff' (if and only if) to be. What kind of conditional is it? In particular, is it one which contraposes? That is, do we have:

- $\neg T \langle A \rangle$ iff $\neg A$

Given that $\neg A$ iff $F \langle A \rangle$, and assuming that the conditional is at least transitive, we then have:

- $\neg T \langle A \rangle$ iff $F \langle A \rangle$ (iff $T \langle \neg A \rangle$)

[9] Spoiler alert: It will turn out, as we will see in the next chapter, that one *can* say something about it (as well). But since whatever is said, is said using language/concepts, what is said is still a conventional truth, even though it is about ultimate reality (and so ultimate, in that sense).

[10] See, e.g., Glanzberg (2013).

[11] 'To say of what is that it is not, or of what is not that it is, is false, while to say of what is that it is, and of what is not that it is not, is true.' Aristotle, *Met.* $1011^{b}25$ff.

[12] For a survey of the area, see Beall and Glanzberg (2011).

[13] I have defended the integrity of the T-schema in many places (e.g. Priest (1987), ch. 1). One should accept it, and the paradoxes to which it gives rise.

One might have thought this held; but not in the land of the catuṣkoṭi. Suppose that A is neither true nor false. Then the left-hand side of this is true, but the right-hand side isn't. That's enough to scupper most conditionals. Or, on the other side of the street, suppose that A is both true and false. Then the right-hand side of the biconditional is true, but the left-hand side isn't.[14]

Given that the T-schema does not contrapose, truth of negation and negation of truth are quite distinct; and the same for falsity. Thus, our four corners of the catuṣkoṭi can be expressed thus:[15]

- A has the value t: $T\langle A\rangle$ but not $F\langle A\rangle$.
- A has the value f: $F\langle A\rangle$ but not $T\langle A\rangle$.
- A has the value b: $F\langle A\rangle$ and $T\langle A\rangle$.
- A has the value n: neither $F\langle A\rangle$ nor $T\langle A\rangle$.

These are all quite distinct. So the space of statements is partitioned as the following diagram shows:

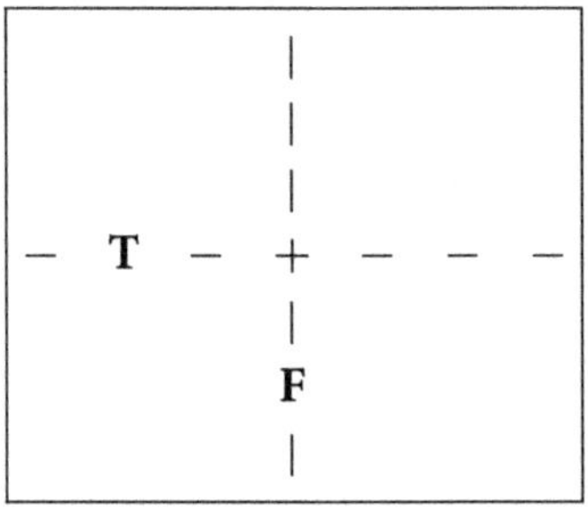

The truths are on the left-hand side; the falsities are in the bottom half. So things in the bottom left-hand quadrant are both true and false; and those in the top right-hand quadrant are neither true nor false. Any quadrant can be non-empty.

5.6 Correspondence

I have left the hardest question about truth till last. Any theory of truth is likely to hold that it satisfies the T-schema. But is there more to truth than this? It is here that the real differences of opinion have arisen in Western philosophy. Some,

[14] The situation concerning truth value 'gluts' is, in fact, more complicated than that concerning gaps, since someone may hold that the left-hand side *is* true. We have both $T\langle A\rangle$ and $\neg T\langle A\rangle$. I am inclined to the view that such is not the best thing to do, since it multiplies contradictions beyond necessity. See Priest (1987), 4.9.

[15] This is a bit swift. The values t, f, b, n, are truth values *in an interpretation*, whereas T is truth *simpliciter*. So what we are really talking about here before the colon is the interpretation which assigns truth values as they really are; that is, in the intended interpretation, as logicians say.

deflationists, say 'no': there is nothing more to truth than the T-schema.[16] That is also a possible choice for Madhyamaka.[17]

Non-deflationary accounts of truth hold that there is more to truth than just the T-schema. This is not the place to go into the many possibilities of what that more is. However, given that states of affairs are on the table, we can now see how to formulate a correspondence theory of truth: to be true is for the state of affairs described to obtain, that is, to be a fact.

To formulate the account more precisely, we will need to be very clear about the difference between sentences and states of affairs—for which I have so far been using the same notation. So in what follows, when I need to be careful about this distinction, I will use underlining to indicate states of affairs. Thus, if A is any sentence, $\underline{A}$ is the state of affairs it describes. Now let us say that $\underline{A}$ is a *fact* iff $\underline{A}$ actually obtains. Then the correspondence theory of truth tells us that $T\langle A\rangle$ iff $\underline{A}$ is a fact.

The four values of the semantic catuṣkoṭi[18] have now become:

- A has the value t: $\underline{A}$ is a fact, but $\underline{\neg A}$ is not.
- A has the value f: $\underline{\neg A}$ is a fact, but $\underline{A}$ is not.
- A has the value b: both $\underline{A}$ and $\underline{\neg A}$ are facts.
- A has the value n: neither $\underline{A}$ nor $\underline{\neg A}$ are facts.

And if we think of our quadrant diagram as partitioning the space of effable states of affairs, rather than the space of sentences, the left-hand side will contain those states of affairs, $\underline{A}$, such that $\underline{A}$ is a fact; and the bottom part will contain those states of affairs, $\underline{A}$, such that $\underline{\neg A}$ is a fact.

5.7 Empty States of Affairs

We have, then, a perfectly precise correspondence theory of truth. At this point, one might well expect an objection from the direction of Madhyamaka. A correspondence theory of truth has always been associated with realism, and Madhyamaka has *rejected* Abhidharma realism. In fact, Madhyamaka is a view which sails between the horns of realism and idealism.[19] But as far as I can see, there is, in fact, no problem about talking of states of affairs for Madhyamaka, provided that these have no svabhāva: they must be as empty as anything else. And the notion of an empty state of affairs makes perfectly good sense. To see this, merely consider the following account of states of affairs.

[16] See, e.g., Horwich (1990).
[17] See Priest, Siderits, and Tillemans (2010).
[18] In the intended interpretation.
[19] See Priest (2014a), ch. 13.

We suppose that we have a domain of objects and a domain of properties. To keep matters simple, let us suppose that the properties are monadic. (Generalization to higher adicities is routine.) Then an atomic state of affairs is a pair (d, π), where d is an object and π is a property. I use round brackets here, note, to indicate ordered pairs. (It would be more normal to use angle brackets, but this would invite confusion with their use as a name-forming device.) Complex states of affairs are given by the following recursion—note that both round and angle brackets are in operation:[20]

- $\underline{\neg A} = (\langle\neg\rangle, \underline{A})$
- $\underline{A \wedge B} = (\langle\wedge\rangle, (\underline{A}, \underline{B}))$
- $\underline{A \vee B} = (\langle\vee\rangle, (\underline{A}, \underline{B}))$

There are many things one might say about this account.[21] For present purposes, the only important thing to note is that all states of affairs have parts, and so, depending on them, are empty.[22] Thus, a complex state of affairs, such as $\underline{\neg A}$, has $\langle\neg\rangle$ and $\underline{A}$ as parts; and an atomic state of affairs, such as Socrates being snub-nosed, has the parts Socrates and snub-nosedness.[23] True, we must take these as having no svabhāva, as well. As far as Socrates goes, we are on familiar Buddhist ground. He was a partite object. What of the universal?

Buddhist nominalists (which is most of them) might reject an appeal to universals. But Buddhists struggled with the question how to understand predication without an appeal to universals. They developed a theory of *apoha*. To say that something is red is to say that it is outwith the not-red things. This doesn't look very promising. What is it so say that something is not red, except to say that it is outwith the red things? We have gone round in a rather unilluminating circle. Much effort was spent by the logician Dharmakīrti (fl. c. seventh century) and others, trying to make sense of the idea.[24] The results are, to put it gently, tangled. But in any case, there is, again as far as I can see, no reason why Madhyamaka *has* to espouse nominalism about universals. The important thing for Madhyamaka

[20] I note that the identity conditions of states of affairs, so construed, are very fine-grained. If A and B are distinct sentences, $\underline{A}$ and $\underline{B}$ are distinct states of affairs. A less fine-grained notion may be obtained by factoring out by the relation of logical consequence. The state of affairs described by the sentence A is then $\{\underline{B}: B \models A \text{ and } A \models B\}$—or if the language contains further suitable operators, as $\{\underline{B}: \models \Box(A \leftrightarrow B)\}$. Employing this more complex construction affects none of the points below.

[21] For example, it is committed to complex states of affairs, such as disjunctive and, especially, negative states of affairs. These are not to everyone's taste. For a discussion, see Priest (2006), 2.7.

[22] The parts of a set may be taken to include its members. See 3.5.

[23] Or alternatively, one could take the second part to be the trope of Socrates' snub-nosedness. But this is empty too, since it depends on Socrates.

[24] See Tillemans (2011), and more generally Siderits, Tillemans, and Chakrabarti (2011).

is that universals, like everything else, must be empty. And it is easy enough to construct a theory of universals according to which this is so. Thus, they can be taken to have parts (and so depend on them): for example, the relevant tropes.[25] And if one is tempted by the thought that universals do not exist because they have no causal impact, this can simply be rejected. Socrates' snub-nosedness does have causal impact: for example, on me when I see it (or, rather, on those who actually did see it).

In any case, mereological considerations aside, the emptiness of atomic states of affairs follows also from quite different considerations. Even if states of affairs are not thought of as partite things, they still have no svabhāva: they are not independent of other such states. So, take the states of affairs of Socrates having a snub nose, and Socrates having an aquiline nose. These are not independent: each rules out the other. This was exactly the consideration which forced Wittgenstein to give up the metaphysical atomism of the *Tractatus*, as I noted in 3.7.

5.8 Conclusion

In this chapter we have seen how, for Nāgārjuna, the catuṣkoṭi has split into two: a four-valued semantic catuṣkoṭi, and a 5-valued ontological catuṣkoṭi—the fifth value in the ontological case being ineffability. We examined the nature of the distinction, and its role in Nāgārjuna's thought.

It might have seemed that Nāgārjuna being committed to both four values and five values in the catuṣkoṭi is a paradoxical feature of his thought. It is not; once the distinction between the two kinds of catuṣkoṭis is made, there is no contradiction here.

But there is a much harder paradox in the wings, which we have already noted. Madhyamaka, following the *Prajñāpāramitā Sūtras*, speaks of the ineffable. That's certainly a contradiction. What is to be made of this? That is the topic of the next chapter.

5.9 Technical Appendix

In this appendix, I will spell out the technical details of FDEe more formally.

FDEe is a many-valued logic. $V = \{t, f, b, n, e\}$; $D = \{t, b\}$. The connectives of the language are the same as those for FDE, and the truth functions for the connectives are also the same as for FDE when none of the inputs is e. (See 2.10.2.)

[25] See, e.g., Priest (2014a), ch. 3.

It remains to say how they behave when the inputs are e. This is as follows. For any value, x:

$$f_{\neg}(e) = f_{\vee}(x, e) = f_{\vee}(e, x) = f_{\wedge}(x, e) = f_{\wedge}(e, x) = e$$

To obtain a sound and complete rule system for FDEe, we take the rule system of FDE (2.10.3), and replace the rule of $\vee$-introduction:

$$\frac{A}{A \vee B}$$

with a restricted version, Weak $\vee$-introduction:

$$\frac{A \quad B^{\dagger}}{A \vee B}$$

where $B^{\dagger}$ is any formula which contains all the propositional parameters in B. (If this has a designated value, none of these can take the value e, so neither can B.)[26]

If one deletes the value n from the semantic values, the rest of the machinery makes perfectly good sense. (The remaining values are closed under the truth functions.) This logic may be found in Oller (1999). A rule system for this is obtained by augmenting the rules for FDEe by Weak Excluded Middle:

$$\frac{A^{\dagger}}{A \vee \neg A}$$

There is no proof of this fact in the literature, that I know of. I have discovered a truly marvellous demonstration of the proposition, but the margin is too narrow to contain it.[27] 空

[26] For further details, see Priest (2010a).

[27] Actually, it's a rather boring proof using the canonical model construction. (It can be found in Priest (2019).) Margins are for more interesting things.

6

Paradox and Ineffability

6.1 Introduction

In the last chapter, we saw how the four corners of the catuṣkoṭi could be augmented with a fifth, which could naturally be interpreted as ineffability, and that this could resolve a puzzle of interpretation concerning the MMK. A bigger puzzle looms. That some things are ineffable is one thing; talking about them is quite another. To talk about the ineffable is obviously a contradiction. That one can do so would clearly seem to be a paradox of some kind. In this chapter we will explore the paradox.

First, we will look at the context of the paradox, and note that paradoxes of the same kind arise also in Western philosophy. Next, we will see how the matter may be handled by a further development of the formal machinery of the catuṣkoṭi. We will then look at another important text, the *Vimalakīrti Nirdeśa Sūtra*, a central concern of which is exactly talking about the ineffable. A final section takes its leave of India.

A brief coda to the chapter describes Jaina logic, for comparison with the Buddhist logic of this chapter.

6.2 The Paradox of Ineffability

In 4.3 and 4.6, we noted that both the *Prajñāpāramitā Sūtras* and Nāgārjuna talk about the ineffable. Indeed, they even indicate *why* it's ineffable. This is clearly paradoxical. To say that something is ineffable is to say that nothing can be (truly) predicated of it. Yet to explain why one can predicate nothing of it clearly requires one to predicate something of it.

What do these texts have to say about the paradox? Nothing, it would seem. Perhaps a discussion of the matter is not to be expected in the *Sūtras*, which are, after all, as much religious documents as philosophical. But Nāgārjuna is a systematic philosopher. Did he not notice the matter? Unlikely: it is hardly recondite. Perhaps the silence is not so surprising, though. After all, he is working in the context of the catuṣkoṭi, where some contradictions can be true. Maybe he thought that this was just one of them. Certainly, though, some later Buddhist philosophers felt discomfort over the matter, and tried to wriggle out of it. One of these is the important Tibetan philosopher Gorampa (1429–89). (As to why he might have felt so inclined, we will see in 6.6.)

Gorampa is as clear as his Mahāyāna predecessors that the ultimate is ineffable. He says in his *Synopsis of Madhyamaka*, 75:[1]

> The scriptures which negate proliferations of the four extremes [GP: of the catuṣkoṭi] refer to ultimate truth but not to the conventional, because the ultimate is devoid of conceptual proliferations, and the conventional is endowed with them.

But he also realizes that he talks about it. Indeed, he does so in this very quote. Gorampa's response to the situation is to draw a distinction. Kassor describes matters succinctly thus:[2]

> In the *Synopsis*, Gorampa divides ultimate truth into two: the nominal ultimate (*don dam rnam grags pa*) and the ultimate truth (*don dam bden pa*). While the ultimate truth . . . is free from conceptual proliferations, existing beyond the limits of thought, the nominal ultimate is simply a conceptual description of what the ultimate is *like*. Whenever ordinary persons talk about or conceptualize the ultimate, Gorampa argues that they are actually referring to the nominal ultimate. We cannot think or talk about the *actual* ultimate truth because it is beyond thoughts and language; any statement or thought about the ultimate is necessarily conceptual, and is, therefore, the nominal ultimate.

It does not take long to see that this hardly avoids contradiction. If all talk of the ultimate is about the nominal ultimate, then Gorampa's own talk of the ultimate is this. And the nominal ultimate is clearly effable. Hence Gorampa's own claim that the ultimate is devoid of conceptual proliferations is just false. This is, hence, no way out of the contradiction: it merely relocates it.

6.3 Interlude: Western Connections

Before we go on, let us pause to look at some Western connections. Some might think that the phenomenon we are dealing with is but a strange feature of Eastern philosophy. Nothing could be further from the truth. In the history of Western philosophy, several philosophers have endorsed the claim that there are things

[1] The translation is taken from Kassor (2013), p. 401.

[2] Kassor (2013), p. 406. Kassor informs me (in correspondence) that the nomenclature for the distinction employed here is not Gorampa's, but is that of another thinker. He himself calls the distinction one between *the ultimate that is realized*, and *the ultimate that is taught*.

that are ineffable, and explained why they are so, putting themselves in precisely the same situation.[3]

Indeed, it is orthodox in Christian philosophy that God is so much greater than his creatures that human language cannot apply to him. To suppose otherwise is almost blasphemy. Yet, as hardly needs to be remarked, Christian philosophers say a great deal about God, applying human concepts in the process. (What others do they have?)

Nor is it just the philosophy of religion that engenders this paradox. In the *Critique of Pure Reason*, Kant says that the categories of thought apply only to phenomena, since the criteria of their application are spatio-temporal; yet he applies the categories to noumena in his remarks about them.

In the *Tractatus*, Wittgenstein tells us that propositions are about objects, but the form of a proposition (or of the state of affairs it describes) is not an object. It is a quite different kind of thing: it is the *way* that objects (or names) are structured into a unity. He concludes, correctly, that one cannot talk about form. But the *Tractatus* is replete with discussion of form.

One more example. At the beginning of *Sein und Zeit*, Heidegger asks the *Seinsfrage*: what is *being*, what is it *to be*? He immediately tells us that there is an important mistake to avoid. Whatever *being* is, it cannot be another being. It is what *gives* beings their being. But to say anything about *being*, one has to say: *being* is such and such. And doing so treats it exactly as a being. One can, then, say nothing about *being*. Of course, *Sein and Zeit* and all of Heidegger's later writings say much about *being*.

Kant, Wittgenstein, and Heidegger are three of the most outstanding Western philosophers, so this is no trivial matter.

Of course, the thinkers we have just looked at realized that they were in this situation. Some bold thinkers did accept the contradiction. Thus, for example, Nicholas of Cusa accepted the claim that God was, indeed, a contradictory object. Most of the thinkers were not game to flout the Principle of Non-Contradiction, however, so orthodox was it. Most of them tried to wriggle out of the problem.

This is not the place to go into all the things that were suggested. However, none of them had any more success than Gorampa. Thus, to take just one example: at the end of the *Tractatus*, Wittgenstein famously declared much of his own book meaningless. One has to admire the chutzpah of this; but the move really does not work. First, the views of the *Tractatus* are not meaningless. We can read the book,

[3] For a more general discussion of the following, see Priest (2005b). For detailed references and discussion, see Priest (2002a): Cusanus: 1.8, 1.9; Kant: ch. 5; Wittgenstein: 12.3–12.9; Heidegger: ch. 15.

understand its claims, argue for and against them. Worse, Wittgenstein is sawing off the very branch on which he is sitting. If the doctrines of the *Tractatus* are meaningless, they cannot establish anything. In particular, they cannot establish that form is ineffable. The motivation for declaring the text meaningless is, therefore, simply undercut.

If one endorses the Principle of Non-Contradiction, there is no easy way out.

I note that it is not just metaphysics that runs into this problem. So does logic. There are paradoxes of self-reference which deliver the same situation. Consider König's paradox.[4] This concerns the ordinals. Ordinals are numbers that extend the familiar counting (natural) numbers, 0, 1, 2, . . . beyond the finite. Thus, after all the finite numbers there is a next, ω, and then a next , $\omega + 1$, and so on. So we have:

$$0,\ 1,\ 2,\ 3,\ \ldots\ \omega,\ \omega+1,\ \omega+2,\ \ldots\ 2\omega,\ 2\omega+1,\ \ldots\ 3\omega,\ \ldots\ 4\omega,\ \ldots\ \omega^2,\ \ldots$$

Crucially, these numbers preserve the property of the natural numbers, that any collection of them has a least member.

How far, exactly, the ordinals go is a somewhat vexed question, both mathematically and philosophically, but it is not contentious that there are many more ordinals than can be referred to by (non-indexical) noun phrases of a language with a finite vocabulary, such as English (as it is at the present moment). This can be shown by a perfectly rigorous mathematical proof. Now, if there are ordinals that cannot be referred to in this way, then, by the properties of the ordinals, there must be a least. Consider the phrase 'the least ordinal that cannot be referred to'. This obviously refers to the number in question. This number, then, both can and cannot be referred to. Moreover, to say something about it one has to refer to it and predicate something of it. Since one cannot refer to it, one can say nothing about it: it is ineffable. But one *can* refer to it and say something about it. For example, one can say that the least ordinal that cannot be referred to is not a natural number.

Again, consistent solutions to the paradox are troubled. Since the demise of hierarchical solutions to the semantic paradoxes,[5] which fragment 'is true', 'denotes', etc., into a hierarchy of distinct predicates, the most popular consistent kind of solution to these paradoxes has been one which rejects the Principle of Excluded Middle ($A \vee \neg A$). Now, this may, *prima facie*, solve the Liar Paradox, since that principle is involved in the standard Liar argument. But whatever else is to be said about this kind of solution, it would seem to fail to deal with

[4] See, e.g., Priest (2002a), pp. 131–4.

[5] As a result of Kripke (1975).

König's paradox, since the principle is nowhere used in the argument for its conclusion—as an inspection of the above argument will show.[6]

6.4 Having More than One Value

But, and to return to Buddhist thought, we are in a context where the Principle of Non-Contradiction is not being assumed. The third koṭi of the catuṣkoṭi violates it. So if $\underline{A}$ is an ineffable state of affairs about which one *can* say something, then the statement '$\underline{A}$ is ineffable' may well be in the third koṭi. This does not get to the root of the matter, however. To say that $\underline{A}$ is ineffable and effable is to say that $\underline{A}$ takes the value e *and* some other value. There is no provision for this in our 5-valued catuṣkoṭi. What is to be done?

In fact, the modification required to accommodate the situation is not difficult. We simply allow bearers of semantic values (in our case, states of affairs) to take more than one value. In 2.6, I noted that FDE could be set up by supposing that there are just two truth values, 1 and 0, but by allowing sentences to have none, one, or both of these values. We may do something similar with our five values.

Recall that our five values may be depicted as follows:

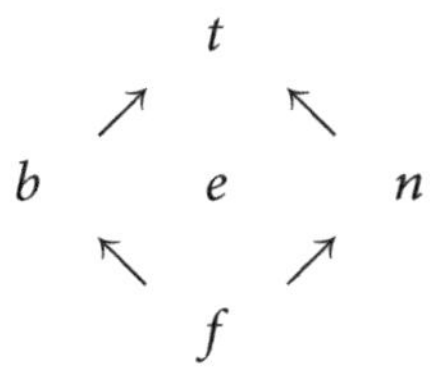

In FDE (formulated as a 4-valued logic) and FDEe, an interpretation is a *function*. That is, it assigns one and only one value to each formula. We now take an interpretation to be a *relation*, which relates each semantic bearer to *at least one* of these values. So if $\rhd$ is such a relation, we may have both of $A \rhd t$ and $A \rhd e$.

The values of compound semantic-bearers can be computed in a very natural way: we simply operate on the values of the parts in all possible ways. For example, if the set of values that A relates to is $\{f, e\}$, we obtain the set of values that $\neg A$ relates to simply by negating each of these, to obtain $\{t, e\}$. And if the sets of values A and B relate to are $\{b, e\}$ and $\{f, e\}$, respectively, we obtain the set of values

[6] It might be suggested that the principle is not used in the argument itself, but in the proof that there are more ordinals than English has noun phrases. For the sake of set theory, I hope not. But in any case, there is a very similar finitary paradox, Berry's. This concerns the least natural number that cannot by referred to by a noun phrase of less than 100 words. A formalization of this paradox demonstrating that it does not use the Principle of Excluded Middle can be found in Priest (1987), 1.8.

$A \wedge B$ relates to by conjoining every possible combination: (i) b, f (ii) b, e (iii) e, f (iv) e, e; giving us $\{f, e, e, e\}$. That is, just $\{f, e\}$, since repetitions don't count.

All that remains is to define validity. Say that a semantic bearer is designated, in a new sense, if it relates to a value that was designated in the old sense, t or b. Then an inference is valid in this logic just if it preserves designation in this new sense.

A logic obtained by starting with a many-valued logic, and then allowing semantic bearers to take one or more of these values in this way is called a *plurivalent* logic. We may therefore call the logic we have just obtained, *plurivalent* FDEe. A perhaps surprising fact is that an inference is valid in plurivalent FDEe iff it is valid in ordinary FDEe.

In fact, we have seen no reason why, in the present context, something should have more than one of the values t, f, b, and n. So we might restrict ourselves to interpretations that have at most two values: e and/or one of these. As a matter of fact, if we do this, the consequence relation obtained is exactly the same. Further details of this can be found in the technical appendix below.

The 5-valued catuṣkoṭi happily resolves the problem with which we started this section. Let $A(u)$ be some statement about the ultimate. Then since one can say nothing about u, $\underline{A(u)}$ is ineffable; but since $A(u)$ says something about it, $\underline{A(u)}$ is effable (as well). To say that $\underline{A(u)}$ is ineffable is to say that it takes the value e; and to say that it is effable is to say that it takes some other value (as well). The plurivalent 5-valued catuṣkoṭi allows for exactly his possibility.[7]

It also provides an elegant representation of the Madhyamaka picture of a bicameral reality. This two-sided nature can be taken as expressed by the fact that a state of affairs can have two values. The conventional side is represented by the state taking one of the conventional values. The ultimate and inexpressable side is represented by its having the value e.

6.5 The *Vimalakīrti Nirdeśa Sūtra*

Philosophically, however, all this is predicated on the assumption that a Buddhist really might endorse the thought that something is both effable and ineffable. Can they?

They certainly can, and we can see this by looking at the *Vimalakīrti Nirdeśa Sūtra* (Sūtra of the Teachings of Vimalakīrti). The sūtra is an Indian Mahāyāna text, of uncertain date, but possibly about the first century CE.

[7] The fact that something can take the value e and some other value, one might note, is a consistent representation of an inconsistency. In the same way, the fact that something can take the values 1 and 0 in the 1/0 semantics of FDE in 2.6 is a consistent representation of an inconsistency.

It is an unusual one, for a number of reasons. First, its hero is neither the Buddha nor a monk, but a layman, Vimalakīrti from Licchavi. Next, a woman—a goddess, no less—plays an important role in it. (Women are notably absent from nearly all classical Buddhist texts.) Third, it has clear moments of humour.

A number of issues are addressed in the sūtra, but a central one is the transcendence of duality—including the dualism which is our central concern at the moment: effability and ineffability. As we saw in 4.3, the *Prajñāpāramitā Sūtras* tell us that the ultimate transcends all dualities. The *Vimalakīrti Sūtra* is much concerned with what that means.

So let us turn to the text. At one point in it, the goddess appears in the room, and causes petals to flutter down. These slide off enlightened people, but stick to people who are unenlightened. The petals stick to Śāriputra (a hero of a number of the pre-Mahāyāna sūtras), and he is not very happy about this. A conversation between him and the goddess ensues:[8]

Then the venerable Śāriputra said to the goddess, "Goddess, how long have you been in this house?"

The goddess replied, "I have been here as long as the elder has been in liberation."

Śāriputra said, "Then, have you been in this house for quite some time?"

The goddess said, "Has the elder been in liberation for quite some time?"

At that, the elder Śāriputra fell silent.

The goddess continued, "Elder, you are 'foremost of the wise!' Why do you not speak? Now, when it is your turn, you do not answer the question."

Śāriputra: Since liberation is inexpressible, goddess, I do not know what to say.

Śāriputra, appealing to the idea that enlightenment, the realization of ultimate reality, is ineffable, takes the 5th Amendment. The goddess is not impressed (*ibid.*):

Goddess: All the syllables pronounced by the elder have the nature of liberation. Why? Liberation is neither internal nor external, nor can it be apprehended apart from them. Likewise, syllables are neither internal nor external, nor can they be apprehended anywhere else. Therefore, reverend Śāriputra, do not point to liberation by abandoning speech! Why? The holy liberation is the equality of all things!

The reply is dark. The thought would appear to be that words are not something over and above ultimate reality, which can be—indeed, must be—peeled off of it. They are part of it, and so can be used to describe it. But whatever the exact

[8] Thurman (2014), p. 59.

meaning of the goddess's words, it is clear that she says that one can speak about ultimate reality.

If one left the text at this point, one might just think that the doctrine of ineffability had been dismissed. But this is not so. Two chapters later there is a chapter entitled 'Entering the Gate of Non-Dualism'. As the title suggests, the topic of discussion turns explicitly to the question of what it means to transcend duality. Many bodhisattvas are brought into the discussion, and each takes it in turn to say what this means. To give just a few examples:[9]

The bodhisattva Sunetra declared, " 'Uniqueness' and 'characterlessness' are two. Not to presume or construct something is neither to establish its uniqueness nor to establish its characterlessness. To penetrate the equality of these two is to enter nonduality."

The bodhisatta Nārāyana declared, "To say, 'This is mundane' and 'That is transcendental' is dualism. The world has the nature of voidness, so there is neither transcendence nor involvement, neither progress nor standstill. Thus, neither to transcend nor to be involved, neither to go nor to stop—this is the entrance into non-duality."

The bodhisattva Priyadarśana declared, "Matter itself is void. Voidness does not result from the destruction of matter, but the nature of matter is itself voidness. Therefore, to speak of voidness on the one hand, and of matter, or of sensation, or of intellect, or of motivation, or of consciousness on the other—is entirely dualistic. Consciousness itself is voidness. Voidness does not result from the destruction of consciousness, but the nature of consciousness is itself voidness. Such understanding of the five compulsive aggregates and the knowledge of them as such by means of gnosis is the entrance into nonduality."

The bodhisattva Satyarata declared, "It is dualistic to speak of 'true' and 'false'. When one sees truly, one does not ever see any truth, so how could one see falsehood? Why? One does not see with the physical eye, one sees with the eye of wisdom. And with the wisdom-eye one sees only insofar as there is neither sight nor insight. There, where there is neither sight nor insight, is the entrance into nonduality."

The last bodhisattva to speak is the most important of them all. This is Mañjuśrī, the Bodhisattva of Wisdom—so he should know what he is talking about:[10]

Mañjuśrī replied, "Good sirs, you have all spoken well. Nevertheless, all your explanations are themselves dualistic. To know no one teaching, to express nothing, to say nothing, to explain nothing, to announce nothing, to indicate nothing, and to designate nothing—that is the entrance into nonduality."

Then, Vimalakīrti, the real hero of the dialogue, is asked what he thinks (*ibid.*):

[9] Thurman (2014), pp. 73ff. [10] Thurman (2014), p. 77.

> Then the crown prince Mañjuśrī said to the Licchavi Vimalakīrti, "We have all given our own teachings, noble sir. Now, may you elucidate the teaching of the entrance into the principle of nonduality!"
>
> Thereupon, the Licchavi Vimalakīrti kept his silence, saying nothing at all.
>
> The crown prince Mañjuśrī applauded the Licchavi Vimalakīrti: "Excellent! Excellent, noble sir! This is indeed the entrance into the nonduality of the bodhisattvas. Here there is no use for syllables, sounds, and ideas."

Vimalakīrti remains silent. But unlike the silence of Śāriputra, this is praised. What is the difference?

The context. The silence of Vimalakīrti acquires its meaning from what Mañjuśrī has just said about transcending duality. (If Vimalakīrti had been silent because he hadn't heard this, or just plain fallen asleep, it could not have had the same significance.) Mañjuśrī has just *said* that you cannot speak about ultimate reality (thereby contradicting himself). Vimalakīrti *shows* the same thing. The sūtra, then, endorses speaking of the ineffable.[11]

From the point of view of our formal semantics, both Mañjuśrī and Vimalakīrti are addressing the same state of affairs. Mañjuśrī expresses the conventional aspect of it; Vimalakīrti expresses the ultimate. Moreover, the interchange may be seen as enacting a transcendence of the duality between effability and ineffability. Describing the ineffable is a contradiction. To have just one of the limbs of the contradiction would be one-sided. Duality is overcome by having both. This is exactly what Mañjuśrī says, and Vimalakīrti shows.

Although the *Vimalakīrti Nirdeśa Sūtra* is an Indian text, it actually had little impact on the development of Indian Buddhism, as judged by the Indian Mahāyāna commentarial tradition. It rapidly became a very well known sūtra in China, however, and exercised an enormous influence on the development of Chinese Buddhism, as we shall see.

6.6 A Farewell to India

Let me conclude with a few words on Buddhism in its last few hundred years in India.

Something of a sea change came over Indian Buddhism in the sixth and seventh centuries CE. At that time, India was a hotbed of philosophical debate between Hindus, Buddhists, Jains—and indeed between the various schools of

[11] See, further, Garfield (2002b).

each. Unsurprisingly, then, a focus of attention turned to the ground-rules of debate. This was the time of the influential Buddhist thinkers Dignāga (fl. sixth century) and Dharmakīrti (fl. seventh century). They are sometimes styled as the Buddhist logicians—though in modern terms, the label *epistemologists* is more apt. And under the influence of the Hindu Nyāya epistemologists, they came to endorse the Principle of Non-Contradiction (and of Excluded Middle). This had a major impact on later Indian and Tibetan Buddhist thought, most thinkers (such as Gorampa) endorsing the principle.[12]

In the light of this, some philosophers have held that Nāgārjuna himself endorsed the principle. The apparent absurdity of this, given that he is working in the context of the catuṣkoṭi, where the third koṭi is *both true and false*, is apparent. However, there are passages in the MMK which can be quoted in support of this. Perhaps the most obvious is XXV: 14, which says:[13]

> How could both non-being and being pertain to nirvāṇa. Just like light and darkness, both are not present in the same place.

But it is not at all clear that what is being appealed to here is the Principle of Non-Contradiction. It is said that light and darkness cannot be in the same place. Even assuming that to be so would be a contradiction (which is not at all obvious), it does not follow that other contradictions must be rejected. Indeed, arguing for a universal principle from one instance is terrible methodology.

One might argue, more generally, that since Nāgārjuna argues by *reductio*, he cannot accept a contradiction: an assumption is shown to entail a contradiction, and so its negation is proved. As noted in 4.4, this is a misunderstanding of how this kind of *reductio* works, however. In it, an assumption is shown to entail something absurd, and so the assumption is rejected. (Whether or not its negation is inferred is another matter, and not so important in the present context.) The *absurdum* might be, but does not have to be a contradiction. It just has to be something that is unacceptable—or, if the argument is *ad hominem*, unacceptable to those against whom the argument is directed.

Perhaps of more interest is whether Candrakīti (who is working at about the same time that the tide of thought is turning against the principle) accepted the Principle of Non-Contradiction. His gloss on the above verse of the MMK goes as follows:[14]

> For being and non-being too, there is no possibility for the two mutually contradictory things (*parasparaviruddha*) to be present in one place—that is, *nirvāṇa*. Thus, "how

[12] See, e.g., Tillemans (2009), p. 80 of reprint.
[13] Tillemans (2009), p. 74 of reprint, cites the passage in this context.
[14] Cited in this way by Tillemans (2009), p. 75.

could could both being and non-being pertain to nirvāṇa?" The point is, they could not at all.

But as the quote makes clear, the point about contradiction is specific to nirvāṇa, something very different from most things. Indeed, we are in the midst here of an argument that it is ineffable.

In another passage of *Prasannapadā*, Candrakīti says:[15]

> You do not accept that there is repeated arising, and you do not accept that there can be an infinite regress. Therefore your argument makes no sense. You have contradicted your own thesis. We have asked about our opponent's account of arising. When the thesis and example are presented together with what follows from them as the argument is set out, the opponent cannot accept them. *If the opponent is willing to contradict his own thesis, we can't argue with madmen.* Therefore, without any embarrassment, we can say that the thesis and example, being contradictory, cannot be advanced.

But this comes immediately after a passage where he has shown that the Sāṃkhya position is committed to an infinite regress. (The Sāṃkhya were a school of orthodox Hindu philosophy.) And the Sāṃkhya ('you') *did* accept the Principle of Non-Contradiction. Hence what we have here can clearly be interpreted as an *ad hominem* argument. There is no need for Candrakīrti himself to accept the principle.[16]

6.7 Conclusion

Be that as it may, after Dignāga and Dharmakīrti, most Indo-Tibet Buddhist thinkers did accept the Principle of Non-Contradiction. Perhaps it was for that reason that no further significant developments concerning the catuṣkoṭi occur in Indo-Tibetan Buddhism. For that we have to go to East Asia, which we do in the next part of the book.

6.8 Coda: Jaina Logic

In this section, I describe another plurivalent logic, that of the Jains, for comparison with the Buddhist one.

Jainism is an Indian philosophy of antiquity comparable to that of Buddhism. It appears to have been founded by Mahāvīra, who flourished some time in

[15] Gelugpa Students' Welfare Committee (2003), p. 10; translation by Jay Garfield; italics mine. This is cited as evidence that Candrakīrti accepted the principle by Tillemans (2013), p. 86 of reprint.

[16] But why should Candrakīrti call his opponent a madman, if he himself is willing to accept a contradiction? Because the opponent takes themself to be advocating a consistent line; and if they think they can do this by endorsing a contradiction, they are indeed mad. For further discussion of these matters, see Deguchi, Garfield, and Priest (2013c).

the fifth or sixth century BCE. Jainism has a very distinctive logic, metaphysics, and ethics. Our concern here will be with only the logic and its metaphysical underpinnings.[17]

6.8.1 Anekānta-Vāda

Any system of logic has various metaphysical presuppositions;[18] and Jainism is no exception. So we need to start with Jaina metaphysics—and, in particular, the theory of *anekānta-vāda*; that is, the doctrine of non-onesidedness, as it is sometimes translated (*ekānta* = one-sided). The Jains believed that truth was not the prerogative of any one school. The views of Buddhists and Hindus, for example, may disagree about crucial matters, such as the existence of an individual soul; each has, nonetheless, an element of truth in it. This can be so because reality itself is multi-faceted. Thus, the doctrine of *anekānta-vāda* is sometimes glossed as the doctrine of 'the many-sided nature of reality'.[19] Reality is a complex, with a multitude of aspects; and each of the competing theories provides a perspective, or standpoint (*naya*), which latches on to one such aspect. As Siddhasena (fl. fifth or sixth century CE) puts it in the *Nyāyāvatāra* (v. 29):[20]

> Since a thing has manifold character, it is comprehended (only) by the omniscient. But a thing becomes the subject matter of a *naya*, when it is conceived from one particular standpoint.

On its own, each standpoint is right enough, but incomplete. To grasp the complete picture, if indeed this is possible, one needs to have all the perspectives together—like seeing a cube from all six sides at once.[21]

It follows that any statement to the effect that reality is thus and such, if taken categorically, will be, if not false, then certainly misleading. Better to express the view with an explicit reminder that it is correct from a certain perspective.[22] This was the function with which Jaina logicians employed the word of 'syāt'. This means something like 'it may be that', 'perhaps', or 'arguably'; but in the technical sense in which the Jaina logicians used it, it may be best thought of as something like 'In a certain way . . . ' or 'From a certain perspective . . . '.[23] So instead of saying

[17] Some of what follows comes from Priest (2008b).

[18] For further discussion of the point, see Priest (2015a).

[19] Matilal (1981), pp. 1, 25. See also Ganeri (2001), 5.2.

[20] Quoted by Matilal (1981), p. 41.

[21] See Ganeri (2001), 5.4. Sometimes different perspectives are described as being obtained by interpreting a single sentence in various ways. (See Ganeri (2001), p. 133, and Matilal (1981), p. 60.) In this case, the facets of reality are accessed by semantic disambiguation.

[22] Matilal (1981), p. 2.

[23] Matilal (1981), p. 52, Ganeri (2001), 5.5, and (2002), sect. 1.

'An individual soul exists', it is better to say 'Syāt an individual soul exists'. This is the Jain method of *syād-vāda*.

6.8.2 *The theory of sevenfold predication*

We are now in a position to look at the Jaina theory of sevenfold division (*saptabhaṇgī*). A sentence may have one of seven truth values; or, as it is often put, there are seven predicates that may describe its semantic status. The matter is explained by the twelfth-century theorist, Vādideva Sūri, as follows:[24]

The seven predicate theory consists in the use of seven claims about sentences, each preceded by 'arguably' or 'conditionally' (*syāt*) [all] concerning a single object and its particular properties, composed of assertions and denials, either simultaneously or successively, and without contradiction. They are as follows:

(1) Arguably, it (i.e., some object) exists (*syād esty eva*). The first predicate pertains to an assertion.

(2) Arguably, it does not exist (*syād nāsty eva*). The second predicate pertains to a denial.

(3) Arguably, it exists; arguably it does not exist (*syād esty eva syād nāsty eva*). The third predicate pertains to successive assertion and denial.

(4) Arguably, it is non-assertable (*syād avaktavyam eva*). The fourth predicate pertains to a simultaneous assertion and denial.

(5) Arguably, it exists; arguably it is non-assertable (*syād esty eva syād avaktavyam eva*). The fifth predicate pertains to an assertion and a simultaneous assertion and denial.

(6) Arguably, it does not exist; arguably it is non-assertable (*syād nāsty eva syād avaktavyam eva*). The sixth predicate pertains to a denial and a simultaneous assertion and denial.

(7) Arguably, it exists; arguably it doesn't exist; arguably it is non-assertable (*syād esty eva syād nāsty eva syād avaktavyam eva*). The seventh predicate pertains to a successive assertion and denial and a simultaneous assertion and denial.

A perusal of the seven possibilities indicates that there are three basic ones, (1), (2), and (4), and that the others are compounded from these.[25] (1) says that the

[24] *Pramāṅa-naya-tattvālokālaṁkāra*, ch. 4, vv. 15–21. Translation from Battacharya (1967).

[25] A referee noted that if one strips off the occurrences of *syād* from (1) to (4), we have something like the cases of the catuṣkoṭi. It might be thought that this provides an interpretation of the Buddhist catuṣkoṭi which does not countenance dialetheism. Perhaps: we still have the value *i* to worry about. More importantly, there is no textual evidence (that I am aware of, anyway) which suggests that Buddhists availed themselves of the consistency-generating *syāt* notion, or the perspectival metaphysics which legitimizes its deployment. True, they do have the distinction between the conventional and the utimate to deploy. However, if the distinction is to be deployed in the third koṭi, this falls apart into two cases (*conventionally true, ultimately false* and *conventionally false, ultimately true*). The catuṣkoṭi would then have five cases. Indeed, matters are worse: the conventional/ultimate distinction would have to be applied in all four cases, splitting each into multiple sub-cases. There is no textual evidence for such multiplication.

statement in question (that something exists) holds from a certain perspective. (2) says that from a certain perspective, it does not. (4) says that from a certain perspective, it has another status, non-assertable. Exactly what this is is less than clear. We will return to the matter in a moment. Let us call these three values t, f, and i.

In understanding the other possibilities we hit a *prima facie* problem. Take (3). This says that from some perspective the sentence is t, and from some perspective it is f. That's intelligible enough, but unfortunately, it would seem to entail both (1) and (2). If it's true from some perspective and false from some perspective, it's certainly true from some perspective.[26]

The solution is straightforward, however. We have to understand (1) as saying not just that the sentence is true from some perspective, but as denying the other two basic possibilities: it is t from some perspective, and there are no perspectives from which it is f or i. (3) is now to the effect that there is a perspective from which the sentence is t, a perspective from which it is f, and no perspective from which it is i. In fact, all the seven cases now fall into place. Each corresponds to a non-empty subset, X, of $\{t, i, f\}$. If $x \in X$, there is some perspective, p, such the sentence has the value x from p; if not, then not. The empty set, $\emptyset$, is ruled out, since there must be at least one perspective, and so X cannot be empty. If we write $\wp X$ for the powerset (set of all subsets) of X, then the cardinality of $\wp\{t, i, f\} = 2^3 = 8$. Hence, there are $2^3 - 1 = 7$ possibilities.

And as should now be clear, we have a basic many-valued logic with three values. But the perspectivalism of Jainism allows sentences to relate to one or more of these values. Thus, it is natural to see Jaina logic as a plurivalent logic based on these three values. The main difference between the Buddhist plurivalent logic and the Jaina one is that Buddhism starts from a 5-valued logic, whereas Jainism starts from three.

6.8.3 *The meaning of i*

What is the basic Jaina 3-valued logic, however? That depends on how i is to be understood. A natural possibility is that i means *both true and false*. That is essentially how Vādideva Sūri glosses case (4) in the quotation above. In this case, i is essentially our value b. Unfortunately, Vādideva Sūri also glosses i as *unassertable*. So the status of i is more like *neither true nor false*. In this case, i is essentially either our value n or our value e.

[26] Ganeri (2002), sect. 1, seems to miss this. However, he goes on to suggest essentially the idea that I describe in the next paragraph.

Which is the most plausible interpretation of i in Jain logic, all things considered, is a moot point. Stcherbatsky (1962), p. 415, Bharucha and Kamat (1984), and Sarkar (1992) argue that i is most plausibly interpreted as *both true and false*. Ganeri (2002), sect. 1, and (2001), 5.6, favours *neither true nor false*.

I will leave it to scholars to argue about how the Jains interpreted i. It may well be that different Jains conceptualized i in different ways, or were even just plain confused about the matter. So I note only the following. If i is b, we have the 3-valued logic given by omitting the values n and e from the 5-valued catuṣkoṭi. (This is the paraconsistent logic LP.) If it is n, it is the logic obtained by omitting the values b and e. (This is the logic K3, usually referred to as *strong Kleene*.) And if it is e, this is the logic obtained by omitting the values b and n. (This is Bochvar's logic B_3, sometimes referred to as *weak Kleene*.)

Jaina logic is, then, the plurivalent logic based on one of these.

6.9 Technical Appendix

In this technical appendix, I spell out plurivalent logic in general, and its applications to the Buddhist and Jaina cases. Further details can be found in Priest (2014c).

6.9.1 *Plurivalent logic*

I adopt the notation of 2.10.1. As in many-valued logic, a plurivalent logic is defined by a structure $\langle V, D, \{f_c : c \in C\}\rangle$. But in a plurivalent logic, an interpretation is a one-many relation, $\rhd$, between propositional parameters and V. That is, every propositional parameter relates to at least one value in V. The relation $\rhd$ is extended to a relation between all formulas[27] and values in V pointwise. That is:

- $c(A_1, \ldots, A_n) \rhd v$ iff $\exists v_1, \ldots v_n(A_1 \rhd v_1, \ldots, A_n \rhd v_n$ and $v = f_c(v_1, \ldots, v_n))$

It is easy to see that since every parameter relates to at least one value, so does every formula.

We will write the plurivalent consequence relation as $\models_p$. Let us say that $\rhd$ *designates* A iff for some v such that $A \rhd v$, $v \in D$. Then:

- $\Sigma \models_p A$ iff for all $\rhd$, if $\rhd$ designates every member of Σ, $\rhd$ designates A

[27] Or whatever the bearers of semantic values are. This qualification should be read into all that follows in this appendix.

A technical note. FDE is *not* plurivalent classical logic, as might have been thought. A simple reason is that, as defined above, every formula must relate to at least one value. This rules out the *neither* case. More importantly, the construction can be liberalized by dropping this constraint;[28] but even in this case, the result is still not FDE. In this kind of plurivalent logic, if a subformula relates to no values, the formula itself relates to no values. Thus in FDE, if A has the value f, and B has the value n, $A \wedge B$ has the value f. But in plurivalent classical logic if A relates to just 0 and B relates to no value, $A \wedge B$ relates to no value. Relating to no value works as does e, not n.

6.9.2 *Plurivalent FDEe*

Plurivalent FDEe is obtained by applying the plurivalent construction to the many-valued semantics of 5.9. The consequence relation of plurivalent FDEe is, in fact, exactly the same at that of FDEe itself.[29]

Let us call a *restricted interpretation* one which has at most two values: e and/or one of t, f, b, and n. Let us write the consequence relation delivered by just the restricted interpretations as $\models^r_p$. Then $\models^r_p = \models_p$. For if designation is preserved in all interpretations, it is preserved in restricted interpretations. Hence:

- if $\Sigma \models_p A$ then $\Sigma \models^r_p A$

Conversely, let us write the consequence relation of FDEe as $\models$. Suppose that it is not the case that $\Sigma \models A$. Let ν be a function that designates the premises, but not the conclusion. Let $\rhd$ be the restricted plurivalent interpretation such that for every propositional parameter, p, $p \rhd x$ iff $\nu(p) = x$ or $x = e$. Then a swift induction shows that for any formula, A, if $\nu(A) = x$, then $A \rhd x$. Hence $\rhd$ designates all premises. But another simple induction shows that if $A \rhd x$, and it is not the case that $\nu(A) = x$, then $x = e$. Hence, the conclusion is not designated. So:

- if $\Sigma \models^r_p A$ then $\Sigma \models A$

Since $\models = \models_p$, the result follows.

6.9.3 *The Jaina version*

If i is interpreted as b, the basic Jaina 3-valued logic is FDE with the value n omitted. This is the paraconsistent logic LP. A rule system for it is obtained from that for FDE by adding Excluded Middle. If i is interpreted as n, the basic Jaina 3-valued logic is FDE with the value b omitted. This is the strong Kleene, logic K_3.

[28] See Priest (2014c).

[29] For the proof, see Priest (2014c).

A rule system for it is obtained from that for FDE by adding Explosion. If i is interpreted as e, the logic is Bochvar's logic B_3, sometimes known as *weak Kleene*. A rule system for this is obtained from that for Oller's system (5.9) by adding Explosion.[30]

The seven-valued logic is obtained by applying the plurivalence construction to these three 3-valued logics. The consequence relation of Plurivalent K_3 is the same as that of FDE. The consequence relation of Plurivalent LP is, in fact, the same as that of LP. The consequence relation of Plurivalent B_3 is the same as that of the logic of Oller's logic (5.9).[31]

[30] The proof of these things can be found in Priest (2019).
[31] For a proof of these facts, see Priest (2014c).

Fig. 3. Dōgen Kigen

PART III

East Asia

7

And So On

7.1 Introduction

So let us cross the Himalayas into China. The third part of the book will concern developments in Buddhist metaphysics and the catuṣkoṭi there. We will meet three Chinese schools, *Sanlun* (Jap: Sanron), *Huayan* (Jap: Kegon), and *Chan* (Jap: Zen). This chapter is concerned with the first of these, and in particular with the thought of arguably the most significant figure in the school: the Chinese monk and systematic philosopher Jizang (549–623). We will look at his views concerning the application of the catuṣkoṭi to the two realities—or better, in this context, the two truths about them. Hegel took Kant's dialectic, and made it dynamic. In the same way, Jizang took the catuṣkoṭi, and made it dynamic. In this chapter, we will see how. What will emerge is a distinctive picture of what it means to transcend dualities, namely, that it is a certain kind of process. But first, some background.

7.2 From Daoism to Buddhism

Ancient Chinese natural philosophy—for example, as underlying the *Yijing* (Book of Changes)—took the phenomenal world to be in a constant flux. There are opposite but co-dependent principles, *yin* ('dark') and *yang* ('light'), one of which waxes while the other wanes, until there is a cyclical reversal.

Classical Daoist texts—or the Neo-Daoist interpretation of these, which will be our concern here—notably the *Laozi*, espy a principle that underlies the phenomenal world, the Dao. In some sense, it is the ground of all we see in that world.[1] Because the Dao is not a thing, but that which underlies all things, one can say nothing about it. It is not a this or a that. It was therefore sometimes described as non-being—nothingness—(Chin: *wu*), contrasted with the beings (Chin: *you*) of the phenomenal world, the 'myriad things'.

[1] For an account of Daoism, see Liu (2006), chs. 6 and 7.

In the second century CE, there was something of a revival of Daoism, as a reaction against the contemporary Confucianism:[2] Neo-Daoism, also known as *Xuanxue* (literally something like 'study of the dark/mysterious/profound').[3] And at this time, there were disputes about which of being and non-being was the more fundamental. Thus, Wang Bi (226–249) took nothingness to be more important, whilst Guo Xiang (d. 312) took being to be more important. As one historian puts the matter:[4]

[W]hile Wang Pi emphasizes non-being, Kuo emphasizes being, and while Wang Pi emphasizes the one, Kuo emphasizes the many.

When Buddhism entered China around the turn of the common era, people's knowledge of it was rather limited, but they were struck by some very apparent similarities with Daoism.[5] Daoist terms were then used to translate Buddhist terms. In particular, people identified the Dao with emptiness, that is, ultimate reality. Both were, in some sense, the realm of non-being, and both were ineffable. Coordinately, the phenomenal world of the myriad things was conventional reality.[6] Moreover, because of the influence of Neo-Daoism, there appear to have been disputes amongst the Buddhists of this period concerning whether being or non-being was the more fundamental.[7]

A turning point in the history of Buddhism in China occurs with the work of the Kuchean monk Kumārājiva (344–413) and his school in Xi'an. Kumārājiva and his students made translations of many Buddhist texts, which became highly authoritative. By this time, though, nothing was going to shake the influence of Daoism on Chinese Buddhist thought.

Perhaps the most influential of the early Buddhist thinkers was one of Kumārājiva's students, Sengzhao (384–414), who helped to establish *Sanlun* Buddhism. Sengzhou was knowledgable of classical Chinese thought, including the Neo-Daoist debates, which he worked into his Buddhist views. However, he adopted a more balanced view of the relationship between being and non-being, placing them on a more equal footing. Again, as one historian tells the story:[8]

Seng-chao was born into a poor family and had to earn his living by repairing and copying books. This enabled him to read extensively in literature and history, and he took a special liking to Lao Tzu and Chuang Tzu. However, after he read the translation of the *Vimilakīrti-nirdeśa sūtra* . . . he was convinced of the superiority of Buddhism . . .

He felt that previous Chinese Buddhist schools were one sided, insofar as they still adhered to being or non-being. This is the gist of his criticism of these schools. To him, substance

[2] See Chan (1963), p. 315. [3] See Chan (2014).
[4] Chan (1963), p. 317. Chan uses Wade-Giles for transliteration.
[5] On the entry of Buddhism into China, see Sharf (2002), pp. 1–27.
[6] See Chan (1963), p. 336. [7] See Chan (1963), p. 337.
[8] Chan (1963), p. 344. Of course, much of this may simply be legend.

and function [GP: the Dao and the phenomenal world] are identical, and activity and tranquility are the same. He believed that the self-nature of things is vacuous, and therefore things defy any determination. All dharmas (elements of reality) are merely temporary names (dependent entities), as they come into existence through causes and conditions and not through any nature of their own. Being temporary names, they are unreal, and being unreal, they are empty.

With this background, let us now turn to Jizang.

7.3 The Two Truths: Stage 1

The Sanlun (Three Treatises) School is so called because it was based on two texts by Nāgārjuna, the MMK and *Dvādaśanikāya Śāstra* (The Twelve Gates Treatise), and one by his disciple Āryadava, the *Śata Śāstra* (One Hundred Verses Treatise). In some sense, then, it was a Chinese version of Madhyamaka. It may be traced back to Sengzhao, but it took on its most distinctive aspects at the hands of Jizang.

In his treatise *Erdi zhang* (Treatise on the Two Levels of Truth), Jizang announces his project and its starting point as follows:[9]

The three kinds of Two Levels of Truth all represent the principle of gradual rejection, like building a framework from the ground. Why? Ordinary people say that dharmas, as a matter of true record, possess being, without realizing that they possess nothing. Therefore the Buddha propounded to them the doctrine that dharmas are ultimately empty and void.

We are to see the construction of a hierarchy of successive stages of rejection, or negation, as Hegel might have put it. The starting point is the claim that dharmas have being (read *svabhāva*), and its negation, that they do not: they have non-being. He goes on to explain this dichotomy in more detail as follows (*ibid.*):

When it is said that dharmas possess being, it is ordinary people who say so. This is worldly truth, the truth of ordinary people. Saints and sages, however, truly know that dharmas are empty of nature. This is absolute truth, the truth of sages. The principle [of worldly versus absolute truth] is taught in order to enable people to advance from the worldly to the absolute, and to renounce [the truth of] ordinary people and to accept that of sages. This is the reason for clarifying the first level of twofold truth.

It is conventional truth that dharmas have being. It is ultimate truth that they do not, that is, they are empty. Let D be 'Dharmas have being'. We have, then, the following picture.

Stage	Conventional Truth	Ultimate Truth
1	D	$\neg D$

[9] Chan (1963), p. 360.

7.4 The Two Truths: Stages 2 and 3

However, this is just a starting point. D and $\neg D$ are a duality, and so need to be transcended. Moreover, they are both expressed in language. So both are merely conventional truths. The ultimate is to reject both. As Jizang puts it (*ibid.*):[10]

Next comes the second stage, which explains that both being and non-being belong to worldly truth, whereas non-duality (neither being nor non-being) belongs to absolute truth. It shows that being and non-being are two extremes, being the one and non-being the other. From these to permanence and non-permanence, and the cycle of life and death and Nirvāṇa are both two extremes, they therefore constitute worldly truth, and because neither-the-absolute-nor-the-worldly, and neither-the-cycle-of-life-and-death-nor-Nirvāṇa are the Middle Path without duality, they constitute the highest truth.

So, at the second stage we have the following picture:

Stage	Conventional Truth	Ultimate Truth
1	D	$\neg D$
2	$D \wedge \neg D$	$\neg D \wedge \neg\neg D$

To a thoughtful eye, there is an obvious problem here. But let us set it aside for the moment.

Jizang has, in effect, taken us through the four stages of the catuṣkoṭi. But we are not finished yet. The situation with respect to the conventional and ultimate at this stage is exactly the same as before. We must therefore make exactly the same move. As Jizang puts it (*ibid.*):

Next comes the third stage in which both duality and non-duality are worldly truth, whereas neither-duality-nor-non-duality is the highest truth. Previously, it had been explained that the worldly and the absolute and the cycle of life-and-death and Nirvāṇa are two extremes and one-sided and therefore constitute worldly truth, whereas neither-the-worldly-nor-the-absolute and neither-the-cycle-of-life-and-death-nor-Nirvāṇa are the Middle Path without duality and therefore constitute the highest truth. But these two are also extremes. Why? Duality is one-sided while non-duality is central. But one-sidedness is an extreme and centrality is also an extreme. One-sidedness and centrality, after all, are two extremes. Being two extremes, they are therefore called worldly truth. Only neither-one-sidedness-nor-centrality can be regarded as the Middle Path or the highest truth.

[10] Note that Jizang identifies the conventional realm with the cycle of birth and death (saṃsāra) and ultimate reality with nirvāṇa. What Chan translates in this quotation and the next as an *extreme* might be better translated as *one side of a duality*.

At the second stage we have duality and non-duality. This is itself a duality, and must itself be *aufgehoben*—to put it in Hegelean terms. Thus we have the following picture:

Stage	Conventional Truth	Ultimate Truth
1	D	$\neg D$
2	$D \wedge \neg D$	$\neg D \wedge \neg\neg D$
3	$(D \wedge \neg D) \wedge (\neg D \wedge \neg\neg D)$	$\neg(D \wedge \neg D) \wedge \neg(\neg D \wedge \neg\neg D)$

At each stage, the conventional and the ultimate at the previous stage both become conventional, and the denial of both becomes ultimate.

7.5 The Problem

But now let us address the problem. Let us write the entries for the conventional and ultimate truths at Stage i as C_i and U_i, respectively. The zig-zagging progression is meant to take us through a series of distinct states. But if we may apply the law of double negation to U_2, it is exactly the same as C_2, $D \wedge \neg D$. C_3 also reduces to C_2. Hence, the whole process grinds to a halt at that stage. Now, the law of double negation holds in all the logics we have looked at till now; and there is no reason to suppose that Jizang did not accept it. Here is the problem.

The way I have represented the progression so far, then, does not work. How better to represent it? As observed, the first four statements in the progression take us through the 4-valued catuṣkoṭi. We might therefore think to employ this machinery. Let us write 'A (or the state of affairs it describes) takes the value v' as: $A \rightsquigarrow v$. Then we might have:

Stage	Conventional Truth	Ultimate Truth
1	$A \rightsquigarrow t$	$A \rightsquigarrow f$
2	$A \rightsquigarrow b$	$A \rightsquigarrow n$
3	?	?

But how to fill in the lines at Stage 3? There is nothing obvious. True, in the 5-valued catuṣkoṣi we have an extra value, e, to play with, but C_3 is a conventional truth, so it cannot be represented as $A \rightsquigarrow e$, since e is ineffability. Perhaps this could represent U_3, but we are still in need of something for C_3. Perhaps we could invent another value, but what this might be, and how, exactly, it is meant to function is unclear. Moreover, whatever takes us from Stage 1 to C_2 is supposed to take us from Stage 2 to C_3. How one might represent this with this formalism is opaque.

But we also have the resources of plurivalent logic to appeal to. C_2 is meant to represent both of C_1 and U_1. So we might think of it as the plurivalent state where A is both t and f. We then have the following picture:

Stage	Conventional Truth	Ultimate Truth
1	$A \rightsquigarrow t$	$A \rightsquigarrow f$
2	$A \rightsquigarrow t$ and $A \rightsquigarrow f$	?
3	?	?

But how to fill in the blanks here is even less clear. There is nothing, as such, in the plurivalent semantics which represents A *not* having those two values. Perhaps we could try: $A \rightsquigarrow b$ or $A \rightsquigarrow n$ or $A \rightsquigarrow e$. But that would make C_3: $(A \rightsquigarrow t$ and $A \rightsquigarrow f) \wedge (A \rightsquigarrow b$ or $A \rightsquigarrow n$ or $A \rightsquigarrow e)$, and so U_3 would be: $\neg(A \rightsquigarrow t$ and $A \rightsquigarrow f) \wedge \neg(A \rightsquigarrow b$ or $A \rightsquigarrow n$ or $A \rightsquigarrow e)$, that is: $A \rightsquigarrow t$ or $A \rightsquigarrow f$. And that cannot be right, since it takes us back to the two possibilities at Stage 1.

In fact, there is a simple way to resolve the problem. Recall from 5.5 the truth predicate, T. This satisfies the T-schema: $T\langle A\rangle$ iff A. Recall, also, that $\neg T\langle A\rangle$ is not equivalent to $F\langle A\rangle$, that is, $T\langle\neg A\rangle$. We might then express U_2, the claim that D is neither true nor false as $\neg T\langle D\rangle \wedge \neg T\langle\neg D\rangle$. Since truth does not commute with negation, the second conjunct is not equivalent to $T\langle\neg\neg D\rangle$, and so to $\neg\neg D$, and so to D. U_3 is also meant to reject both of the conjuncts of C_3 in the same way. We can therefore apply the same move there. This gives us the following:

Stage	Conventional Truth	Ultimate Truth
1	D	$\neg D$
2	$D \wedge \neg D$	$\neg T\langle D\rangle \wedge \neg T\langle\neg D\rangle$
3	$(D \wedge \neg D) \wedge (\neg T\langle D\rangle \wedge \neg T\langle\neg D\rangle)$	$\neg T\langle D \wedge \neg D\rangle \wedge$ $\neg T\langle\neg T\langle D\rangle \wedge \neg T\langle\neg D\rangle\rangle$

Recall that C_2 is meant to represent the thought that D is both true and false. We might therefore represent this as $T\langle D\rangle \wedge T\langle\neg D\rangle$, which is, in any case, equivalent to $D \wedge \neg D$, by the T-schema. If we make this replacement, and do the same thing at C_3, we obtain:

Stage	Conventional Truth	Ultimate Truth
1	D	$\neg D$
2	$T\langle D\rangle \wedge T\langle\neg D\rangle$	$\neg T\langle D\rangle \wedge \neg T\langle\neg D\rangle$
3	$T\langle T\langle D\rangle \wedge T\langle\neg D\rangle\rangle \wedge$ $T\langle\neg T\langle D\rangle \wedge \neg T\langle\neg D\rangle\rangle$	$\neg T\langle T\langle D\rangle \wedge T\langle\neg D\rangle\rangle \wedge$ $\neg T\langle\neg T\langle D\rangle \wedge \neg T\langle\neg D\rangle\rangle$

So we now have a simple pattern. If C and U are the conventional and ultimate statements at some stage, the conventional truth at the next stage is just $T\langle C\rangle \wedge T\langle U\rangle$, and the ultimate truth at the next stage is $\neg T\langle C\rangle \wedge \neg T\langle U\rangle$. So we have the following pattern:

Stage	Conventional Truth	Ultimate Truth
1	$C_1 = D$	$U_1 = \neg D$
2	$C_2 = T\langle C_1\rangle \wedge T\langle U_1\rangle$	$U_2 = \neg T\langle C_1\rangle \wedge \neg T\langle U_1\rangle$
3	$C_3 = T\langle C_2\rangle \wedge T\langle U_2\rangle$	$U_3 = \neg T\langle C_2\rangle \wedge \neg T\langle U_2\rangle$

And this is a pattern, moreover, which takes us though distinct stages, because of the relationship between truth and negation.

But now an obvious question arises. The pattern could obviously be continued. Why stop there?[11]

7.6 Pseudo Jizang

Light is thrown on the matter by another San Lun text. This is the text *Dasheng xuanlun* (The Profound Meaning of Mahāyāna). Traditionally, this text was taken to have been written by Jizang; but more recent scholarship suggests that it is by a later writer (or writers), of unknown name(s). By analogy with the practice of referring to some medieval European whom history has placed in a similar invidious situation, let us call this voice *Pseudo Jizang*.[12]

One reason that Pseudo Jizang is interesting is that he explicitly endorses the Paradox of Ineffability, which we met in Chapter 6. As he puts it:[13]

Since effability is effability-as-ineffability, effability is ineffability. Since ineffability is ineffability-as-effability, ineffability is always effability.

However, that is not an aspect of his thought we need to go into here. What we are concerned with are his remarks on Jizang's progression.

Taking us through the first three stages of Jizang's hierarchy, Pseudo Jizang writes as follows:[14]

[11] In his comment on this passage, Chan notes the similarity between Jizang's dialectic and that of Hegel, and notes that it may be be continued indefinitely. (Chan (1963), p. 361.) A similar point is made by Liu (1003), p. 666.

[12] For discussion and references, see Deguchi (forthcoming), Section 1. The terminology 'Pseudo Jizang' is Deguchi's.

[13] Takakusu and Watanabe (1924), p. 24. Translation by Yasuo Deguchi.

[14] I take the text from Garfield (2015), pp. 257ff. The translation is Deguchi's.

Stage 1: Other schools take only Being as conventional truth, and 'Emptiness' as ultimate truth, and claim nothing else.

Stage 2: Now let me make clear that either of them, whether it is Being or Emptiness, is conventional truth, and Non-Emptiness and Non-Being can be first named as ultimate truth.

Stage 3: Thirdly—let us call Emptiness and Being 'Two' and Non-Emptiness and Non-Being 'Non-two'—all of Two and Non-two are conventional truth, whereas Non-two and Non-non-two can be first named as ultimate truth.

But Pseudo Jizang then adds a fourth stage, according to the same formula.

Stage 4: Fourthly, all of these three sorts of two truths are mere doctrines. Those three are preached only for making people understand Non-three. Having no foundation is alone named as way of things.

Let us add this to our diagram.

Stage	Conventional Truth	Ultimate Truth
1	$C_1 = D$	$U_1 = \neg D$
2	$C_2 = T\langle C_1\rangle \wedge T\langle U_1\rangle$	$U_2 = \neg T\langle C_1\rangle \wedge \neg T\langle U_1\rangle$
3	$C_3 = T\langle C_2\rangle \wedge T\langle U_2\rangle$	$U_3 = \neg T\langle C_2\rangle \wedge \neg T\langle U_2\rangle$
4	$C_4 = T\langle C_3\rangle \wedge T\langle U_3\rangle$	$U_4 = \neg T\langle C_3\rangle \wedge \neg T\langle U_3\rangle$

But then he, too, stops. Why?

The text continues:

QUESTION: Do you take all the former three as conventional truth and Non-three as ultimate truth?

ANSWER: Yes, I do.

QUESTION: Then why do doctrine and the way of things differ with each other?

ANSWER: I take Two truths as doctrines and Non-Two (truths) as way of things. But the distinction between them is merely superficial and occasional, and there is no barrier between them.

QUESTION: Why do you claim this Fourfold Two Truth?

ANSWER: Against the Abhidharma's two truths of phenomena and truth, the first two truths, i.e., Emptiness and Being, is claimed.

Against people who are based on Vasubandhu's *Thirty Verses* and uphold two truths of Emptiness and Being, I claim that since your truths of Emptiness and Being are merely our conventional truth, Non-emptiness and Non-Being are really ultimate truth. That's why I made the second set of two truths.

Thirdly, against people who are based on Asaṇga's *Anthology of Mahayana* (*Mahāyāna-saṃgraha*) and take 'Two'; i.e., interdependent nature and discriminative nature as conventional truth, and non-interdependent nature and non-discriminate nature; that is to say true nature as 'Non-two' as ultimate truth, I

> claim that either of the 'Two' or 'Non-two' is merely our conventional truth and 'Non-two and Non-non-two' is ultimate truth. Hence we have the third of two truths.
>
> Fourthly, other Mahāyāna people say that Yogācāra's three are conventional and the three naturelessnesses or non-firmly established truth is ultimate truth. That is why I claim that either of your two truths, i.e., interdependent nature and discriminative nature; or two truth that is not two, or firmly-establish truth on the one hand, and 'Non-two and Non-non-two'; i.e., three non-nature or non-firmly-established truth on the other hand, is merely my conventional truth, whereas 'Forgetfulness of words and annihilation of thoughts' is really ultimate truth.

What is going on here is as follows. The Chinese Buddhists had a problem. They inherited many texts from India. These all arrived at about the same time, and obviously contradicted each other, since they came from different schools of Buddhism. How could these be reconciled? They came up with the ingenious solution of a *panjiao* (classification of doctrines).[15] Buddhist doctrine is difficult, and getting one's head around it is hard. So during his ministry the Buddha taught it in stages. Each stage prior to the final one was not exactly right, but once one grasped that stage, it was easier to understand the next stage, and so on, till one gets to the correct view. The previous stages, though not actually correct, were skilful means of teaching (*upāya*). (The doctrine of upāya is a familiar Indian doctrine. Much is made of it in the sūtra commonly known as the *Lotus Sūtra*,[16] which was very familiar to the Chinese.) Each Chinese school had it's own panjiao; and each, of course, put its own view as the highest teaching, normally the last stage of the panjiao. What we have here is Pseudo Jizang's panjiao. (Later schools of Chinese Buddhism tended to have more complex panjiaos, simply because they had to accommodate the other schools of Chinese Buddhism as well.)

The stages of Pseudo Jizang's dialectic are, then, the stages of his panjiao. The texts that he cites which express the views of the first three stages are:[17]

- Stage 1: Abhidharma texts
- Stage 2: Vasubandhu's *Thirty Verses*
- Stage 3: Asaṇga's *Anthology of Mahāyāna*

Stage 4—or at least the ultimate at this stage—is, naturally, his own view. At each stage, the view of the previous stage is rejected and replaced by a more accurate

[15] See Mun (2006).

[16] *Suddharma Puṇḍarika Sūtra* (literally: Sūtra of the White Lotus of the Supreme Dharma).

[17] Of course, these are not sūtras, that is, texts attributed to the Buddha; but each is drawing from certain sūtras taken to be canonical.

view, until we arrive at the last stage. Whether or not Pseudo Jizang does justice to the texts in question may well be dubious. However, at least we see why he stopped at Stage 4.

7.7 The Jizang Hierarchy

Once one sees the pattern, it is clear that it can continue indefinitely, however. There is an infinite number of stages, S_n, one for every positive integer n. Each stage is a pair, the first member of which is C_n, the things held to be conventionally true, and the second member of which is U_n, things held to be ultimately true. These may be defined by recursion:[18]

- $C_1 = D$ and $U_1 = \neg D$
- $C_{n+1} = T\langle C_n \rangle \wedge T\langle U_n \rangle$ and $U_{n+1} = \neg T\langle C_n \rangle \wedge \neg T\langle U_n \rangle$

Call this the *Jizang Hierarchy*. Clearly, the move that takes us from one stage of the progression to the next is the same every time, as is its rationale: what is held to be ultimately true at a stage is expressed in language, and so is really conventionally true. Thus, at the next stage it is added to the things that are conventionally true. And what is ultimately true at this stage is a denial of both.

One might wonder whether the progression, as I have defined it, really does produce something different at each stage, or whether at some point it collapses into mere repetition, as my original formulation of Jizang's view did. It can be shown that it does not, but I defer the proof to a technical appendix to the chapter.

Supposing that the progression does go on to infinity in the way I have indicated, what has been achieved? Since there is no terminus to the progression, the import is in the journey, not the destination. (Unless, that is, one simply gives up when one comes to see the infinite game of tail-catching in play. I will come back to this briefly in Chapter 9.) Each stage is a duality of conventional and ultimate truth. The duality is unacceptable, and must be transcended. This is done at the conventional level of the next stage: we have both conjuncts. This is the third koṭi of the catuṣkoṭi. But this itself is a duality of two conjuncts; and so is transcended in the ultimate truth at the same level, where neither conjunct is true. This is the fourth koṭi of the catuṣkoṭi. Thus, the whole progression is one

[18] If we have a suitable infinitary language, we could, if we wished, iterate the stages into the transfinite. At limit ordinals, λ, we would have $C_\lambda = \bigwedge_{\alpha<\lambda} (T\langle C_\alpha \rangle \wedge T\langle U_\alpha \rangle)$ and $U_\lambda = \bigwedge_{\alpha<\lambda} (\neg T\langle C_\alpha \rangle \wedge \neg T\langle U_\alpha \rangle)$.

of successively transcending dualities, alternately applying the third and fourth corners of the catuṣkoṭi to do so.

According to this picture, then, transcending dualities is not a final state but a *process* involving the successive rejection of dualities that arise, employing these two koṭis. As Liu puts matters, this is a:[19]

> method of making use of one standpoint to undermine another standpoint, the final goal being the transcending of all specific standpoints, that is, the realization of the truth of nonduality.

This is not an entirely happy way of putting matters. If the process does, indeed, go on to infinity, there is no final goal—at least, if this is understood as a last state. Perhaps, then, we might understand the thought as being that the whole process *shows* us something about ultimate reality: that it is ineffable, this being the 'final goal'.

7.8 Conclusion

In this chapter we have looked at the thought of Jizang and Pseudo Jizang, the hierarchies they deliver, and the infinite progression this generates when shorn of the termination required to put a certain view last. What emerges is the importance, not of a state, but of a process: the process of duality-transcendence.

For the next developments in our subject, we will look at how the topic of the two realities which are one plays out in later Chinese Buddhisms, and particularly in the Huayan tradition.

7.9 Technical Appendix

In this appendix I will prove that the Jizang Hierarchy generates novel states at every stage.

First, we need a language in which to express the sentences of the hierarchy. For this, take a language with one propositional parameter, D, a monadic predicate T, and a name-forming operator $\langle . \rangle$. The syntax of the language is defined recursively: D is a formula; if A is any formula, $T\langle A \rangle$ is a formula; if A, B are formulas, so are $A \wedge B$, $A \vee B$, $\neg A$.

A four-valued FDE interpretation, with values $V = \{t, f, b, n\}$, is a structure, $\langle X, \delta \rangle$, such that X is a non-empty set, and:

[19] Liu (1993), p. 663.

- $\delta(D) \in V$
- for every A, $\delta(\langle A \rangle) \in X$
- $\delta(T)$ is a function such that if $d \in X$, $\delta(T)(d) \in V$

The truth/falsity conditions for the connectives are as usual in FDE. (See 2.10.2.)

We will say that A *entails* B iff, if A is designated then so is B, in every interpretation which validates the T-scheme. (That is, for any formula, C, C is designated iff $T\langle C \rangle$ is designated.)

Now, it is clear that any for $i > 1$, C_{i+1} entails C_i, since C_{i+1} entails $T\langle C_i \rangle$. It follows that if $j > i$, C_j entails C_i. We show that the converse is not true.

Define the *order* of a sentence to be the length of the greatest chain of nested Ts *plus* 1. A simple induction on i shows that C_i and U_i have order i. Write the order of A as $|A|$. Note that, given an interpretation, to evaluate the value of a formula of order i, one needs to know the value of $\delta(T)$ only for formulas, A, of order $< i$.

Next we show:

Lemma(*): For every i, C_i does not entail U_i.

Proof: This is obviously true for $i = 1$. So let $i = j + 1$. Take an interpretation, I, where X is the set of formulas, $\delta(\langle A \rangle) = A$, $\delta(D) = b$, and $\delta(T)$ is defined by recursion on the order of A, thus:

- if $|A| < j$, $\delta(T)(A) = b$
- if $|A| = j$, $\delta(T)(A) = t$
- if $|A| > j$, $\delta(T)(A)$ is the value of A

The last clause makes sense, since to evaluate A one has to have only the values of $\delta(T)$ for things of order less than that of A.

It is now not difficult to show the following, which establish the result.

- I verifies the T-schema. (If $|A| < j$, both A and $T\langle A \rangle$ have the value b. If $|A| = j$, A has the value b and $T\langle A \rangle$ has the value t. If $|A| > j$, A and $T\langle A \rangle$ have the same value.)
- If $|A| \leq j$ then the value of A is b. In particular, then, C_j and U_j have the value b.
- C_{j+1}, which is $T\langle C_j \rangle \wedge T\langle U_j \rangle$, takes the value t; and U_{j+1} which is $\neg T\langle C_j \rangle \wedge \neg T\langle U_j \rangle$ takes the value f. ■

Corollary(**): For any $i \geq 1$, C_i does not entail C_{i+1}. For $C_{i+1} = T\langle C_i \rangle \wedge T\langle U_i \rangle$, and C_i does not entail $T\langle U_i \rangle$ (and so, U_i), by Lemma (*). ■

We can now prove the main:

Theorem: For all $j > i$, C_i does not entail C_j.

Proof: The proof is by induction on j. For $j = 1$, this clear. So suppose it proved for j, that $i < j + 1$, and that C_i *does* entail C_{j+1}. i cannot be j—by Corollary (**). So $i < j$. But by assumption, C_i entails $C_{j+1} = T\langle C_j\rangle \wedge T\langle U_j\rangle$. So C_i entails C_j, contrary to induction hypothesis. ■

So for every $i \neq j$, C_i and C_j are logically distinct. We now show the same for U_i and U_j.

Theorem: If $i < j$, U_i does not entail U_j, and U_j does not entail U_i.

Proof: That U_i does not entail U_j is shown by the interpretation defined in Lemma (*). For the reverse, consider the interpretation I, where X is the set of formulas, $\delta(\langle A\rangle) = A$, $\delta(D) = n$, and $\delta(T)$ is defined by recursion on the order of A, thus:

- if $|A| < j$, $\delta(T)(A) = n$
- if $|A| = j$, $\delta(T)(A) = f$
- if $|A| > j$, $\delta(T)(A)$ is the value of A.

It is now not difficult to show the following, which establish the result.

- I verifies the T-schema. (If $|A| < j$, both A and $T\langle A\rangle$ have the value n. If $|A| = j$, A has the value n and $T\langle A\rangle$ has the value f. If $|A| > j$, A and $T\langle A\rangle$ have the same value.)
- If $|A| \leq j$ then the value of A is n. In particular, then, C_j and U_j have the value n.
- U_{j+1}, which is $\neg T\langle C_j\rangle \wedge \neg T\langle U_j\rangle$, takes the value t. (So U_{j+1} does not entail U_i for any $i \leq j$.) ■

8

The Golden Lion

8.1 Introduction

In the 5-valued catuṣkoṭi, the bearers of semantic values are states of affairs. Each may have two aspects, a conventional one and an ultimate one. The former is effable; the latter is ineffable. As will probably have been clear to the reader a long time ago, the distinction between the conventional and ultimate aspects of reality is clearly a duality. And Buddhism, as we have already seen, is committed to overcoming all dualities. How should one do so in this case? In this chapter we will look at how the matter is handled in one of the very distinctive forms of Chinese Buddhism, Huayan. Huayan Buddhism paints a striking picture of reality as a totality of interpenetrating elements, each of which has a fractal quality, reflecting each of the other elements, as well as the whole itself. The relationship between conventional and ultimate reality plays a central role in this. Getting clear on the matter will deliver an answer to the question at hand.

We will start by going back to India, to look at two of the important Indian ideas that fed into Chinese Buddhism, and which we have not looked at so far. We will then turn to the Daoist influence on the issue at hand in Chinese Buddhism. This will provide the background necessary to discuss Huayan. The second part of the chapter will discuss the Huayan picture, including the question of the exact relationship between the two realities.[1] Central to the account presented here is a use of some elementary graph theory. This will deliver exactly what is required.

8.2 *Ālaya-Vijñāna*

First, then, to some Indian developments, which are relevant to the Chinese evolution.[2] Madhyamaka has been of much concern to us in previous chapters.

[1] And at this point, let me remind the reader, again, of the warning of §0.3 of the Preface: disagreements about the interpretation of the texts we are concerned with in the chapter are certainly possible.

[2] Some of the material in the next few sections is drawn from Priest (2010b).

We now need to look briefly at the other Indian Mahāyāna school: Yogācāra. Another name for the school was *Cittamātra*—mind only. And this is a much more accurate name for the school, since, unlike Madhyamaka, it was idealist (at least according to the most natural understanding of the school). That is: there is no mind-independent reality. The 'external world' exists only in one's mind.[3]

Being idealist, Yogācāra was particularly interested in the way that the mind works, and it gave a very distinctive analysis of this. There are eight sorts of consciousness. Six of these are those to do with sensation: the consciousnesses of sight, hearing, touch, taste, smell, and introspection. The first five of these are, of course, standard from Western thought. The sixth is pretty standard in Indian thought as well: it is our consciousness of 'internal' events, such as pains and emotions. The seventh kind of consciousness is *kliṣṭa-manas*.[4] This is a level of consciousness interposed between the first six and the eighth. Its function is somewhat debatable. However, it is not really relevant to our story here.

What is highly relevant is the eighth sort of consciousness, the *ālaya-vijñāna*. This is the deepest level of consciousness. Indeed, we might call it the unconscious; and in many ways it is somewhat similar to the unconscious of Freud.[5] The Sanskrit term means *storehouse consciouness*; and it is called this because it stores the 'seeds' of karma. When we act, there are effects—seeds—which can manifest later. The seeds are stored in the ālaya, bubbling up at a later time to disturb the top six levels of consciousness, generating the phenomenal world we experience. The ālaya is often likened to the water of an ocean, and the top six levels of consciousness to the waves on its surface.

In his *Trisvabhāvanirdeśa* (Treatise on the Three Natures), Vasubandhu ties these things to the matter of non-duality. As an object is imagined in the external world, there is a subject/object duality; but this is not real. As he puts it:[6]

> If anything appears, it is imagined.
> The way it appears is as duality.
> What is the consequence of its nonexistence?
> The fact of nonduality.

[3] For a general introduction to Yogācāra, see Siderits (2007), ch. 8, and Williams (2008), ch. 4.

[4] Also called *manas-vijñāna*, or sometimes simply *manas*.

[5] Not only are both unconscious, but both store things—in the case of Freud, painful memories and experiences—which can eventually work their way to the surface and have effects on the conscious part of the mind.

[6] The following are vv. 4, 29, and 34. See Garfield (2002a), pp. 131–4.

The apparent duality is generated by the effect of the ālaya (the root consciouness) on the sense-consciousnesses, causing the 'perception':

> Through the root consciousness
> The nonexistent duality appears.
> But since the duality is completely nonexistent,
> This is only a percept.

When one grasps the illusory nature of the imagined object, the subject/object duality vanishes:

> In the same way[7] through the non-perception of duality
> There is the vanishing of duality.
> When it vanishes completely,
> Nondual awareness arises.

An analysis of consciousness, then, leads to the transcendence of this duality.

8.3 *Tathāgata-Garbha*

The second Indian matter we need to look at is a certain kind of sūtra that appeared, which was, at least initially, orthogonal to both Madhyamaka and Yogācāra. These were the *Tathāgata-Garbha Sūtras*.[8] The name means *womb* or *seed* (garbha) *of Buddhahood* (tathāgata). The thought expressed by this term is that in each person there is a part that can generate enlightenment. Indeed, one might think of it as the part that is already enlightened. When joined with Yogācāra thought, it was natural to see the tathāgata-garbha as the ālaya, at least in its pure form. Normally, it is impure, 'tainted' by the karmic seeds. The point of the Buddhist path is to eliminate these seeds. The tathāgata-garbha/ālaya then manifests as Buddhahood.[9]

In the early *Tathāgata-Garbha Sūtras*, the garbha, whose nature it is to be a Buddha, is very much an individual matter: each consciousness has a different one (ālaya). But in later sūtras it morphs into something much more grandiose: something like a universal Mind, or Buddha nature (Chin: *Foxing*). (For comparison, think of Hegel's *Geist*, and how it manifests in individual subjective consciousnesses.) In the process, it loses most of its mind-like qualities—the ālaya had few enough of these anyway. But the Yogācāra thought, that it is the ground of the phenomenal world, is retained, as is the idea that this phenomenal world is its manifestation.

[7] This refers to a conjuring trick in which a magician produces an illusory elephant.
[8] See Williams (2009), ch. 5.
[9] Further on the 'transformation of the basis,' see Park (1983), pp. 126–32.

One of the *Tathāgata-Garbha Sūtras*, *The Awakening of Faith in Mahāyāna* (*Dasheng qixinlun*), puts matters like this:[10]

In the one soul we may distinguish two aspects. The one is the soul as suchness (*bhūtatathatā*), the other is the soul as birth-and-death (*samsāra*). Each in itself constitutes all things, and both are so closely interrelated that one cannot be separated from the other.

What is meant by the soul as suchness (*bhūtatathatā*) is the oneness of the totality of things (*dharmadhātu*), the great all-including whole, the quintessence of the Doctrine. For the essential nature of the soul is increate and eternal.

All things, on account of our confused subjectivity (*smṛti*), appear under the form of individuation. If we could overcome our confused subjectivity, the signs of individuation would disappear, and there would be no trace of the world [of isolated individual objects].

Therefore, all things in their fundamental nature are not namable or explicable. They cannot be adequately expressed in any form of language . . . They possess absolute sameness. They are subject neither to transformation, nor to destruction. They are nothing but the one soul, for which suchness is another designation.

The Chinese character translated as 'soul' here is *xin* (mind/heart), which, in this context, it is just another name here for the tathāgata-garbha writ large. Traditionally, the *Awakening of Faith* is attributed to the Indian philosopher Aśvaghoṣa (fl. second century). But it is almost certainly, in fact, an apocryphal text, composed in China, perhaps around the sixth century.[11] At any rate, though the text had little influence on Indian Buddhism, it had an enormous influence on Chinese Buddhism. And central to this was the idea that Mind is a single thing, with a pure side, tathāta, which is ultimate reality, and an impure side which is the conventional world, saṃsāra.

8.4 China and the Two Realities

So back to China.

As we noted in 7.2, in the early years of Buddhism in China, ultimate reality came to be identified with the Dao, and conventional reality with phenomenal reality. This played a significant role in how the relationship between the two realities was thought of in Chinese Buddhism. The relationship between the Dao and the 'myriad things' is not at all that between appearance and reality. The myriad things are the manifestations of the Dao, roughly in the same way that your actions are the manifestation of your personality. One cannot have a manifestation without the something of which it is a manifestation. Conversely, the form of being of the Dao is precisely in its activity (which is a non-activity, in the sense that

10 Suzuki (no date), pp. 55–7.

11 Williams (2009), p. 115.

it is just happens—like normal breathing); so one cannot have the Dao without its manifestations. So things came to be seen in the following way:

$$\frac{\text{Dao}}{\text{manifestations}} = \frac{\text{non-being } (wu)}{\text{beings } (you)} = \frac{\text{ultimate reality}}{\text{conventional reality}}$$

This provided a way of understanding the relationship between the two realities which resonated with the developments in tathāgata-garbha thought described in the last section. Reality (Mind) is two-sided, one conventional side of tathāta, and one ultimate side of saṃsāra. It also articulates an answer to the question, posed by Madhyamaka, of what ultimate reality, being empty, depends upon. (See 4.6.)

In Huayan, a striking metaphor for this picture is to be found in the *Jin shizi zhang* (Treatise on the Golden Lion)[12] by Fazang, traditionally the third Huayan Patriarch, but arguably the most systematic of the Huayan thinkers. Fazang uses a golden statue of a lion to illustrate the relationship in question. He likens ultimate reality to the gold out of which the lion is made, and phenomenal reality to the lion, or its shape. So we have the following analogy:

$$\frac{\text{gold}}{\text{lion}} = \frac{\text{ultimate reality}}{\text{phenomenal reality}}$$

On this model, there is, again, only one reality: there is only one thing—the golden lion. The gold and the lion are nonetheless distinct. (The gold could be melted down and refashioned into the statue of the Buddha. The lion would then cease to exist, but the gold would not.) But one cannot have the lion without the something of which it is made, the gold; conversely, the gold must manifest itself in some form or other, in this case, that of a lion. Neither has self-nature.[13]

An aside: this is clearly a monism of some kind. It is interesting to compare it with the monism of Spinoza. For him there is only one substance, but it may have different modes: mind/matter. This is not unlike there being a unique Dao (or ultimate reality), which manifests in different ways. However, there is a crucial difference between Spinoza's picture and the one here. For him, modes depend on a substance in a way in which the substance does not depend on its modes.[14] It is, after all, a substance—something, if you like, with svabhāva. By contrast, the Dao is just as empty as its manifestations, and depends for being what it is on them.

[12] See, e.g., Chan (1963), pp. 409–14.

[13] For some further discussion of the relationship between the two realities in Chinese Buddhism, and especially Huayan, see Perkins (2015), sec. 6.

[14] As he says in Part I of the *Ethics*: 'Proposition III: By *substance* I mean that which is in itself, and is conceived of through itself; in other words, that of which a conception can be formed independently of any other conception.' 'Proposition V: By *mode*, I mean the modifications of a substance, or that which exists in, and is conceived thorough, something other than itself.' (Quotations from Elwes (1956), p. 45.)

Let me end this section by highlighting some contrasts between the picture of the two aspects of reality and the relationship between them that has emerged, by comparing it with that delivered by Candrakīrti, as discussed in 4.6.

For a start, Candrakīrti's understanding of the distinction is tied closely to perception. The two aspects are two ways that the same thing can be perceived, or maybe dispositional properties of the thing to be perceived in two ways. In the Chinese picture, the distinction has little explicitly to do with perception: it is to do with the distinction between something whose nature it is to manifest in a certain way and those manifestations. Chinese Buddhists had not, of course, forgotten the mind, and it is related to the distinction between conventional and ultimate reality, but its relationship to the two aspects of reality is very different from that in Candrakīrti's account. Mind is the whole of reality, with two interrelated aspects: an ineffable something and its manifestations.

Secondly, and more importantly for what is to follow: for Candrakīrti, each thing has two aspects, and there is no suggestion that the ultimate aspects of two distinct things are the same. But in the Chinese picture, there is one single thing which is the ultimate aspect of all things, the ineffable something, whether one wishes to call it: Dao, Buddha nature, non-being, emptiness, or whatever.

8.5 *Li*, *Shi*, *Ji*

Which brings us to Huayan itself. Though this kind of Buddhism flourished for only a short time in China, it was, perhaps, the most theoretically sophisticated form of Chinese Buddhism, and it had an enormous impact on other Buddhisms, such as Chan (and indeed, on Chinese Neo-Confucianism).[15] The school is named after the sūtra which it took to be most important, the *Huayan Sūtra*. It is also know by its Sanskrit name, the *Avataṃsaka Sūtra*.[16] The Chinese *Huayan* and Sanskrit *Avataṃsaka* both translate into the English *Garland of Flowers*. The sūtra is a very long one, composed of a number of originally independent pieces, probably written in Central Asia in the early part of the common era, possibly the third and fourth centuries. It is certainly available in Chinese translation by the early fifth century.

We can start to understand Huayan by looking at some of its key terms, and especially *li*, *shi*, and *ji*.

[15] Commentators differ over some details of the interpretation of Huayan philosophy—though not the ones that will concern us here. Various accounts can be found in Chan (1969), Introduction; Chang (1972); Cook (1977); Cleary (1983), Introduction; Lusthaus (1998), sec. 8; Liu (2006), ch. 10; Williams (2009), ch. 6. The Lusthaus is a good concise statement of the matters that will concern us here. The Chan and Cleary references translate some of the most important Huayan texts. But as yet, few Huayan texts have been translated into English.

[16] One standard translation is Cleary (1993a).

The easiest is *li*. This means, literally, *principle*, and it is simply the Huayan name for ultimate reality, emptiness, Buddha nature.

Shi is more complicated. Its basic meaning is *affair* or *event*. But in various contexts, it can mean any of: situation, event, thing, manifest phenomenon, topic, state, scene—and maybe other things as well. The Huayan use it as a term for the elements of phenomenal reality. One might ask whether these are objects such as mountains and molehills, or situations, such as mountains being above sea level or molehills being made by moles. The answer is probably *both*. I suspect that the Chinese didn't place much importance on this conceptual difference. Indeed, the Chinese language might well make the distinction difficult to see. For a single character, say that for a horse, *ma*, might well mean, *a horse*, *this is a horse*, *a horse is the kind of thing in question*, depending entirely on the context. Indeed, maybe there is not that much difference anyway. Situations are, after all, objects of a certain kind. And with a bit of juggling, we can simply identify an object *a* with the situation of *a*'s being an object, or of *a*'s being the very object it is.

Crucially for present purposes, however, shi includes states of affairs—or better, their phenomenal manifestations. This is important because our present inquiry concerns the relationship between the two aspects of the semantic bearers in the 5-valued catuṣkoṭi, and these are states of affairs.

Finally, *ji* (Jap: *soku*). This is the hardest matter of all. In the vernacular, ji means something like *is the same as*. It is clear, however, that the Huayan philosophers use it as something of a term of art. The notion is translated into English in various ways, such as *mutual identification*, *mutual containment*, *interconnectedness*, *interpenetration*, *non-obstruction*, *non-interference*. I will stick with 'interpenetration'.[17]

This is a start to understanding ji, but does not get us very far. In what follows we will find a very precise understanding of the relationship involved. And since this is exactly the relationship between li and shi, it will provide, amongst other things, exactly the answer to the question of the relationship between the two realities in Huayan which we are looking for.

8.6 The Net of Indra

Let us approach the matter via the metaphor of the Net of Indra,[18] alluded to many times in the *Huayan Sūtra*.[19] This concerns a net that a god, Indra, has

[17] It is worth noting that in the Chinese text of the *Heart Sūtra* (4.2), in the lines translated as 'form is emptiness; emptiness is form', the character translated as 'is' is exactly ji.

[18] Much of what follows comes from Priest (2015b).

[19] Another beautiful metaphor used in the sūtra to illustrate the same phenomenon is the Tower of Maitreya, a nesting of towers and their contents, possessing a fractal quality.

spread through space. At every interstice of the net, Indra has placed a jewel which reflects every other jewel. Fazang himself puts matters as follows:[20]

It is like the net of Indra which is entirely made up of jewels. Due to their brightness and transparency, they reflect each other. In each of the jewels, the images of all the other jewels are [completely] reflected. This is the case with any one of the jewels, and will remain forever so. Now, if we take a jewel in the southwestern direction and examine it, [we can see] that this one jewel can reflect simultaneously the images of all other jewels at once. It is so with the one jewel, and is also so with each of all the others. Since each of the jewels simultaneously reflects the images of all other jewels at once, it follows that this jewel in the southwestern direction also reflects all the images of the jewels in each of the other jewels [at once]. It is so with this jewel, and is also so with all the others. Thus, the images multiply infinitely, and all these multiple infinite images are bright and clear inside this single jewel. The rest of the jewels can be understood in the same manner.

Thus, each jewel reflects each other jewel; but it reflects each other jewel reflecting each other jewel; and each other jewel reflecting each other jewel reflecting each other jewel; and so on. The relationship between each jewel is rather like that which obtains if one puts two mirrors opposite each other. If one then looks into either, one can (in principle) see each mirror reflecting the other to infinity.

In the metaphor, the jewels represent the elements of reality, and what the metaphor indicates is that each encodes every other, in some sense. This is exactly the relationship *ji*. The metaphor is certainly beautiful and suggestive. What we are after, however, is a non-metaphorical understanding of the notion.[21]

8.7 Identity

A somewhat flat-footed interpretation of the notion is simply as one of numerical identity. Thus Fazang says—or is translated as saying:[22]

If we take ten coins as symbolizing the totality of existence, and examine the relationship of existence amongst them, then, according to Huayan teaching, coin one will be seen as identical with the other nine coins.

[20] Quoted in Liu (1982), p. 65.

[21] Western philosophers who meet the Net of Indra for the first time are often struck by the similarity between this and Leibniz's account in the *Monadology*. For him, reality is composed of an infinitude of monads. Each monad is 'windowless'; that is, what goes on in each has no effect on what goes on in any other. But God has prearranged things in such a way that what goes on in each coordinates with what goes on in the others. The jewels in the net might be thought of as rather like Leibniz's monads. Indeed they are, to a certain extent. But there is a major difference. As Leibniz tells us right at the start of the *Monadology*, each of the monads is a substance. But whatever each jewel represents in reality is precisely *not* a substance, just because it is empty, and so has its nature only in relation to other things.

[22] Cook (1977), p. 2. The coins are clearly metaphors for the elements of reality.

And his commentator, Cook, says, concerning another passage by Fazang:[23]

This passage makes it clear that Fazang does in fact assert the identity of the rafter and the building, or, in other words, the part and the whole, or the particular and the universal.

Now, a feature of identity is that it is normally taken as supporting the substitution of identicals: if x and y are identical, then anything true of x is true of y. And we do indeed find Fazang reasoning sometimes in a way that suggests this:[24]

Question: since the building is identical with the rafter, then the remaining planks, tiles, and so on, must be identical with the rafter, aren't they? *Answer*: generally speaking, they are all identical with the rafter.

The reasoning here would appear to be that if r is any rafter, p is any plank, and b is the whole building, then since $r = b$ and $p = b$, $r = p$. This is an instance of the substitution of identicals.

Note that Fazang endorses the interpenetration between the part and the whole. This, itself, would seem to rule out the interpretation of interpenetration as identity. A car is not identical with its steering wheel. But worse follows. The interpretation quickly collapses into what amounts, effectively, to trivialism: nearly everything is true. Consider me. Take any property, P, and some object with that property. Then since I am that thing, I have the property P. This seems far too strong. There is clearly some sense in which I am not a slice of toast; and for all that George Bush and I may be one, I am not responsible for the invasion of Iraq and its disastrous consequences in the way that he is. Indeed, the passage just quoted does not, in fact, require the relation to be identity. Any transitive relation will do. So it would seem that whatever the notion is, it is not one of literal identity.[25]

8.8 Emptiness

Cook himself gestures at another understanding of what the relation might be. We often say that things are the same, meaning by this that they have a property in common. The ripe strawberry and the top traffic light are the same in that they are both red. In the present case, this seems far too weak an understanding, however. Any two things have some properties in common—for example, the property of being one thing. So this is to reduce the relation in question to a banality.

[23] Cook (1977), p. 79. The rafters and planks here are metaphors for the elements of reality; the building is a metaphor for the totality.

[24] Cook (1977), p. 82.

[25] Interestingly, Ziporyn (2013) does defend a trivialist interpretation of the closely related school of Chinese Buddhism, Tianti. This is discussed and rejected in Deguchi, Garfield, and Priest (2013a).

But maybe, says Cook, to say that things are related in the way we seek, is to say that they have some *really important* property in common. What? Says Cook:[26]

First, we must accept the basic concept of emptiness itself. Second, we must consider emptiness to be so fundamental to the being of things that despite their obvious and real differences, they are alike in a more essential way in being empty. If we can accept these premises, then the claim that all things are identical does not seem quite so improbable, because identity is claimed on the basis of this common emptiness.

As we have seen, emptiness, or being empty, is the central notion in the analysis of reality in Indian Madhyamaka Buddhism, and it was certainly taken over by Chinese Buddhism in general, and Huayan in particular. As Fazang himself puts it:[27]

The all is the one, for both are similar in being non-existent in Nature [GP: svabhāva].

[Things] are produced by the mind and have no self-nature at all. This is called the absence of characters. The scripture says, "All dharmas are originally empty in their nature and have not the least character".

Now, according to Cook, to say that all things are one is to say that they share this one important property. They are the same in this most fundamental of ways.

That all things are one, in this sense, is stating an important truth of Buddhism, and one of the appropriate profundity. However, it really doesn't seem to do justice to the metaphor of the Net of Indra. According to the metaphor, all things interpenetrate with all other things. To grasp one is, in some sense, to grasp all. This seems to go a lot further than the simple claim that all things share the same fundamental property. You can know everything about *a* and know that *a* and *b* share this most fundamental property without knowing much else about *b*.

8.9 ... and its Structure

But Cook's insight, that emptiness is important to what is going on, at least takes us in the right direction. To understand how, let us go back to the discussion of emptiness in 4.5. As we saw there, if something is empty, its being is determined by its locus (location) in a network of relations. Something's being the thing that it is, is its bearing a bunch of relations to other things.

We may represent this graphically. Suppose, for the sake of illustration, that the being of something, *x*, is constituted by its relationship to three things, *a*, *b*, and *c*. Then we might depict the situation thus:

[26] Cook (1977), p 62.

[27] Chang (1969), pp. 410, 416. See also Liu (2006), p. 251.

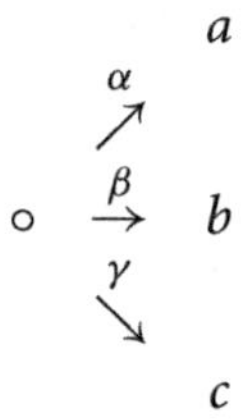

where the labels on the arrows indicate the relations in question. Anything at the spot marked ○ would be x.

Note that relations have a direction, marked by the direction of the arrow. (Brutus killing Caesar is not the same as Caesar killing Brutus.) It will be helpful in what follows to arrange for all the arrows to point in the same direction.[28] One can do this because every relation, ρ, has a converse, $\breve{\rho}$, which expresses the same thing, since $y\rho x$ iff $x\breve{\rho}y$. (To say that Brutus killed Caesar is the same as saying that Caesar was killed by Brutus.) So we can always replace an arrow pointing in the wrong direction, $x \stackrel{\rho}{\leftarrow} y$, with one pointing in the right direction, $x \stackrel{\breve{\rho}}{\rightarrow} y$.[29]

Of course, since a, b, and c are empty, the same analysis must be applied to them. They themselves are nothing more than loci in a field of relations. We might depict this (using the magic number three again, and ignoring the superscripts on the arrows) as follows:

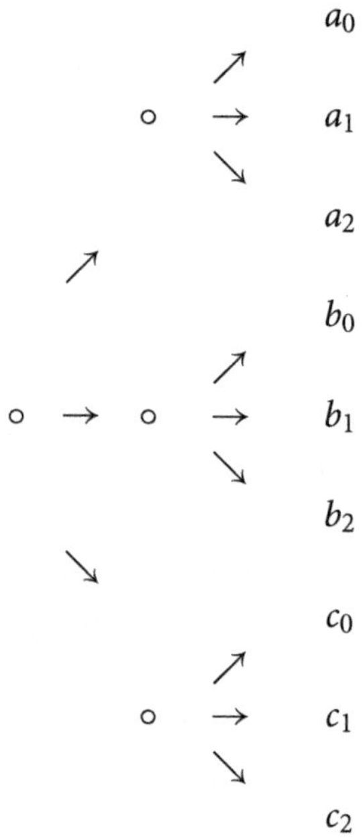

[28] This is not essential, but it makes it much easier to picture what is going on.

[29] Relations can also have more than two places. However, we can think of the relation $\rho x_1 \dots x_n$, where $n > 2$, as a binary relation between x_1 and an ordered $(n-1)$-tuple, thus: $x_1 \rho \langle x_2, \dots, x_n \rangle$.

Each of the a_is, b_is, and c_is, must be treated in the same way, of course; and so on for everything generated in this way. On ultimate analysis, then, the original element, x, turns out to be the locus which is the root of a tree which is infinite along every branch, of the following kind:

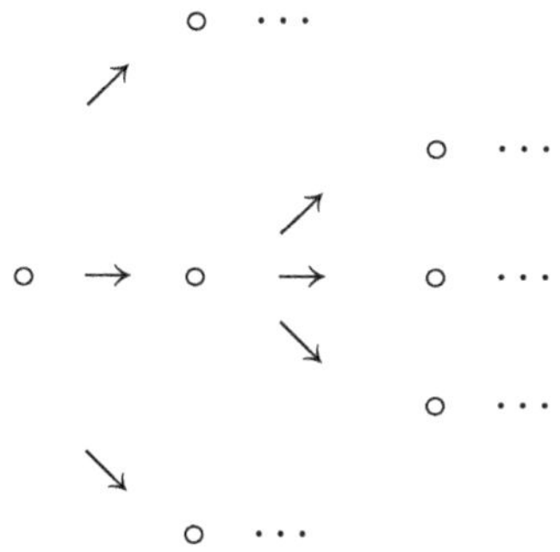

In the end, all content has disappeared. What is left is pure form—structure.[30] Indeed, what the tree gives is exactly the ontological structure of x.[31]

And now, something interesting can happen. Consider, say, being the north pole, n, of a magnet. It is a north pole only because there is a south pole, s, which it relates to in a certain way, π. We may depict matters as follows. (I record which object is at each node, so that one may keep track of matters, but label only the relation π to avoid clutter.)

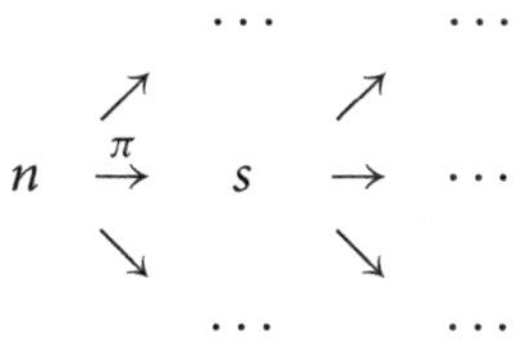

[30] The situation is, in fact, more complex than described, since the relations in the tree must themselves be analysed as having merely relational nature. This gives rise to another kind of non-well-founded tree. The details are given in Priest (2009). However, the level of analysis given here will suffice for present purposes.

[31] One might worry at this point that there are enough different tree structures to provide sufficient discrimination between objects, especially when one notes that the relations themselves are empty, and so must be individuated by their own structural trees (and so on indefinitely). A simple model showing this to be possible is as follows. Take a model, M, of ZF set theory, including the Axiom of Foundation. And let s be the sets of some level, l, in the cumulative hierarchy in M. Take any member of this, x, and consider its membership tree. That is, x is at the root; and the descendants of any node in the tree are its members. Distinct members of s have distinct trees, and so can be individuated by these trees. Moreover, the membership relation restricted to s is a set of pairs which occurs a few levels up from l in the cumulative hierarchy. This can therefore be individuated by its membership tree in exactly the same way—and so on up. One might think that the branches of each of these trees are finite, because of the Axiom of Foundation, and that this finitude is playing an essential role in this argument. It is not. We can take M to be a non-standard model in which the membership relation is not well founded (despite the fact that this is a model of Foundation). The branches of the membership tree may then be infinite.

As one might expect, the tree for being s is a part of the tree for being n.

But of course, s is symmetrically related to n. So if we fill out the tree a little further, we will get the following:

$$
\begin{array}{ccccccc}
 & & \ldots & & \ldots & & \ldots \\
 & \nearrow & & \nearrow & & \nearrow & \\
n & \overset{\pi}{\rightarrow} & s & \overset{\pi}{\rightarrow} & n & \rightarrow & \ldots \\
 & \searrow & & \searrow & & \searrow & \\
 & & \ldots & & \ldots & & \ldots
\end{array}
$$

The tree for being n is part of the tree for being s as well![32] The two things intermingle in the most intimate way. The structure of each is literally a part of the other. Note that this can happen only because the trees for both n and s are infinite. If either were finite, the situation could not arise.

At any rate, one could not hope for a nicer representation of the idea that the two objects 'interpenetrate'. The ontological structure of each contains (encodes) the ontological structure of the other. The relation of two trees each being a sub-tree of the other is obviously a symmetric and transitive relation. (It does no harm to allow sub-trees to be improper, making the relationship reflexive as well, and so an equivalence relation.) The Huayan notion of interpenetration may be taken to be exactly this.

8.10 Tying Everything Together

So far so good. But now come back to li, the ultimate aspect of reality. This is as empty as everything else. So it has only relational nature, and so is at the root of its own tree. What does it have its nature in relation to? As we saw in 8.4, it has this by relating to the objects of conventional reality. So if we write u for the ultimate aspect of reality, and the (three) shi of conventional reality as a, b, and c, the tree for u will look like this (I label the nodes for easy reference):

$$
\begin{array}{ccccc}
 & & & \nearrow & \ldots \\
 & & a & & \\
 & \nearrow & & \nearrow & \ldots \\
u & \rightarrow & b & \rightarrow & \ldots \\
 & \searrow & & \searrow & \ldots \\
 & & c & & \\
 & & & \searrow & \ldots
\end{array}
$$

[32] To be a bit more precise, this is up to isomorphism. The tree for n has a sub-tree which is isomorphic to the tree for s (which tree has, therefore, sub-trees which are isomorphic to the whole tree). But we may simply identify isomorphic trees.

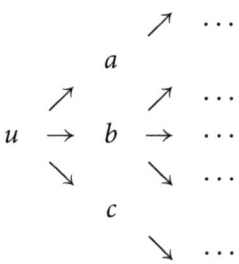

But each shi is what it is by relating to *u*. (Remember the metaphor of the golden lion.) So if we take one of the shi, say *b*, and look at the descendants on its tree, we will find *u*. And the same, of course, for every other shi. We have, then, the following picture:

$$
\begin{array}{ccccccccc}
 & & & \nearrow & \cdots & & & \nearrow & \cdots \\
 & & a & & & & a & & \\
 & \nearrow & & \nearrow & \cdots & \nearrow & & & \\
u & \rightarrow & b & \rightarrow & u & \rightarrow & b & \rightarrow & \cdots \\
 & \searrow & & \searrow & \cdots & \searrow & & & \\
 & & c & & & & c & & \\
 & & & \searrow & \cdots & & & \searrow & \cdots
\end{array}
$$

For future reference, call this **diagram *D***. What we see is that *u* and each shi play north and south to each other. That is, they interpenetrate.

Huayan metaphysics is often encapsulated in four principles. These are:[33]

- The existence of shi
- The existence of li
- The interpenetration of li and shi (*lishi wuai*)
- The interpenetration of shi and shi (*shishi wuai*)

What we have here is exactly *lishi wuai* (literally, the non-obstruction of li and shi).

Lishi wuai is expressed by Dushun (557–640), the First Patriarch of Huayan, in his *Huayan fajie xuanjing* (Meditation on the Dharmadhātu—*Dharmadhātu* is the realm of all dharmas), as follows:[34]

> Li, the law that extends everywhere, has no boundaries or limitations, but shi, the objects that are embraced by li, have limitations and boundaries. In each and every shi, the li spreads all over without omission or deficiency. Why? Because the truth of li is indivisible. Thus, each and every minute atom absorbs and embraces the infinite truth of li in a perfect and complete manner.
>
> Shi, the matter that embraces, has boundaries and limitations, and li, the truth that is embraced [by things], has no boundaries or limitations. Yet this limited shi is completely identical [GP: ji], not partially identical, with li. Why? Because shi has no substance [GP: svabhāva]—it is the selfsame li. Therefore, without causing the slightest damage to itself, an atom can embrace the whole universe. If one atom is so, all other dharmas should also be so. Contemplate on this.

We now have everything we need to answer the question concerning the duality of the conventional and ultimate. I will come back to that at the end of the chapter; but let us finish off the Huayan story first.

[33] See Lusthaus (1998), sec. 8. [34] Chang (1972), pp. 144–5.

If *a* and *b* are shi, then *a* interpenetrates with *u*, and *u* interpenetrates with *b*. But, as we saw in 8.4, it is the self-same *u* in every case. Moreover, interpenetration is, as I noted, transitive. It follows that every shi interpenetrates with every other shi. One can see this diagrammatically. Refer to the **diagram *D***. As this shows, the tree of *c* is a sub-tree of the tree of *b*. Symmetrically, of course, the tree of *b* is a sub-tree of *c*—though this goes off the diagram. (The tree for *b* is a sub-tree of the tree for *u*, which is a sub-tree of the tree for *c*.) Hence, all shi interpenetrate. This is the fourth Huyan principle, shishi wuai (literally, the non-obstruction of shi and shi).

Chengguan (738–839?), the Fourth Patriarch of Huayan, puts it thus:[35]

Because they have no Selfhood [GP: svabhāva], the large and the small can mutually contain each other... Since the very small is very large, Mount Sumeru is contained in a mustard seed; and since the very large is the very small, the ocean is included in a hair.

And Fazang thus:[36]

[A particle of dust] has the characters of roundness and smallness. This is a fact [shi]. Its nature is empty and non-existent. This is principle [li]. Because facts have no substance [GP: svabhāva] they merge together in accordance with principle. And because the dust has no substance, it universally penetrates everything. For all facts are no different from principle and they are completely manifested in the dust.

And as both Chengguan and Fazang say, and **diagram *D*** shows, all this is possible only because all things are empty—and so have infinite structural trees.[37]

Note that if all shi interpenetrate, then any shi interpenetrates with any of its parts.[38] Moreover, the whole which is the whole Net of Indra can be thought of as itself a shi. It is, after all, reality as described by Huayan; and because it is described, it is part of conventional reality, that is, a shi—the maximal state of affairs. The whole Net of Indra is a node in its own net![39] So the (whole) whole interpenetrates with each part. The all is (ji) each one. As Fazang says:[40]

[35] Chang (1972), p. 165. [36] Chan (1969), p. 420.

[37] Fazang again: 'Only when we understand that [dharmas] have no nature [of their own] can we have wisdom about the one and the many.' (Chan (1969), p. 423.)

[38] For a discussion of the Huayan view that a whole interpenetrates with any part, see Jones (2009).

[39] Representing this fact would seem to outstrip the mathematical machinery at hand, but it does not. It cannot be represented using standard set-theory, but it can be represented using the mathematics of non-well-founded sets. Given this apparatus, a node on the tree can be the whole tree. Thus, for example, given a tree, t (which is a set of ordered pairs) with root, r. The set, x, which is a solution to the equation $x = \{\langle x, r\rangle\} \cup t$ is a tree which is its own root. See, e.g., Barwise and Etchemendy (1987), ch. 3, or Aczel (1988), ch. 1.

[40] Chan (1969), p. 410.

All phenomena are in great profusion, and are interfused but not mixed (losing their identity). The all is [GP: ji] the one, for both are similar in being non-existent in nature [GP: having no svabhāva]. And the one is the all for the relation of cause and effect are perfectly clear. As the power [of the one] and the function [of the many] embrace each other, their expansion and contraction are free and at ease.

8.11 The Net Emerges

To finish the Huayan story, let us, finally, return to the Net of Indra. Consider once more the **diagram *D***. *u* is its root; but as we know, the tree for *u* is also a sub-tree of other trees. We may therefore extend the picture indefinitely to the left as well (though the result is no longer a tree). If we do so, we get:

$$
\begin{array}{cccccccccccccc}
 & & & & \nearrow & \cdots & & & \nearrow & \cdots & & & \nearrow & \cdots \\
 & & & a & & & & a & & & & a & & \\
 & & \nearrow & & \nearrow & \cdots & \nearrow & & \nearrow & \cdots & \nearrow & & & \\
\cdots & u & \rightarrow & b & \rightarrow & u & \rightarrow & b & \rightarrow & u & \rightarrow & b & \rightarrow & \cdots \\
 & & \searrow & & \searrow & \cdots & \searrow & & \searrow & \cdots & \searrow & & & \\
 & & & c & & & & c & & & & c & & \\
 & & & & \searrow & \cdots & & & \searrow & \cdots & & & \searrow & \cdots
\end{array}
$$

or, to reorient the arrows a bit, and ignore some repetitions:

$$
\begin{array}{ccccccccc}
 & & \vdots & & & & \vdots & & \\
 & & a & & \vdots & & a & & \\
 & & \uparrow & & \uparrow & & \uparrow & & \\
\cdots & \rightarrow & u & \rightarrow & b & \rightarrow & u & \rightarrow & \cdots \\
 & & \downarrow & & \downarrow & & \downarrow & & \\
 & & c & & \vdots & & c & & \\
 & & \vdots & & & & \vdots & &
\end{array}
$$

The Net or Indra literally appears, a graphic depiction of the great Dharmadhātu.

As Fazang puts it, again in the *Treatise on the Golden Lion*:[41]

In each of the lion's eyes, ears, limbs, joints, and in each and every hair, there is the golden lion. All the lions embraced by all the single hairs simultaneously and instantaneously enter into a single hair. Thus in each and every hair is an infinite number of lions, and in addition all the single hairs, together with the infinite number of lions, in turn enter into

[41] Chan (1969), p. 412.

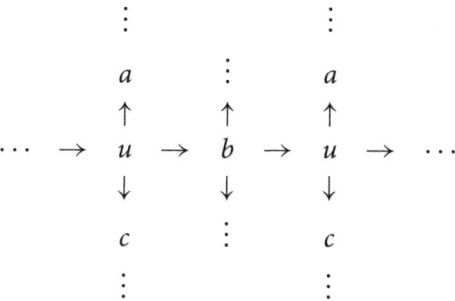

a single hair. In this way, the geometric progression is infinite, like the jewels of Celestial Lord Indra's Net.

8.12 Interpenetration and Duality

And now let us return to the question of the relationship between the conventional and the ultimate, raised in 8.1. Our concern was with the two aspects of the semantic bearers of the 5-valued catuṣkoṭi; that is, between the conventional aspect of a state of affairs and its ultimate aspect. In Huayen, this is exactly the relationship between li and shi, lishiwuai. We saw what this is in 8.10: interpenetration, ji. We have also seen how to understand this in a perfectly precise manner.

Moreover, the worry was that the two realities provide an untoward duality. Interpenetration can be seen as a natural understanding of what it means to transcend this duality. Each side of the duality is not distinct from the other, but intermingles with it in a most intimate way.

8.13 Conclusion

So much for this aspect of the catuṣkoṭi. There is one more episode in the development of the catuṣkoṭi to be looked at. This is its relationship to the notion of enlightenment, a notion absolutely central to Buddhist thought. In the next chapter, we will turn to this, and then, with the help of Dōgen, tie together a number of strands in the book.

9

Enlightenment

9.1 Introduction

In this chapter, we turn the focus of our articulation of the catuṣkoṭi onto the Buddhist doctrine of awakening (enlightenment). How to understand this notion varies from tradition to tradition. Here, we will be concerned with the way it is understood in the Chinese *Chan* tradition, or *Zen* as it is known in Japan. After a general background to the topic, we look at this Chan understanding. We will see how the 5-valued catuṣkoṭi, and the view of the two aspects of reality built into this, can be used to provide a formal model of the process—not, this time, with a single structure, but with a sequence of structures.

By way of illustrating some of this, we will then look at the Japanese Zen philosopher Dōgen Kigen, and his thoughts on enlightenment and related matters. Finally, with this material under our belt, we will return to the question of transcending dualities, and draw together a number of the threads of the book.

9.2 Enlightenment

In Buddhist thought, the understanding of enlightenment evolves, just as much as the metaphysics does. In early Indian Buddhism, enlightenment involves the elimination of tṛṣṇa, and the extinction (nirvāṇa) of duḥkha. It is possible to achieve this in this life, though in practice it will take many (many, many) rebirths before it is achieved. After enlightenment, a person is no longer reborn. What happens then? As we saw in 2.2, this is one of the questions the Buddha refused to answer.

In Indian Mahāyāna thought, progress along the enlightenment path (the Bodhisattva way) is more complex, and comes in stages. At a certain point, one has achieved enlightenment in the older sense, but because one has sworn to help all other sentient beings to achieve enlightenment, one is reborn voluntarily (though this may be in a 'celestial realm'—another planet—from which one can emanate many avatars, and so help even more people). At this stage, the awakened being could enter the final stage *parinirvāṇa* (ultimate nirvāṇa) if they so chose, but, out of compassion, they refrain from doing so until *all* can do so—if, indeed, that ever happens. (No one goes till we can all go together.)

Things change again when Buddhism goes into China. Daoism has a notion of a sage. This is a person who 'goes with the flow'. They act naturally, simply in tune with the Dao. They are detached, and not upset by the ups and downs of life. The Chinese Buddhist conception of enlightenment imports these elements of thought into the understanding of an enlightened person. This happens in perhaps its most distinctive form in Chan.

9.3 Chan

Against this background, let us now turn to Chan itself.[1] According to legend, this was brought to China by an Indian or Central Asian missionary, Bodhidharma (Chin: *Damo*; Jap: *Daruma*), some time in the fifth or sixth century. The Chan tradition therefore takes Bodhidharma to be the first Patriarch of Chan Buddhism (and the twenty-eighth of Buddhism itself). What truth there is in these matters is debatable. What is more certain is that Chan owes a good deal to Huineng (traditionally dated as 638–713), who is reckoned the sixth Patriarch. The *Liu tan-jing* (Platform Sūtra) traditionally attributed to him is one of the most significant documents in the tradition.

The first chapter of this tells the story of how Huineng became the sixth Patriarch—his version (or his school's version) of it, of course. The fifth Patriarch, Hongren, decided that it was time to appoint his successor. He asked his monks to write a poem expressing the Dharma, so that he could decide who would be best. Shenxiu, the head monk, wrote the following poem:[2]

> The body is the bodhi tree.
> The mind is like a bright mirror (stand).
> Constantly strive to keep it pure,
> And never let the dust collect.

Huineng, who was an illiterate and menial labourer in the temple, composed a reply:

> From the beginning bodhi has no tree.
> The luminous mirror also has no stand.
> Buddha nature is always pure.
> Where could dust settle?

[1] For a general account of Chinese Chan and Japanese Zen, see, respectively, Hershoc (2015) and Nagatomo (2015).

[2] The translations are taken from Gregory (2012), p. 9.

Hongren judged Shenxiu's verse to be pretty good, but Huineng's, he thought, really hit the mark. Hongren made Huineng the sixth Patriarch—though he advised him to flee, because the monks of the temple wouldn't like it!

The meanings of the poems, and the difference between them, is a matter of scholarly debate.[3] But one way to look at the matter is as follows. The mind (bright mirror) in question is the two-sided tathāgata garbha of the *Awakening of Faith* (8.3). Shenxiu describes it as polluted by impurities, which have to be extirpated. He, then, describes the conventional side of its nature. Huineng, by contrast, points out that ultimately none of these things exist, playing the ultimate side.

Whatever one makes of this, much can be learned about Chan from the meaning of its name. The Sanskrit for meditation is *dhyāna*. When pronounced by the Chinese tongue, this becomes *channa*, which becomes abbreviated to *chan*, the name of the school. This becomes *zen* to the Japanese tongue.[4] So, as its name says, this is a school of Buddhism which takes meditation to be absolutely central to Buddhist practice—not that it is unimportant in other schools. And it is central because meditation is taken to be the vehicle for enlightenment—in Chinese, *wu*; in Japanese, *satori*. Satori is also often glossed as *kenshō* ('seeing into one's true nature').

In addition to traditional techniques of meditation, different Chan practitioners developed many other techniques aimed at producing enlightenment. Some of these were highly unorthodox and opportunistic, such as shouting, striking, and doing bizarre things.

The most systematic novel technique, however, was *gong'an* (Jap: *kōan*) practice. A kōan is a sort of verbal puzzle, with which the student is meant to wrestle. (Well-known, indeed hackneyed, examples are: 'does a dog have Buddha nature?', 'what is the sound of one hand clapping?') The student tries to find an answer, but no answer is possible. In the process of wrestling, the student comes to understand the inadequacy of conceptual thought in grasping reality.[5] It is worth noting that the story of the wordless transmission from the Buddha to Kāśyapa, which we met in 5.2, is itself used as a kōan. It is the sixth in the thirteenth-century compilation *Wumenguan* (Gateless Gate)—though, as in all kōan, it is not to be taken at face value there.[6] Unorthodox as the thought is, one might also take the process

[3] See Gregory (2012) for an excellent account, which stresses, amongst other things, the relationship between this sūtra and the *Vimalakīrti Nirdeśa Sūtra*.

[4] Or perhaps this was just the way that the Chinese character was pronounced in Chinese when Chan entered Japan.

[5] For a much more deflationary interpretation of the koān tradition in particular, and Chan more generally, see Sharf (forthcoming).

[6] Wumen's comment: 'Gautama Buddha acted shamelessly; he pressed the free into slavery. Hanging out mutton, he sold dog meat, as if it were so wonderful. Suppose everyone had smiled at that moment? How could the treasury of the eye of truth be transmitted? And if Kasyapa had not

involved in Jizang Hierarchy of 7.6 as a sort of kōan: in trying to catch one's own tail, at a certain point one comes to understand the inadequacy of conceptual thought to grasp the ultimate, and so gives the whole game away.

Whatever the technique employed, however, the aim of Chan was to get the student to cast off language, and see reality for what it really is. One might note, here, a shift of emphasis from the Indian perspective on matters. In India, enlightenment is the elimination of suffering, and experiencing ultimate reality is a major vehicle for this. In China, by contrast, enlightenment is the experiencing of ultimate reality, and the elimination of suffering is a concomitant of this.

9.4 The Ox-Herding Pictures

The process involved in obtaining enlightenment in Chan is often depicted in a series of pictures called the *Ox-Herding Pictures*. One version of them can be found in Fig. 4.

The pictures depict a character—let's call them Jo—and Jo's enlightenment path. The Ox, also depicted, is a metaphor for the ultimate. The first picture shows Jo living an ordinary existence in conventional reality, confused, but thinking there must be more to life than this. In the second, Jo sees the footprints of the Ox, and so gets the idea of what this might be. The next five pictures show Jo seeking the Ox, capturing it, and taming it. These represent the discipline by which one tames the mind and approaches a grasp of ultimate reality. In Chan, these would be the textual study and meditative practices employed by the school in question. Picture eight represents the enlightenment experience. It is blank because it represents the grasp of an ineffable reality.

The Chan thinker Zhaozhou (Jap: Jōshu) (778–897) calls this stage the 'Great Death',[7] and it is sometimes likened to leaping off a cliff into a void, since the familiar and comfortable everyday world disappears. Most importantly, the illusion of self disappears. There is no subject, and no object either—just thusness. All dualities of thought have disappeared.

One might have expected the pictures to end here. But they do not. The final two pictures show Jo returning to daily life. This is the return to the ordinary. However, the ordinary is now seen in a quite new way, the illusion of the substantial world

smiled, how could the treasury of eye of truth be transmitted? If you say there is any transmitting the treasure eye of truth, Buddha is fooling villagers; if you say there is no transmitting it, why does he only approve of Kasyapa?' (Clearly (1993b), p. 33).

7 The term is taken up by some Japanese thinkers, including Dōgen and Hakuin Ekaku (1686–1768).

Fig. 4. The Ox-Herding Pictures

of common sense has disappeared, and the phenomenal world is seen as the conceptual construction it is, as *merely* conventional.

Commenting on one of Dōgen's essays (*Kaiin Zanmai,* Ocean Seal Concentration), Cleary explains the way of perceiving reality in the post-enlightenment state as follows:[8]

[8] Cleary (1986), p. 77.

The notion of phenomena arising and vanishing depends on discriminating thought. In terms of the treatise of the *Awakening of faith in Mahāyāna*, popular in both Zen and Kegon [GP: Huayan] schools awareness has two aspects: awareness of thusness and awareness of birth and death. Delusion means being trapped in the latter, in discriminating thought, which singles out things as discrete entities and thus is a linear, sequential way of perceiving, marking beginnings and ends. This is called delusion when it is believed—implicitly or explicitly—to be all there is, to be the only way of seeing, to be the true description of reality. This kind of awareness is by nature restrictive and exclusive (and for that reason may be useful and practically necessary at times while being harmful and counterproductive at others); to put it in a wider perspective the awareness of thusness (being-as-it-is, without conceptual gloss) is cultivated in Buddhism. Ultimately, enlightenment includes both aspects, so that one is neither forced to feel that thought and discrimination reveal the whole of reality, or rendered incapable of ordinary perception and discursive reasoning.

In virtue of this enlightenment experience, Jo, as the pictures show, leads a happy life, unconcerned by the cares of the world. Here, note, the influence of the Daoist sage has entered the picture. The awakened state is not doing anything different, it is just doing it in a different way. Just as in Daoism, the sage acts by spontaneously manifesting being in tune with the Dao, so, in Chan, the awakened person's acts spontaneously manifest their awakened state.[9]

9.5 Mountains Are Not Mountains

Naturally, in reality, the post-enlightenment state is a bit more nuanced than this simplified picture tells. In particular, one would expect the practices which generated the enlightenment experience to continue in the third phase, giving rise to further enlightenment experiences (possibly of a more intense nature), reinforcing and strengthening the post-enlightenment state. As Cleary reports:[10]

The celebrated Zen master Hakuin said, "Without cultivation and practice after enlightenment, many who have seen the essence miss the boat"; and Hakuin's assistant, Tōrei [GP: Enji], said, "Lesser enlightenment turns out to be a hindrance to greater enlightenment. If you give up lesser enlightenments and don't cling to them, greater enlightenment will surely be realized."

[9] The Chan and Zen philosophers never, as far as I know, explicitly repudiated the Indian doctrine of rebirth. (Piety, perhaps, made this impossible.) But in their thinking, it ceases to have much significance. All the action is on the present moment and one's immersement in it. The Indians, after all, could point to only one actual person who had achieved enlightenment, the Buddha himself. It had to be possible to think in the very long term if the Buddhist teachings were to make sense. But Chan could point to many actual people who had achieved enlightenment: all the Chan masters.

[10] Cleary (1986), p. 30.

In principle, though, we have a procedure with three moments: pre-enlightenment, enlightenment, post-enlightenment. As we saw in 6.4, the bicameral nature of reality can be represented in the plurivalent 5-valued catuṣkoṭi by states of affairs having two values. This can now be deployed to represent the stages of enlightenment.[11]

Each stage involves an assignment of values to states of affairs. These represent the states of affairs in the world as Jo grasps them. In the first stage, the appropriate conventional value is assigned, one of: t, f, b, or n. Thus, an evaluation assigns only *one* of these values to a state of affairs. This is the conventional side of a state of affairs that Jo sees. In the second stage, the enlightenment experience, again only one value is assigned, but this is the value e. Jo grasps the ultimate and ineffable aspect of each state of affairs. But in the third stage, a state of affairs is assigned *two* values: both the original conventional value, *and* the value e. Jo has grasped both the conventional and the ultimate aspect of things, and the relationship between them. If one wishes to add a Huayan element to the relationship between the two realities, one may take this to be one of interpenetration, as discussed in the previous chapter.

The whole process can, then, be modelled by a sequence of three interpretations of the kind we looked at in 6.4. In the first, the interpretation, though a relation, relates every state of affairs to just one value: its conventional value. In the second, it likewise assigns only one value, but this is ineffability. In the third, it assigns two values: whatever the original value was, plus ineffability. Thus, the whole process can be modelled by a series of three interpretations of the kind we met in 6.4, $\rhd_1$, $\rhd_2$, $\rhd_3$. If the conventional value (t, f, b, or n) of the state of affairs $\underline{A}$ is c_A, then we have:

Stage 1: $\underline{A} \rhd_1 c_A$
Stage 2: $\underline{A} \rhd_2 e$
Stage 3: $\underline{A} \rhd_3 c_A$ and $\underline{A} \rhd_3 e$

Each of $\rhd_1$ and $\rhd_2$ has, as it were, a partial, one-sided, take on reality. $\rhd_3$ overcomes this duality, encompassing both.

The three-stage process is captured in a saying that one finds in many places in the Chan/Zen literature:[12]

[11] A different model is given in Garfield and Priest (2009). I think the present analysis a much better one.

[12] The first known attribution appears to be to Qingyuan Xingsi in the *Compendium of the Five Lamps* (*Wudeng Huiyuan*, 1252), and goes as follows:

> Thirty years ago, before I practiced Chan, I saw that mountains are mountains and rivers are rivers. However, after having achieved intimate knowledge and having gotten

Before I studied Zen, mountains were mountains, and water was water.

After studying Zen for some time, mountains were no longer mountains, and water was no longer water.

But now, after studying Zen longer, mountains are just mountains, and water is just water.

Prior to Buddhist reflection, mountains and water[13] are taken to be substantially existent and independent entities. Buddhist analysis (one of the things going on before the eighth Ox-herding picture), however, shows these phenomena to be empty of inherent existence; to be insubstantial and to fail to exist ultimately. Were one to stop here, while the error of taking things to be inherently existent—primal ignorance, as it is sometimes put—would have been expurgated *conceptually*, awakening would not have been achieved. For this, one has to have an experience of ultimate reality, in a conceptually unmediated way—the eighth picture. This is what the pre-enlightenment meditative practices are designed to induce.

However, one cannot stop there either. The final stage, the return to the ordinary, is the return to where one started, the assignment of conventional truth values, but now in the knowledge that they are *merely* conventional, a conceptual superposition on the ultimate: the value e is also present. Mountains and waters are *just* mountains and waters. They have no reality over and above this: they exist interdependently and conventionally. That is, the third moment differs from the first just in that the realization of emptiness that mediates them has stripped away the imputation of inherent existence from the apprehension of the conventional, leaving the conventional just as conventional, and transforming the world as seen through primal ignorance into the world as seen through awakened awareness.

As T. S. Eliot puts it in 'Little Gidding', one of his *Four Quartets*:[14]

> We shall not cease from exploration
> And the end of all our exploring
> Will be to arrive where we started
> And know the place for the first time.

One may hear, here, a way of understanding Nāgārjuna's cryptic remark at MMK XXV: 19–20, that nirvāṇa and saṃsāra are the same (see 4.8). Nirvāṇa and saṃsāra are exactly the same—just experienced in different ways. In particular, the ultimate has been there all along, just cloaked by cognitive overlay.

> a way in, I saw that mountains are not mountains and rivers are not rivers. But now that I have found rest, as before I see mountains are mountains and rivers are rivers.

(App (1994), pp. 111–12, n. 2).

13 In Chan thought, these are often used as metonyms for the objects and events (respectively) of phenomenal reality.

14 Eliot (1943).

9.6 Dōgen and the *Shōbōgenzō*

Which brings us to Dōgen. The Japanese Zen thinker and practitioner Dōgen Kigen (1200–1253) is one of the most intriguing Zen philosophers. He was ordained as a Buddhist (Tendai) monk in Japan.[15] According to tradition, he became dissatisfied with what he had been taught, however. He travelled to China to study, where he studied with Ruijing, who taught Caodong Zen. In this, he found what he was looking for. Dōgen then returned to Japan where he initiated the Japanese version of Caodong, Sōtō.[16] He placed great stress on the practice of sitting meditation (*zazen*); but he also lectured to his monks. The lectures are preserved in his *Shōbōgenzō* (Treasury of the True Dharma Eye). The lectures, often taking off from a koān, are difficult to interpret, especially without a knowledge of the many textual allusions he makes.[17] His thought is expounded, but this is usually done with metaphors and twists. He delights in taking Chinese texts and reinterpreting them in unusual and unexpected ways. The lectures seem to be designed to disturb both familiar patterns of conceptual thought, and pat understanding of Chan doctrines, as much as to expound Dōgen's own Zen views. In the second half of this chapter, we will look at his views.[18]

9.7 Dōgen and Huayan

Let us start by noting that Dōgen does indeed import the Huayan picture into his account. In his introduction to Dōgen's essay *Zenki* (The Whole Works), Cleary puts it like this:[19]

> The distinction of existence and emptiness, the noncontradiction and mutual interpenetration of existence and emptiness, and thereby the transcendence of existence and emptiness—these are traditional steps of Mahāyāna Buddhist dialectic. In this essay they are presented by Dōgen in his subtle, almost covert way, evidently to induce the reader to search out these insights by personal contemplation. The ultimate vision of totality, in which the whole and the individuals foster each other—the crown of Kegon Buddhist metaphysics—is one of the fundamental themes of Dōgen's philosophical writings, to be met with time and time again in various guises.

[15] Tendai (Chin: Tientai) is another of the distinctively Chinese forms of Buddhism.

[16] A little earlier, another Tendai monk, Myōan Eisai (1141–1215), also went to China to study. He, too, returned under the influence of Chan, and established the other main school of Japanese Zen, Rinzai (Chin: *Linji*). Rinzai Zen places much more emphasis on kōan practice than does Sōto Zen.

[17] So let me remind the reader for a final time of the warning of §0.3 of the Preface.

[18] A warning: there seems to be scholarly agreement that Dōgen's views evolved during the years of his teaching. Exactly how and why, are, however, matters of scholarly contention. For a discussion, see Heine (2006).

[19] Cleary (1986), p. 44.

Dōgen expresses the matter in the essay in question as follows. One should note that *birth and death* is the standard expression for saṃsāra (the realm of death and rebirth), meaning, in this case, the unenlightened state:[20]

... the principle of *in life the whole works appears* has nothing to do with beginning and end; though it is the whole earth and all space, not only does it not block *the appearance of the whole works in life*, it doesn't block *the appearance of the whole works in death* either. When *the whole works appears in death*, though it is the whole earth and all space, not only does it not block *the appearance of the whole works in death*, it doesn't block *the appearance of the whole works in life* either. For this reason, life doesn't obstruct death, death doesn't obstruct life. The whole earth and all space are in life and death too. However, it is not fulfilling the potential of one whole earth and one whole space in life and fulfilling their potential in death too. Though they are not one, they are not different; though they are not different, they are not identical; though they are not identical, they are not multiple. Therefore, in life there are myriad phenomena of the appearance of the whole works, and in death too there are myriad phenomena of the appearance of the whole works. There is also the manifestation of the whole works in what is neither life nor death.

All phenomena interpenetrate, in the earth, in space, in life, and in death, in the whole works.

9.8 Dōgen on Saṃsāra and Nirvāṇa

Let us now turn to what Dōgen has to say about the relationship between saṃsāra and nirvāṇa.[21]

The *Shōbōgenzō* lecture *Shōji* (Life and Death, that is, Saṃsāra) begins by reporting the interchange between the Chan masters Kassan (Chin: Jiashan, 805–81) and Jōzan (Chin: Dingshan, fl. ninth century):[22]

Because in life-and-death there is buddha, there is no life and death.
Because in life-and-death there is no buddha, we are not deluded in life-and-death.

Dōgen then comments:

[These] are the words of the two Zen Masters; they are the words of the people who had got the truth, and so they were decidedly not laid down in vain. A person who wishes to get free from life and death should just illuminate this truth. If a person looks for Buddha outside of life-and-death, that is like pointing a cart north and making for [the south country of]

[20] Cleary (1986), p. 46.

[21] The interpretation of the passages in this section is defended by Deguchi, Garfield, and Priest (2013b) against a critique by Tanaka (2013).

[22] Nishijima and Cross (1994–9), Vol. 4, p. 197. The translators put the second 'buddha' in scare quotes for no reason that I can see.

Ersu, or like facing south and hoping to see the North Star. It is to be amassing more and more causes of life and death, and to have utterly lost the way of liberation. When we understand that only life-and-death is itself nirvāṇa, there is nothing to hate as life and death and nothing to aspire to in nirvāṇa. Then, for the first time, the means exist to get free from life and death.

Dōgen is making the clearly paradoxical point (following the contradictory utterances attributed to Jiashan and Dingshan) that the only way to be free of saṃsāra is simply to accept that one is in it.[23] He continues:

To understand that we move from birth to death is a mistake. Birth is a state at one moment; it already has a past and will have a future. For this reason, it is said in the Buddha-Dharma that appearance is just non-appearance. Extinction also is a state at one moment; it too has a past and a future. This is why it is said that disappearance is just non-disappearance.

In other words, mountains are just non-mountains.

Dōgen takes up the contradiction involved in this matter in another lecture from the *Shōbōgenzō, Genjō kōan* (The Issue at Hand), where he says:[24]

When all dharmas are . . . the Buddha-Dharma, then there is delusion and realization, there is practice, there is life, there is death, there are buddhas and there are ordinary beings. When the myriad dharmas are each not of self, there is no delusion and no realization, no buddhas and no ordinary beings, no life and death.

Of course, all elements of reality have Buddha nature ('all dharmas are the Buddha-Dharma'), so there is delusion, practice, etc. But each has no self—svabhāva ('the myriad dharmas are each not of self'), so there is no delusion, practice, etc.[25] Such is the contradictory nature of things.

9.9 Dōgen and Zazen

Next, we turn to Dōgen and practice. In Indian Buddhism, the practice of meditative techniques is important because it leads to the enlightened state. For Dōgen it is important because practice *is* the enlightened state.

[23] Tanahashi (1985), p. 74, translates the last four sentences as: 'Just understand that birth-and-death is itself nirvana. There is nothing such as birth and death to be avoided. There is nothing such as nirvana to be sought. Only when you realize this are you free from birth and death.'

[24] Nishijima and Cross (1994–9), Vol. 1, p. 33. In the ellipsis, the translators insert the words 'seen as', which are not in the text.

[25] Tanahashi (1985), p. 69, translates this as: 'As all things are Buddha-dharma, there is delusion and realization, practice, birth and death, and there are Buddhas and sentient beings. As the myriad things are without an abiding self, there is no delusion, no realization, no Buddha, no sentient beings, no birth and death.'

This is most evident in Dōgen's account of zazen. Kasulis puts the matter as follows:[26]

> ... meditation had been taken to be a *means* to an end, a technique by mean of which one might achieve enlightenment or satori. This distinction between methods and goals, Dōgen came to believe, was erroneous: zazen is not a technique by which to achieve enlightenment; it is enlightenment itself. Consequently, the hallmark of Dōgen's Zen is *shikantaza*—"nothing but sitting" or, more simply, "just sitting".

As Dōgen himself puts it in the *Zazengi* (Instructions for Zazen) lecture of the *Shōbōgenzō*:[27]

> Once you have adjusted your posture, take a deep breath, inhale and exhale, rock your body right and left and settle into a steady immobile sitting position. Think of not thinking. How do you think of not-thinking? Without thinking. That is the art of zazen.
>
> The zazen I speak of is not learning meditation. It is simply the Dharma-gate of response and bliss, the cultivation-authentification of totally culminated enlightenment. It is the presence of things as they are.

The cryptic discussion of not thinking is taken further in *Genjō kōan*, where he says:[28]

> To model yourself after the way of the Buddha is to model yourself after yourself. To model yourself after yourself is to forget yourself. To forget yourself is to be authenticated by all things. To be authenticated by all things is to effect the molting of body mind, both yours and others'. The distinguishing marks of enlightenment dissolve and [the molting of body-mind] causes the dissolving distinguishing marks of enlightenment to emerge continuously.

What Dōgen is describing here is exactly the disappearance of any subject/object duality.

9.10 Dōgen and the Return to the Ordinary

One should not think that Zen practice is simply restricted to zazen, however. Practice to be found in quite ordinary activity. As Dōgen puts it in the lecture *Hosshō* (The Nature of Things):[29]

> ... the *here* of the immediate present is the *nature of things*; the *nature of things* is the *here* of the immediate present. *Wearing clothes and eating food* is the *wearing clothes and eating food of absorption in the nature of things*. It is the manifestation of the *nature of things* in

[26] Kasulis (1981), p. 67. [27] Quoted in Kasulis (1981), p. 71.
[28] Quoted in Kasulis (1981), p. 87. [29] Cleary (1986), p. 39.

food, it is the manifestation of the *nature of things* of eating, it is the manifestation of the *nature of things* of clothing, it is the manifestation of the *nature of things* of wearing. If one does not dress or eat, does not talk or answer, does not use the senses, does not act at all, it is not the *nature of things*, it is *not entering the nature of things*.

These rather dark words of the *Shōbōgenzō* can be illuminated by reference to another text by Dōgen. This is *Tenzo kyōkun*, a set of instructions for the person who is in charge of the preparation and serving of food for the monks in a temple, the *tenzo*. Compared with the *Shōbōgengenzō* lectures, the text is notable for its directness and simplicity. The tenzo was an important position in the monastery, but not a specifically Buddhist one: it was not a position that was responsible for teaching meditation or textual analysis. But for Dōgen it was a paradigm of what the ordinary should be; and the tenzo should engage in it with the same sort of mindfulness required of zazen. For example:[30]

Handle every single leaf of a green in such a way that it manifests the body of the Buddha [GP: ultimate reality]. This in turn allows the Buddha to manifest through the leaf. This is a power you cannot grasp with your rational mind. It operates freely, according to the situation, in a most natural way. At the same time, this power functions in our lives to clarify and settle activities and is beneficial to all living beings.

He illustrates with an autobiographical story. I quote at length:[31]

. . . in the fifth month of the sixteenth year of the Jiading era [1223], I was on the ship at Qingyuan. While I was talking with the Japanese captain, there was an old monk who arrived. He was about sixty years old. He came directly onto the ship and inquired of the Japanese passengers if he could buy Japanese mushrooms. I invited him to drink tea and asked where he was from. He was the cook of the monastery on Mount Ayuwang. He said, "I come from Sichuan, but I left my home village forty years ago. This year I am sixty-one years old. In the past I have trained in quite a few different monasteries. In recent years, I stayed for a while with Guyun. I was able to register at Yuwang [monastery], but for some time I felt out of place. At the end of the summer retreat last year, however, I was appointed cook of that monastery. Tomorrow is the fifth day [feast], but the entire menu does not yet include a single delicacy. I need to cook noodle soup, but still have no mushrooms, and thus have made a special trip here to try to buy mushrooms to offer to the monks of the ten directions."

I asked him, "What time did you leave there?" The cook replied, "After the midday meal." I inquired, "How long is the road from Yuwang to here?" He said, "Thirty-four or thirty-five li." I asked, "When will you return to the monastery?" He said, "If I can buy the mushrooms now, I will set off right after that." I said, "Today I did not expect to meet you and have a

30 Wright (2005), pp. 7f.

31 The translation is from Eihei (2016). An alternative translation is given in Wright (2005), pp. 10ff.

conversation on this ship. It is most fortunate, is it not, to form this karmic bond? Dōgen [I] will treat the cook Zen master [you] to a meal." The cook said, "It is impossible. If I do not oversee the preparations for tomorrow's meal offering, it will not turn out well." I said, "Are there not co-workers in the monastery who understand the meals? What will be deficient if only one officer, the cook, is not present?" The cook said, "I took up this position in my later years; it is this old man's pursuit of the way. How could I hand it over to others? Besides, when I came I did not ask to stay away overnight."

I again asked the cook: "You are venerable in years; why don't you sit in meditation to pursue the way or contemplate the words of the ancients? It is troublesome being cook; all you do is labor. What good is that?" The cook laughed and said, "My good man from a foreign country, you do not yet understand pursuit of the way and do not yet know about written words." When I heard him speak in this manner, I suddenly felt ashamed and taken aback. I asked him, "What are written words? What is the practice of the way?" The cook said, "If you do not slip up and pass by the place you ask about, how could you not be a man [GP: of the way]?" At the time, I did not understand. The cook said, "If you still don't understand, come to Yuwang Mountain at some other time, in the future. On that occasion we can discuss the principle of written words." Having spoken thus, the cook got up and said, "It is late in the day and I am in a hurry, so I am going back now."

In the seventh month of the same year, I registered at Tiantong [Monastery]. While I was there, that cook came to meet me and said, "At the end of the summer retreat I retired as cook and am now returning to my home village. I happened to hear a disciple say that you were here; how could I not come to meet you?"

I jumped for joy and was very grateful. In the ensuing conversation that I had with him I brought up the karmic conditions of written words and pursuit of the way that we had discussed previously on the ship. The cook said, "The study of written words is to understand the purpose of written words. Exertion in pursuit of the way requires an affirmation of the purpose of pursuing the way." I asked him, "What are written words?" The cook answered, "One, two, three, four, five." I also asked, "What is pursuit of the way?" He said, "In the whole world, it can never be hidden."

Although there was a great variety of other things that we discussed, I will not record them at this point. The little I know about written words and understand about pursuing the way is due to the great kindness of that cook. I told my late teacher Myōzen about the things that I have just related here, and he was very happy to hear of them.

Later I saw a verse that Xuedou wrote to instruct the monks:

> One letter, seven letters, three letters, or five;
> Investigating myriads of images, one reaches no basis.
> In the depth of night, the moon sets into the dark sea;
> Seeking the black dragon's pearl, one finds there are many.

What that cook said some years before and what Xuedou expresses in this verse clearly coincide. More and more I understand that the cook was a true man of the way.

To practise is not just to practise zazen. It is to practise the ordinary in a certain way. Indeed, this is the third and most important stage of the way. Ultimate reality shines through each ordinary shi.

9.11 Dōgen on Language

Finally, let us turn to the question of language itself, and what Dōgen has to say about it. He addresses the matter in a lecture of the *Shōbōgenzō* called *Katto* (Kudzo and Wisteria),[32] where he elucidates the symbiotic relationship between the two.

In Zen thought there is a familiar story about how Bodhidharma elected his successor, Huike, which Dōgen relates as follows:[33]

The twenty-eighth patriarch said to his disciples, "As the time is drawing near [for me to transmit the Dharma to my successor], please tell me how you express it."

Daofu responded first, "According to my current understanding, we should neither cling to words and letters, nor abandon them altogether, but use them as instruments of the Dao (*dō-yō*)."

The master responded, "You express my skin."

Then the nun Zongzhi, said, "As I now see it [the Dharma] is like Ānanda's viewing the Buddha-land of Akshobhya, seeing it once and never seeing it again."

The master responded, "You express my flesh."

Daoyu said, 'The four elements are emptiness, and the five *skandhas* are non-being. But in my view, there is not a single dharma to be expressed."

The master said, "You express my bones."

Finally, Huike prostrated himself three times and stood [silently].

The master said, "You express my marrow."

The standard interpretation of the story is that each of the respondents says something acceptable, but each gets closer to the essence of things. Huike indicates the ultimate, and so ineffable. On the basis of this, Bodhidharma makes him his successor.

Dōgen's interpretation of the story, however, is quite different. He says:[34]

You should realize that the first patriarch's expression, "skin, flesh, bones, marrow," does not refer to the superficiality of depth [or understanding]. Although there may remain a [provisional] distinction between superior and inferior understanding, [each of the four disciples] expressed the first patriarch in his entirety. When Bodhidharma says "you express my marrow" or "you express my bones", he is using various pedagogical devices that are pertinent to particular people, or methods of instruction that may or may not be apply to different levels of understanding.

It is the same as Śākyamuni's holding up the udambarra flower [to Mahākāśyapa], or the transmission of the sacred robe [symbolic of the transmission of enlightenment].

[32] For the botanically challenged (like me) these are both plants that grow vines, which climb by wrapping themselves round other things.

[33] Heine (2009), pp. 151–2. [34] Heine (2009), p. 152.

What Bodhidharma said to the four disciples is fundamentally the selfsame expression. Although it is fundamentally the selfsame expression, since there are necessarily four ways of understanding it, he did not express it in one way alone. But even though each of the four ways of understanding is partial or one-sided, the way of the patriarchs ever remains the way of the patriarchs.

Dōgen's point is that the replies of each of the disciples do not indicate any real differences of depth, but merely different ways of saying the same thing (and each might be appropriate on different occasions). The speech of the first three disciples and the silence of Huike, then, are all equivalent. So silence is not privileged over speech.

After all, a body is an integrated whole, and each part of it is necessary for the others. The Dharmas (sayings) of the disciples are mutually co-dependent, like the parts of the body. One might say that these interpenetrate. Indeed, Dōgen goes on to put a Huayan spin on the interchange between master and disciples as follows:[35]

You should realize that when you express me, then I express you, expression expresses both me and you, and expression expresses both you and me. In studying the mind of the first patriarch, you must realize the oneness of the interior and exterior [dimensions]. If we do not realize that the whole body permeates his body, then we have not realized the domain of the manifestation of the Buddhas and the patriarchs. Expressing the skin is expressing the bones, flesh, marrow. Expressing the bones, flesh, and marrow is expressing the skin, flesh, face, and eyes. It is none other than the awakening of the true body experienced throughout the entire ten direction of the universe, and [the realization of] the skin, flesh, bones, and marrow. In that way, you express my robe and express the Dharma.

So what has this to do with kudzo and wisteria? The whole lecture takes off from the following:[36]

My late master [Ruijing] once said: "The vine of a gourd coils around the vine of a[nother] gourd like a wisteria vine." I have never heard this saying from anyone else of the past or the present. The first time I heard this was from my late master. When he said, "the vine of a gourd coils round the vine of a[nother] gourd," this refers to studying the Buddhas and patriarchs directly from the Buddhas and partriarchs, and to the transmission of the Buddhas and patriarchs directly to the Buddhas and patriarchs. That is, it refers to the direct transmission from mind-to-mind (*ishin-denshin*).

The direct transmission is the silence of Hiuke and Kāśyapa. That is the vine of one gourd. Language is the vine of the other. The being of each of these is necessary for the being of the other. And both, in their way, say the same thing.

[35] Heine (2009), p. 153. [36] Heine (2009), p. 151.

We are back, here, to the *Vimalakīrti Nirdeśa Sūtra* (see 6.5). It is exactly the point that the goddess is making when she says that words are not internal, not external, and not anywhere else; and it is exactly the final entanglement between Mañjuśrī and Vimalakīrti.

9.12 On Transcending Dualities

With Dōgen in mind, and by way of drawing the threads of the book together, let us return to the question of transcending dualities.

As early in our story as the *Prajñāpāramitā Sūtras* (4.3), the thought was broached that to understand the ultimate aspect of reality requires one to transcend all dualities. What this means is not, of course, entirely clear. Indeed, in the discussion from the *Vimalakīrti Nirdeśa Sūtra* of 6.5 we saw a number of bodhisattvas putting the matter in different ways. Although the chapter in question ends by praising one particular understanding of the matter, there is no reason to suppose that the others are wrong. There may well be many legitimate ways of understanding the matter. Perhaps, transcending duality is not a univocal notion. After all, transcending the effable/ineffable duality is not obviously the same as transcending the subject/object duality. On the other hand, if we take a leaf out of Dogen's *Katto* of the last section, one might think of all these things as different ways of getting at the same point.

Throughout the course of the book, we have, in fact, seen a number of ways in which one might articulate the thought of what it is to transcend a duality—and all of these find resonances in Dōgen.

In Chapter 7, we saw that transcending duality may be thought of, not as a state, but as a process. This finds echoes in Dōgen's view of 9.9 of practice as realization. The processes involved in the Jizang Hierarchy and Dōgen's zazen are obviously not the same; but, as noted, both are practices that may be thought of as revealing the ultimate aspect of reality.

In Chapter 8, we saw that interpenetration can be seen as a way of transcending dualities. This finds direct uptake in Dōgen's adoption of Huayan thought, as we saw in 9.7.

In Chapter 9, we saw (9.5) that the progression to the post-enlightenment state can be seen as a way of transcending the duality of the two partial ways of apprehending reality. This also appears in Dōgen's thought about how the ultimate shines through the ordinary.

Of course, there is an even more straightforward way of understanding the notion of duality-transcendence. A and $\neg A$ form a duality. To endorse just one of these is obviously to endorse a duality. One way to overcome this is, then, to assert both; that is, to put ourselves in the third koṭi of the catuṣkoṭi.[37] In a quite different context, Hegel makes the point as follows:[38]

> The commonest injustice done to a speculative content is to make it one-sided, that is, to give prominence only to one of the propositions into which it can be resolved. It cannot then be denied that this proposition is asserted; but the statement is just as false as it is true, for once one of the propositions is taken out of the speculative content, the other must be equally considered and stated.

Dōgen has this way of transcending duality in his tool box as well, as we saw with his endorsement of the contradictory nature of saṃsāra, that is, nirvāṇa, in 9.8.

So much for our four-cornered catuṣkoṭi. The duality which has concerned us more than any other in this book, however, is the duality between effability and ineffability. Again, to have only one of these is to be 'one-sided', and the duality is transcended by having both: the Paradox of Ineffability. This is the locus of the five-cornered catuṣkoṭi—and specifically its plurivalent form, which allows for something to be both effable and ineffable. In 6.5 we saw how the *Vimalakīrti Nirdeśa Sūtra* allowed for this possibility—indeed, not only allowed for it, but required it. As we saw in 9.11, Dōgen has his own way of making this point as well.

Dōgen is, then, a focal point of all the rays of our narrative. Of course, rays of light may go beyond a focal point; and the story of Buddhist philosophy does not end with Dōgen; indeed, it has not ended yet.

9.13 Conclusion

There is more to be said. The rest is silence.

[37] Of course, employing the fourth koṭi can also be seen as a way of duality-transcendence. Thus, we have in Huineng's *Platfrom Sūtra* (Price and Wong (1990), p. 77):

> [GP: In the *Mahāparinirvāṇa Sūtra*, the Buddha says,] 'There are two kinds of elements of goodness, the eternal and the non-eternal. Since buddha-nature is neither eternal nor non-eternal, therefore their element of goodness is not eradicated.' Now Buddhism is known as having no two ways. There are good ways and evil ways, but since buddha-nature is neither, therefore Buddhism is known as having no two ways.

[38] Miller (1969), p. 91.

Fig. 5. Ensō: the Zen character for enlightenment

After the End

10

A Methodological Coda

This book tells a story. It is the story about Buddhist metaphysics, the catuṣkoṭi, and the interlaced evolution of the two. As for Dōgen's vines, these twine around each other. The point is not to advocate any particular view—though views are certainly interrogated along the way. It is to show the integrity of the process. The techniques of contemporary non-classical logic are employed to help do so. Philosophical ideas are slippery; mathematical ideas much less so.

So as will be clear to anyone who reads this book, the methodology is somewhat unusual. I am working with ancient and medieval Buddhist texts, not from a religious, textual, or philological point view, but as part of a live contemporary philosophical discussion. Moreover, I am applying techniques of contemporary formal logic in the process. One might have some reservations about this methodology. The point of this coda is to address some such concerns.

First, Buddhism is a religion.[1] I have been concerned with but one aspect of it: its philosophy. It might be suggested that one cannot do justice to this if one is not a Buddhist, or at least, without taking other aspects of the religion into account. Now, it is absurd to suppose that one cannot engage with the philosophical basis of a religion if one is not a believer. That is like saying that one cannot engage with the philosophy of Plato, Aquinas, or Kant if one is not a Platonist, Thomist, or Kantian: you do not have to believe to understand. Nor does it do violence to the philosophy if one disengages it from its rituals, practices, power structures. The philosophical views have to stand on their own two feet. Indeed, it is not at all clear that these things could be germane in any way to an analysis of the philosophical basis of Buddhism.

There is one aspect of Buddhism that might give one pause here, though. In most Buddhisms, meditation—in some form or forms—is an important practice.

[1] Though I have heard this denied by some Western thinkers who (parochially) cannot believe that a religion can have no god. However, Buddhism, like all religions, has its world view, ethics, sacred texts, sacred places, practices, rituals, priesthoods, hierarchies, soteriology. I defy anyone to engage with Buddhist institutions, rituals, and practices and still claim that this is not a religion.

Indeed, most Buddhists hold that it is only with this that one can come face to face with ultimate reality (whatever that is supposed to be in the form of Buddhism in question). Now, I do not want to deny that meditative experience may be an important part of Buddhist *religion*. Perhaps it might even be used as an argument for the existence of ultimate reality.[2] However, what I would contest is that it is necessary to have such an experience to understand Buddhist *philosophy*.[3] You do not have to have an experience of something to understand that there might be such a thing, or to appreciate the arguments for there being such a thing, or the consequences of there being such a thing. Thus, I have never been a woman or an Australian Aboriginal. So perhaps I cannot really know how it *feels* to be marginalized by a white male society; but I understand patriarchy and racism very well: how they work, and their effects. Or again, I have never experienced a Christian miracle; but I understand very well what such things are supposed to be, the arguments for their existence, and their supposed consequences. Nor does this lack of experience imply that I cannot judge that there are no such things. That belief, if rational, can be formed on quite other bases.

Let us turn to a more substantial matter: my philosophical methodology itself. One might hold that the use of contemporary formal methods is temporally incongruous. Of course it is, in one sense. These techniques are far beyond the conceptual horizon of the actors in our drama. But the question is whether the use is objectionably so. I think not. Philosophy is a dynamically evolving enterprise, and we are just a lot clearer nowadays about a number of things than historical philosophers were. This is not because we are smarter, but because we have had longer to think about these things. We have also developed new and useful tools—such as those of contemporary formal logic. These can be helpful in analysing philosophical views and arguments, both to help articulate them more clearly, and to analyse their pros and cons. Refusing to use these insights and tools when they are available is perverse. It's like refusing to use DNA analysis when analysing some historical situation, just because those involved in it had no knowledge of DNA. Neither is there anything special about Asian philosophy in this regard. Philosophers can, and frequently do, use contemporary ideas and techniques in the investigation of Plato, Aquinas, Kant, and a whole host of other Western philosophers and philosophical traditions.

[2] Though I am dubious of this. No religious experience is self-certifying. Believers may interpret it in certain ways, but there is always a question of the correctness of their interpretation.

[3] And it can hardly be claimed that an understanding of philosophy is irrelevant to Buddhist religion. After all, *right view* is the first of the octet of the Fourth Noble Truth; and all schools of Buddhism—even Zen—study texts and their meanings.

Would the actors in the drama of this book have used those insights and tools had they been available to them? I see no reason why not. They were all thoughtful people, and were certainly not averse to novelty. Indeed, many of them were responsible for developing novelties of their own. I might add, also, that the benefit of the engagement here is not unidirectional. The issues that our historical philosophers were dealing with can certainly benefit from engagement with the novel. But the novel also benefits by engagement with history. We can and do come to see new aspects of contemporary ideas and tools—in formal logic and elsewhere[4]—in the process.

Recall that my project here is not simply one of describing what is in texts—though the book clearly engages in this. I am taking ideas arguably to be found in the texts, and articulating, analysing, and evaluating them, employing all the resources of modern logic and philosophy at my disposal.

This bring us to the third concern one might have. I am taking ideas in Asian philosophy and treating them as a contemporary Western philosopher does. One might be concerned that I am committing the sin of what Edward Said (1978) called Orientalism. Orientalism is an attitude of paternalism and systematic misrepresentation of Asia, in the cause of privileging things Western over things Eastern. It is often connected with colonial and imperialistic attitudes. Am I doing this? Not at all.

First, I do not want to deny for a moment that European powers have a grim history when it comes to other cultures (and many other things for that matter). It is clear to anyone who has a knowledge of some basic facts of history that the European countries have often invaded, subjugated, and colonized other parts of the world. They have committed genocide; they have used its peoples; they have taken its wealth; they have appropriated whatever they wished to help themselves to. The attitude that the oppressors had a superior culture was certainly an integral part of the legitimation of this.

But that is no part of what is going on here. I am certainly engaging with Asian ideas, and from the perspective of a contemporary Western philosopher. I cannot do otherwise. I cannot change the facts concerning the place in which I was born, the culture in which I grew up, the education I received. And in some sense, I suppose, one might say that I am appropriating Asian ideas:[5] I am certainly deploying them, discussing them, sometimes criticizing them. But my attitude

[4] See, for example, Bliss and Priest (2018).

[5] The *Oxford English Dictionary* defines *to appropriate* as follows: 'to take something for one's own use, typically without the owner's permission'. There is no way, of course, I can seek the permission of those who came up with the ideas I have been discussing: they are long since dead. In my work I have frequently appropriated the ideas of many Western philosophers in exactly the same way.

is anything *but* one of devaluation and patronization. I am engaging with these views precisely because I find them important, interesting, and worthy of thought and investigation. I would hardly write a book about them otherwise.

Naturally, being a philosopher, I am critical of some of these views. Does this show a lack of respect? Not at all. The way one shows respect in philosophy is precisely by engaging with ideas: not by ignoring them; not by mothballing them; but by treating them as part of an ongoing philosophical investigation and dialogue. That is how philosophy, both East and West, has always been done. I might point out that this is exactly how I (and many other philosophers) treat ideas from the history of Western philosophy too. And the culture, language, social institutions, etc., of ancient Greece and medieval Europe are just as alien to me as those of ancient India and China. In no way does that show a lack of respect for the philosophy that comes from *those* times and places. On the contrary, it shows that I value its importance.

After many decades, if not centuries, when Western philosophers had a somewhat lamentable knowledge of the Asian philosophical traditions—if any at all—and it was common to hear Western philosophers declaim (largely out of ignorance) that such things were not philosophy at all, but religion, mysticism, simply oracular pronouncements, things are slowly changing. Western philosophers are starting to engage with Asian texts, learn the languages in which they are written, and integrate the ideas contained into their philosophical thinking. (Such, of course, is a commonplace with respect to ancient and medieval Western philosophy.) This is a development highly to be welcomed. It does not privilege Western ideas. On the contrary: both Eastern and Western ideas are developed in a conversation of equal respect and mutual benefit. (Asian philosophers themselves have been engaged in this inter-cultural process for at least a century.) This book is part of that process.

Sino-Japanese Glossary

Note: Where Chinese/Japanese pronunciations are given, the Chinese is first.

Amituofo:	阿彌陀佛
Caodong/Sōtō:	曹洞
Chan/Zen:	禪
Chengguan:	澄觀
Damo/Daruma:	達摩
Dao:	道
Daode jing:	道德經
Daofu:	道副
Daoyu:	道育
Dasheng qixinlun:	大乘起信論
Dasheng xuanlun:	大乘玄論
Dingshan/Jōzan:	定山
Dōgen Kigen:	道元希玄
Dōyō:	道用
Dushun:	杜順
Erdi zhang:	二諦章
Fazang:	法藏
Foxing:	佛性
Genjō kōan:	現成公案
Gong'an/kōan:	公案
Guo Xiang:	郭象
Hakuin Ekaku:	白隠慧鶴
Hongren:	弘忍
Hossō:	法相
Huayan/Kegon:	華嚴
Huayan fajie xuanjing:	華嚴法界玄鏡
Huike:	慧可
Jiashan/Kassan:	夾山
Jin shizi zhang:	金獅子章
Jingtu/Jōdo:	淨土

Jizang:	吉藏
Kaiin zanmai:	海印三昧
Kattō:	葛藤
Kenshō:	見性
Kong/kū:	空
Kongfuzi:	孔夫子
Laozi:	老子
Li:	理
Linji/Rinzai:	臨済
Lishi wuai:	理事無礙
Liuzu tanjing:	六祖壇經
Lunyu:	論語
Ma:	馬
Myōan Eisai:	明菴榮西
Myōzen:	明全
Panjiao:	判教
Qingyuan Xingsi:	青原行思
Rujing:	如淨
Sanlun/Sanron:	三論
Sengzhao:	僧肇
Shenxiu:	神秀
Shi:	事
Shikantaza:	只管打坐
Shintō:	神道
Shishi wuai:	事事無礙
Shōbōgenzō:	正法眼藏
Shōji:	生死
Tenzo kyōkun:	典座教訓
Tiantai/Tendai:	天台
Tōrei Enji:	東嶺圓慈
Wang Bi:	王弼
Weixin:	唯心
Wu:	無
Wu/satori:	悟
Wudeng huiyuan:	五燈會元
Wumenguan:	無門關

Xuanxue:	玄學
Xuedou:	雪竇
Xin:	心
Yang:	陽
Yijing:	易經
Yin:	陰
You:	有
Zazen:	坐禪
Zazengi:	坐禪儀
Zenki:	全機
Zhaozhou/Jōshū:	趙州
Zhuangzi:	莊子
Zi:	子
Zongzhi:	總持

Bibliography

Aczel, P. (1988), *Non-Well-Founded Sets* (CSLI Lecture Notes 14), Chicago, IL: University of Chicago Press.

App, U. (1994), *Master Yunmen: From the Record of the Chan Teacher Gate of the Clouds*, New York, NY: Kodansha International Press.

Ariew, R., and Garber, D. (eds.) (1989), *Leibniz: Philosophical Essays*, Indianapolis, IN: Hackett Publishing Company.

Armstrong, D. M. (1997), *A World of States of Affairs*, Cambridge: Cambridge University Press.

Barwise, J., and Etchemendy, J. (1987), *The Liar: An Essay on Truth and Circularity*, Oxford: Oxford University Press.

Battacharya, H. S. (ed. and tr.) (1967), *Pramāṇa-naya-tattvālokālaṁkāra*, Bombay: Jain Sahitya Vikas Mandal.

Battacharya, K., Johnston, E. H., and Kunst, A. (trs.) (1978), *The Dialectical Method of Nāgārjuna's Vigrahvyāvartanī*, Delhi: Motilal Banarsidass.

Beall, J., and Glanzberg, M. (2011), 'The Liar Paradox', in E. Zalta (ed.), *Stanford Encyclopedia of Philosophy*, http://plato.stanford.edu/entries/liar-paradox/.

Belnap, N. D. (1977), 'A Useful Four-Valued logic', pp. 8–37 of J. M. Dunn and G. Epstein (eds.), *Modern Uses of Multiple-Valued Logics*, Dordrecht: Reidel.

Bharucha, F., and Kamat, R. V. (1984), '*Syādvāda* Theory of Jainism in Terms of Deviant Logic', *Indian Philosophical Quarterly* 9: 181–7.

Bliss, R., and Priest, G. (2018), 'Metaphysical Dependence: East and West', pp. 63–85 of S. Emmanuel (ed.), *Buddhist Philosophy: A Comparative Approach*, Hoboken, NJ: Wiley Blackwell.

Carpenter, A. (2014), *Indian Buddhist Philosophy*, Durham: Acumen.

Chalmers, A. (2013), *What Is This Thing Called Science?*, 4th edn, Brisbane: University of Queensland Press.

Chan, A. (2014), 'Neo-Daoism', in E. Zalta (ed.), *Stanford Encyclopedia of Philosophy*, https://plato.stanford.edu/entries/neo-daoism/.

Chan, W. T. (ed. and tr.) (1963), *A Source Book in Chinese Philosophy*, Princeton, NJ: Princeton University Press.

Chang, G. C. C. (1972), *The Buddhist Teaching of Totality: The Philosophy of Hwa Yen Buddhism*, London: George Allen & Unwin Ltd.

Cleary, T. (tr.) (1983), *Entry into the Inconceivable: An Introduction to Hua-yen Buddhism*, Honolulu, HI: University of Hawai'i Press.

Cleary, T. (ed. and tr.) (1986), *Shōbōgenzō: Zen Essays by Dōgen*, Honolulu, HI: University of Hawai'i Press.

Cleary, T. (tr.) (1993a), *The Flower Ornament Scripture: A Translation of the Avatamsāka Sūtra*, Boston, MA: Shambala Publications.

Cleary, T. (tr.) (1993b), *No Barrier: Unlocking the Zen Koan*, New York, NY: Bantham Books.

Conze, E. (tr.) (1973), *The Perfection of Wisdom in Eight Thousand Lines and its Verse Summary*, Delhi: Sri Satguru Publications.

Conze, E. (tr.) (1979), *The Large Sutra on Perfect Wisdom*, Delhi: Motilal Banarsidass Publishers Pvt Ltd.

Cook, F. H. (1977), *Hua-yen Buddhism: The Jewel Net of Indra*, University Park, PA: Pennsylvania State University Press.

Cowherds, The (2010), *Moonshadows: Conventional Truth in Buddhist Philosophy*, New York, NY: Oxford University Press.

De La Vallée Poussin, L., and Sangpo, G. L. (trs.) (2012), *Abhidharmakośa-Bhāṣya of Vasubandhu*, Delhi: Motilal Banarsidass Publishers Private Limited.

Deguchi, Y. (forthcoming), 'Contradictions in the Sanlun School? Is Pseudo Jizang a Dialetheist?', to appear in H. R. Kantor and M. Salvini (eds.), *Language in the Traditions of Madhyamaka Thought*, Vienna: Austrian Academy of Sciences Press.

Deguchi, Y., Garfield, J., and Priest, G. (2008), 'The Way of the Dialetheist: Contradictions in Buddhism', *Philosophy East & West* 58: 395–402.

Deguchi, Y., Garfield, J., and Priest, G. (2013a), 'Two Plus Two Equals One: A Response to Brook Ziporyn', *Philosophy East & West* 63: 353–8.

Deguchi, Y., Garfield, J., and Priest, G. (2013b), 'A Mountain by Any Other Name: A Response to Koji Tanaka', *Philosophy East & West* 63: 335–43.

Deguchi, Y. Garfield, J., and Priest, G (2013c), 'How We Think Mādhyamikas Think: A Response to Tom Tillemans', *Philosophy East & West*, 63: 462–35.

Dennett, D. (1982), 'The Self as a Center of Narrative Gravity', ch. 6 of F. Kessell, P. Cole, and D. Johnson (eds.), *Self and Consciousness: Multiple Perspectives*, Hillsdale, NJ: Erlbaum.

Dennett, D. (1993), *Consciousness Explained*, London: Penguin Books.

Duerlinger, J. (ed. and tr.) (2003), *Indian Buddhist Theories of Persons: Vasubandhu's 'Refutation of the Self'*, London: Routledge Curzon.

Dumont, H. (1963), *A History of Zen Buddhism*, New York, NY: Random House.

Eihei, S. (trs.) (2016), *Instructions for the Cook*, https://web.stanford.edu/group/scbs/sztp3/translations/eihei_shingi/translations/tenzo_kyokun/translation.html.

Elliot, T. S. (1943), *Four Quartets*, San Diego, CA: Harcourt.

Elwes, R. H. M. (tr.) (1955), *Works of Spinoza*, Vol. 2, New York, NY: Dover Publications.

Foucault, M. (1988), 'Technologies of the Self', pp. 16–49 of L. H. Martin, H. Gutman, and P. H. Hutton (eds.), *Technologies of the Self*, Amherst, MA: University of Massachusetts Press.

Ganeri, J. (2001), *Philosophy in Classical India*, London: Routledge.

Ganeri, J. (2002), 'Jaina Logic and the Philosophical Basis of Pluralism', *History and Philosophy of Logic* 23: 267–81.

Garfield, J. (tr.) (1995), *The Fundamental Wisdom of the Middle Way*, New York, NY: Oxford University Press.

Garfield, J. (2002a), 'Vasubandhu's Treatise on Three Natures', pp. 128–51 of Garfield (2002c).

Garfield, J. (2002b), 'Sounds of Silence: Ineffability and the Limits of Language in Madhyamaka and Yogācāra', pp. 170–86 of Garfield (2002c).

Garfield, J. (2002c), *Empty Words*, New York, NY: Oxford University Press.

Garfield, J. (2015), *Engaging Buddhism: Why it Matters to Philosophy*, New York, NY: Oxford University Press.
Garfield, J. (2016), *The Heart Sūtra: Bhagavatī-Prajñāpāramitā-Hṛdaya-Sūtra*, https://jaygarfield.files.wordpress.com/2016/08/heart-sutra.pdf.
Garfield, J., and Priest, G. (2003), 'Nāgārjuna and the Limits of Thought', *Philosophy East & West* 53: 1–21; this also appeared as ch. 16 in Priest (2002a).
Garfield, J., and Priest, G. (2009), 'Mountains are Just Mountains', pp. 71–82 of J. Garfield and M. D'Amato (eds.), *Pointing at the Moon: Buddhism, Logic and Analytic Philosophy*, New York, NY: Oxford University Press.
Gelugpa Students' Welfare Committee (2003), *dBu ma rtsa ba'I 'grel ba tshig gsal ba zhes bya ba gzhugs so*, Sarnath: Gelugpa Students' Welfare Committee.
Glanzberg, M. (2013), 'Truth', in E. Zalta (ed.), *Stanford Encyclopedia of Philosophy*, http://plato.stanford.edu/entries/truth/.
Gregory, P. (2012), 'The *Platform Sūtra* as the Sudden Teaching', pp. 77–108 of M. Schlütter and S. F. Teiser, *Readings on the Platform Sūtra*, New York, NY: Columbia University Press.
Hanson, N. R. (1958), *Patterns of Discovery: An Inquiry into the Conceptual Foundations of Science*, Cambridge: Cambridge University Press.
Harvey, P. (2000), *Buddhist Ethics*, Cambridge: Cambridge University Press.
Heine, S. (2006), *Did Dōgen Go to China? What He Wrote and When He Wrote it*, New York, NY: Oxford University Press.
Heine, S. (tr.) (2009), 'Dōgen's *Shōbōgenzō* Fascicles "Katto" and "Ōsukasendaba"', pp. 149–58 of W. Edelglass and J. Garfield (eds.), *Buddhist Philosophy: Essential Readings*, New York, NY: Oxford University Press.
Hershoc, P. (2015), 'Chan Buddhism', in E. Zalta (ed.), *Stanford Encyclopedia of Philosophy*, http://plato.stanford.edu/entries/buddhism-chan/.
Horwich, P. (1990), *Truth*, Oxford: Basil Blackwell.
Jayatilleke, K. N. (1963), *Early Buddhist Theories of Knowledge*, London: George Allen and Unwin Ltd.
Jones, N. (2009), 'Fazang's Total Power Mereology: An Interpretive Analytic Reduction', *Asian Philosophy* 19: 199–211.
Jones, N. (2015), 'Buddhist Reductionism and Emptiness in Huayen Perspective', ch. 6 of K. Tanaka, Y. Deguchi, J. Garfield, and G. Priest (eds.), *The Moon Points Back*, New York, NY: Oxford University Press.
Kassor, C. (2013), 'Is Gorampa's "Freedom from Conceptual Proliferations" Dialetheist? A Response to Garfield, Priest, and Tillemans', *Philosophy East & West* 63: 399–410.
Kasulis, T. P. (1981), *Zen Action Zen Person*, Honolulu, HI: University of Hawai'i Press.
Kemp Smith, N. (tr.) (1933), *Immanuel Kant's Critique of Pure Reason*, 2nd edn, London: Macmillan & Co.
Keown, D. (2003), *Dictionary of Buddhism*, Oxford: Oxford University Press.
Koller, J. M. (2002), *Asian Philosophies*, 4th edn, Upper Saddle River, NJ: Prentice Hall.
Koller, J. M., and Koller, P. (1991), *A Sourcebook in Asian Philosophy*, Upper Saddle River, NJ: Prentice Hall.
Kripke, S. (1975), 'Outline of a Theory of Truth', *Journal of Philosophy* 72: 690–716.

Ladyman, J., and Ross, D., with Spurrett, D., and Collier, J. (2007), *Every Thing Must Go: Metaphysics Naturalized*, Oxford: Oxford University Press.

Latta, R. (ed.) (1898), *Leibniz: The Monadology and other Philosophical Writings*, Oxford: Oxford University Press.

Lewis, D. K. (1991), *Parts of Classes*, Oxford: Basil Blackwell.

Liu, J. L. (2006), *An Introduction to Chinese Philosophy*, Oxford: Blackwell.

Liu, M. W. (1982), 'The Harmonious Universe of Fazang and Leibniz', *Philosophy East & West* 32: 61–76.

Liu, M. W. (1993), 'A Chinese Madhyamaka Theory of Truth: The Case of Chi-tsang', *Philosophy East & West* 43: 649–73.

Lusthaus, D. (1998), 'Buddhist Philosophy, Chinese', in E. Craig (ed.), *Routledge Encyclopedia of Philosophy*, Vol. 1, London: Routledge.

Matilal, B. K. (1981), *The Central Philosophy of Jainism (Anekānta-Vāda)*, Ahmedabad: L. D. Institute of Indology.

Miller, A. V. (tr.) (1969), *Hegel's Science of Logic*, London: George Allen & Unwin Ltd.

Mitchell, D. (2002), *Buddhism: Introducing the Buddhist Experience*, Oxford: Oxford University Press.

Mun, C. (2006), *The History of Doctrinal Classification in Chinese Buddhism: A Study of the Panjiao Systems*, Lanham, MD: University Press of America.

Nagatomo, S. (2015), 'Japanese Zen Buddhist Philosophy', in E. Zalta (ed.), *Stanford Encyclopedia of Philosophy*, https://plato.stanford.edu/entries/japanese-zen/.

Ñāṇamoli, Bikkhu, and Bodhi, Bikkhu (trs.) (1995), *The Middle Length Discourses of the Buddha*, Somerville, MA: Wisdom Publications.

Nishijima, G. W., and Cross, C. (1994–9), *Master Dogen's Shobogenzo*, Woods Hole, MA: Windbell Publications.

Oller, C. (1999), 'Paraconsistency and Analyticity', *Logic and Logical Philosophy* 7: 91–9.

Padmakara Translation Group (trs.) (2004), *Introduction to the Middle Way: Candrakīrti's Madhyamakāvatāra with a Commentary by Jamgön Mipham*, Boston, MA: Shambala.

Park, S. (1983), *Buddhist Faith and Sudden Enlightenment*, New York, NY: SUNY Press.

Perkins, F. (2015), 'Metaphysics in Chinese Philosophy', in E. Zalta (ed.), *Stanford Encyclopedia of Philosophy*, https://plato.stanford.edu/entries/chinese-metaphysics/#BudMetChi.

Prawitz, D. (1965), *Natural Deduction: A Proof-Theoretical Study*, Stockholm: Almqvist & Wiksell.

Price, A. F., and Wong M. L. (trs.) (1990), *The Diamond Sūtra and the Sūtra of Hui-Neng*, Boston, MA: Shambala.

Priest, G. (1987), *In Contradiction*, The Hague: Martinus Nijhof; 2nd edn, Oxford: Oxford University Press, 2006.

Priest, G. (2002a), *Beyond the Limits of Thought*, 2nd edn, Oxford: Oxford University Press.

Priest, G. (2002b), 'Paraconsistent Logic', Vol. 6, pp. 287–393 of D. Gabbay and F. Guenthner (eds.), *Handbook of Philosophical Logic*, 2nd edn, Dordrecht: Kluwer Academic Publishers.

Priest, G. (2005a), *Towards Non-Being*, Oxford: Oxford University Press; 2nd edn, 2016.

Priest, G. (2005b), 'The Limits of Language', Vol. 7, pp. 156–9, 2nd edn, of K. Brown (ed.), *Encyclopedia of Language and Linguistics*, Amsterdam: Elsevier.

Priest, G. (2006), *Doubt Truth to be a Liar*, Oxford: Oxford University Press.
Priest, G. (2008a), *Introduction to Non-Classical Logic*, 2nd edn, Cambridge: Cambridge University Press.
Priest, G. (2008b), 'Jaina Logic: A Contemporary Perspective', *History and Philosophy of Logic* 29: 263–78.
Priest, G. (2009), 'The Structure of Emptiness', *Philosophy East & West* 59: 467–80.
Priest, G. (2010a), 'The Logic of the *Catuṣkoṭi*', *Comparative Philosophy* 1: 32–54.
Priest, G. (2010b), 'Two Truths: Two Models', ch. 13 of Cowherds (2010).
Priest, G. (2011), 'Four Corners—East and West', pp. 12–18 of M. Banerjee and A. Seth (eds.), *Logic and Its Applications*, Berlin: Springer.
Priest, G. (2013a), 'Between the Horns of Idealism and Realism: The Middle Way of Madhyamaka', ch. 13 of S. Emmanuel (ed.), *A Companion to Buddhist Philosophy*, Hoboken, NJ: Wiley-Blackwell.
Priest, G. (2013b), 'Nāgārjuna's *Mūlamadhyakamakārika*', *Topoi* 32: 129–34.
Priest, G. (2014a), *One*, Oxford: Oxford University Press.
Priest, G. (2014b), 'Speaking of the Ineffable . . .', ch. 7 of J. Lee and D. Berger (eds.), *Nothingness in Asian Philosophy*, London: Routledge.
Priest, G. (2014c), 'Plurivalent Logic', *Australasian Journal of Logic* 11, article 1, http://ojs.victoria.ac.nz/ajl/article/view/1830.
Priest, G. (2015a), 'Alethic Values', *Newsletter of the APA, Asian and Asian-American Philosophers and Philosophies* 14: 2–4.
Priest, G. (2015b), 'The Net of Indra', pp. 113–27 of K. Tanaka, Y. Deguchi, J. Garfield, and G. Priest (eds.), *The Moon Points Back*, New York, NY: Oxford University Press.
Priest, G. (2019), 'Natural Deduction for Systems in the *FDE* Family', to appear in H. Omori and H. Wansing (eds.), *New Essays in Belnap-Dunn Logic*, Dordrecht: Springer.
Priest, G., and Berto, F. (2013), 'Dialetheism', in E. Zalta (ed.), *Stanford Encyclopedia of Philosophy*, http://plato.stanford.edu/entries/dialetheism/.
Priest, G., Siderits, M., and Tillemans, T. (2010), 'The Truth(s) about the Two Truths', ch. 8 of Cowherds (2010).
Raju, P. (1954), 'The Principle of Four-Cornered Negation in Indian Philosophy', *Review of Metaphysics* 7: 694–713.
Rhys Davids, T. W. (tr.) (1890), *The Questions of King Milinda*, Oxford: Oxford University Press.
Robinson, R. (1957), 'Some Logical Aspects of Nāgārjuna's System', *Philosophy East & West* 6: 291–308.
Ronkin, N. (2014), 'Abhidharma', in E. Zalta (ed.), *Stanford Encyclopedia of Philosophy*, http://plato.stanford.edu/entries/abhidharma/.
Ruegg, D. (1977), 'The Uses of the Four Positions of the *Catuṣkoṭi* and the Problem of the Description of Reality in Mahāyāna Buddhism', *Journal of Indian Philosophy* 5: 1–71.
Russell, B. (1912), *The Problems of Philosophy*, Oxford: Oxford University Press.
Said, E. (1978), *Orientalism*, New York, NY: Random House.
Sarkar, T. (1992), 'Some Reflections on Jaina *Anekāntavāda* and *Syādvada*', *Jadavpur Journal of Philosophy* 2: 13–38.
Selby-Bigge, L. A. (ed.) (1978), *David Hume: A Treatise on Human Nature*, 2nd edn, Oxford: Oxford University Press.

Sharf, R. (2002), *Coming to Terms with Buddhism: A Reading of the Treasure Store Treatise*, Honolulu, HI: University of Hawai'i Press.

Sharf, R. (forthcoming), 'Chan Cases', ch. 6 of Y. Deguchi, J. Garfield, G. Priest, and R. Sharf, *Whereof One Cannot Speak*.

Siderits, M. (2007), *Buddhism as Philosophy*, Aldershot: Ashgate.

Siderits, M. (2015), 'Buddha', in E. Zalta (ed.), *Stanford Encyclopedia of Philosophy*, http://plato.stanford.edu/entries/buddha/.

Siderits, M., and Katsura, S. (trs.) (2013), *Nāgārjuna's Middle Way*, Boston, MA: Wisdom Publications.

Siderits, M., Tillemans, T., and Chakrabarti, A. (eds.) (2011), *Buddhist Nominalism and Human Cognition*, New York, NY: Columbia University Press.

Staal, F. (1975), *Exploring Mysticism*, London: Penguin Books.

Stcherbatsky, F. T. (1962), *Buddhist Logic*, New York, NY: Dover Publications.

Suzuki, D. T. (tr.) (No date), *Asvaghosha's Discourse on the Awakening of Faith in Māhāyana*, Fremont, CA: Asian Humanities Press.

Tahko, T. E., and Lowe, E. J. (2015), 'Ontological Dependence', in E. Zalta (ed.), *The Stanford Encyclopedia of Philosophy*, http://plato.stanford.edu/entries/dependence-ontological/.

Takakusu, J., and Watanabe, K. (eds.) (1924), *The Taisho Shinshu Daizokyo*, Tokyo: Taisho Shinshu Daizokyo Kanko Kai.

Tanahashi, K. (tr.) (1985), *Moon in a Dewdrop: Writings of Zen Master Dōgen*, San Francisco, CA: North Point Press.

Tanaka, K. (2013), 'Contradictions in Dōgen', *Philosophy East & West* 62: 322–34.

Taylor, B. (1985), *Modes of Occurrence*, Oxford: Basil Blackwell.

Thurman, R. (2014), *The Holy Teachings of Vimalakīrti*, University Park, PA: Pennsylvania State University.

Tillemans, T. (1999), 'Is Buddhist Logic Non-classical or Deviant?', ch. 9 of *Scripture, Logic, Language: Essays on Dharmakīrti and His Tibetan Successors*, Boston, MA: Wisdom Publications.

Tillemans, T. (2009), 'How Do Mādhyamikas Think? Notes on Jay Garfield, Graham Priest, and Paraconsistency', pp. 83–100 of J. Garfield, W. D'Amato, and T. Tillemans (eds.), *Pointing at the Moon: Buddhism, Logic, Analytic Philosophy*, New York, NY: Oxford University Press; reprinted as ch. 3 of Tillemans (2016).

Tillemans, T. (2011), 'Dharmakīrti', in E. Zalta (ed.), *Stanford Encyclopedia of Philosophy*, http://plato.stanford.edu/entries/dharmakiirti/.

Tillemans, T. (2013), '"How Do Mādhyamikas Think?" Revisited', *Philosophy East & West* 63: 417–25; reprinted as ch. 4 of Tillemans (2016).

Tillemans, T. (2016), *How Do Mādhyamikas Think? And Other Essays on the Buddhist Philosophy of the Middle*, Somerville, MA: Wisdom Publications.

Varzi, A. (2009), 'Mereology', in E. Zalta (ed.), *Stanford Encyclopedia of Philosophy*, http://plato.stanford.edu/entires/mereology.

Varzi, A. (2011), 'Boundaries, Conventions, and Realism', pp. 129–53 of J. Campbell, M. O'Rourke, and M. Slater (eds.), *Carving Nature at its Joints*, Cambridge, MA: MIT Press.

Westerhoff, J. (2010), *Nāgārjuna's Metaphysics: A Philosophical Introduction*, Oxford: Oxford University Press.

Williams, P. (2009), *Mahāyāna Buddhism: The Doctrinal Foundations*, 2nd edn, London: Routledge.

Wittgenstein, L. (1929), 'Some Remarks on Logical Form', *Proceedings of the Aristotelian Society, Supplementary Volumes* 9: 162–71.

Wright, T. (tr.) (2005), *How to Cook Your Life: From the Zen Kitchen to Enlightenment*, Boulder, CO: Shambala Publications.

Ziporyn, B. (2013), 'A Comment on "The Way of the Dialetheist: Contradictions in Buddhism", by Yasuo Deguchi, Jay L. Garfield, and Graham Priest', *Philosophy East & West* 63: 344–52.

Index of names

Abhayadeva 18
Ānanda 139
Aquinas, T. 147–8
Ariew, R. 37n.15
Aristotle 17, 19, 42, 69
Armstrong, D. M. 39
Āryadava 97
Asaṅga 5
  Anthology of Mahayana 102–3
Aśvaghoṣa 111
Avalokiteśvara 50

Battacharya, H. S. 87n.24
Beall, J. 69n.12
Belnap, N. D. 25n.21
Bharucha, F. 89
Bliss, R. 56n.18, 149n.4
Bodhi, B. 16n.2, 27n.23, 28n.25
Bodhidharma (Damo, Daruma) 7, 126, 139–40

Candrakīrti 58, 59, 84, 113
  Prasannapadā 85
Carpenter, A. 8n.12, 13n.22, 15n.24
Chakrabarti, A. 72n.24
Chalmers, A. 43n.31
Chan, A. 96n.3
Chan, W. T. 95, 96nn.2,4,6–8, 97n.9, 98n.10, 101n.11, 112n.12, 113
Chang, G. C. C. 113n.15, 121n.34, 122n.35
Chengguan 122, 151
Cleary, T. 64n.1, 113nn.15–16, 129–30, 133, 136n.29
Confucius (Kongfuzi) 6
Conze, E. 52nn.7–8, 53n.10, 65n.2
Cook, F. H. 113n.15, 115n.22, 116–17

Damo (Bodhidharma, Daruma) 7, 126, 151
Daofu 139, 151
Daoyu 139, 151
Daruma (Bodhidharma, Damo) 126, 151
De LaVallée Poussin, L. 33n.6
Deguchi, Y. 85n.16, 101nn.12–14, 116n.25, 134n.21
Dennett, D. 12
Dharmakīrti 72, 84–5
Dignāga 84–5
Dingshan (Jozan) 134, 151
Dōgen Kigen 7–8, 92, 124, 138, 139–41, 142, 147, 151
  Genjō kōan 135–6, 151
  Hosshō 136, 151
  Kaiin Zanmai 129, 152
  Katto 139, 141
  Shōbōgenzō 133, 134–7, 139, 152
  Shōji 134
  Tenzo kyōkun 137, 152
  Zazengi 136, 153
  Zenki 133, 153
Duerlinger, J. 13n.20, 13n.22
Dunn, J. M. 25n.21
Dushun 7, 151
  Huayan fajie xuanjing 121, 151

Eihei, A. 137n.31
Eliot, T. S.
  Four Quartets 132
Elwes, R. H. M. 112n.14

Fazang 7, 115–17, 122–3, 151
  Jin shizi zhang (*Treatise on the Golden Lion*) 112, 123, 151
Foucault, M. 9

Gadamer, H. G. 54
Ganeri, J. 33n.4, 86nn.19,21,23, 88n.26, 89
Garber, D. 37n.15
Garfield, J. 50nn.5–6, 54n.12, 57n.21, 65n.3, 83n.11, 85n.15, 101n.14, 109n.8, 116n.25, 131n.11, 134n.21
Glanzberg, M. 69nn.10,12
Gorampa 77, 84
  Synopsis of Madhyamaka 76
Gregory, P. 126n.2, 127n.3
Guo Xiang 96, 151
Guyun 137

Hakuin Ekaku 128n.7, 130
Hanson, N. R. 43n.31
Harvey, P. 8n.12
Hegel, G. W. F. 95, 97, 101n.11, 110, 142
Heidegger, M.
  Sein und Zeit 77
Heine, S. 133n.18, 139nn.33–4, 140nn.35–6
Hershoc, P. 126n.1
Hongren 126–7, 151
Huike 139–40, 151

Huineng 127
Liuzū tanjing (Platform Sūtra) 7, 126, 142n.37, 152
Hume, D. 13, 43
Treatise on Human Nature 12

Jayatilleke, K. N. 18n.7, 20, 21n.13
Jiashan (Kassan) 134–5, 151
Jizang 95, 98–9, 101, 105, 152
Erdi zhang 97, 151
Jones, N. 42n.28, 122n.38
Jozan (Dingshan) 134, 151

Kant, I. 11, 56, 59, 95, 147–8
Critique of Pure Reason 36, 77
Kassan (Jiashan) 134, 151
Kassor, C. 76
Kasulis, T. P. 136
Kāśyapa 64, 127, 128n.6, 140
Katsura, S. 28n.26, 61n.28
Kemp Smith, N. 36n.12
Keown, D. 50n.4
King Milinda 11n.16
Koller, J. M. 18n.5–6, 37n.14
Koller, P. 18n.5–6
Kongfuzi 6, 152
Kripke, S. 78n.5
Kumārajīva 7, 96

Ladyman, J. 56n.17
Leibniz, G. W. 37–8, 56
Monadology 115n.21
Lewis, D. K. 41
Liu, J. L. 95n.1, 101n.11, 105, 113n.15, 117n.27
Liu, M. W. 115n.20
Lowe, E. J. 44n.34
Lusthaus, D. 113n.15, 121n.33

Mahāvīra 85
Mañjuśrī 82–3
Matilal, B. K. 86nn.19–23
Mitchell, D. 3n.1
Mun, C. 103n.15
Myōan Eisai 8, 133n.16, 152
Myōzen 138, 152

Nāgārjuna 5, 11n.16, 35, 46, 49, 53–8, 60, 62–6, 68, 73, 75, 84, 97, 132
Nagatomo, S. 126n.1
Ñāṇamoli, B. 16n.2, 27n.24, 28n.25
Nārāyana 82
Newton, I. 56
Nicholas of Cusa 77
Nishijima, G. W. 134n.22, 135nn.22,24

Oller, C. 74, 91

Park, S. 110n.9
Perkins, F. 112n.13
Plato 147–8
Phaedrus 40
Price, A. F. 61n.29, 142n.37
Priest, G. 3n.3, 8n.13, 16n.1, 22n.17, 29nn.27–30, 31, 34–5, 36n.12, 37n.16, 41n.24, 42n.29, 50, 53n.11, 56n.18, 57, 67n.7, 69n.13, 70n.14, 71nn.17,19, 72n.21, 73n.25, 74nn.26–7, 77n.3, 78n.4, 79n.6, 85n.16, 86nn.17–18, 89, 90nn.28–9, 91nn.30–1, 108n.2, 114n.18, 116n.25, 119n.30, 131n.11, 134n.21, 149n.4
Priyadarśana 82

Qingyuan Xingsi
Wudeng huiyuan 131n.12, 152

Raju, P. 17n.3, 61n.27
Rhys Davids, T. W. 11n.16
Robinson, R. 19
Ronkin, N. 32n.1
Ruegg, D. 17n.3, 27n.23
Ruijing 133
Russell, B. 67n.5

Said, E. 149
Sangpo, G. L. 33n.6
Sañjaya 17
Śankara 61n.27
Śāntarakṣita 5–6
Śāntideva 6
Śāriputra 50–2, 81, 83
Sarkar, T. 89
Selby-Bigge, L. A. 12n.19
Sengzhao 96–7, 152
Shenxiu 126–7, 152
Siddhasena
Nyāyāvatāra 86
Siderits, M. 8n.12, 10n.15, 13n.21, 15n.25, 28n.26, 32n.1, 53n.11, 61n.28, 71n.17, 72n.24, 109n.3
Socrates 23, 34n.7, 67, 72–3
Spinoza, B.
Ethics 112
Staal, F. 21
Stcherbatsky, F. T. 89
Sunetra 82
Suzuki, D. T. 111n.10

Tahko, T. E. 44n.34
Takakusu, J. 101n.13

Tanahashi, K. 135nn.23,25
Thurman, R. 81n.8, 82nn.9–10
Tillemans, T. 20, 71n.17, 72n.24, 84nn.12–13, 85n.15
Tōrei Enji 130, 152

Vādideva Sūri 87–8
Varzi, A. 32n.2, 36n.11, 39n.21
Vasubandhu 5, 13, 33, 34n.7, 109
  Abhidharmakośa-Bhāṣya 13n.22, 33
  Thirty Verses 102–3

Wang Bi 96, 152
Watanabe, K. 101n.13
Westerhoff, J. 21–2, 34n.7, 44n.33, 54n.13, 55n.16
Williams, P. 49, 53n.11, 109n.3, 110n.8, 111n.11, 113n.15
Wittgenstein, L.
  Investigations 54
  Tractatus 43, 73, 77–8
Wong, M. L. 61n.29, 142n.37
Wright, T. 137nn.30–1

Xuedou 138, 153

Zhaozhou 128, 153
Ziporyn, B. 116n.25

General Index

Abhidharma 4, 38, 41, 50, 102
  dharmas 58
  literature 36
  mereology 32
  metaphysics 29, 32, 49, 63
  philosophers 32–3, 35, 37n.14, 43, 44n.33
  realism 71
  taxonomy 51
  texts 33, 103
  tradition 5, 43–4
  view of causation 55
action 9, 42, 130n.9
Advaita Vedānta 61n.27
Afghanistan 6
Agivacchagotta Sutta 16, 26–7
Ājīvikas 18
ālaya (ālaya-vijñāna) 108–10
Amitābha 7n.11
Amituofo 7n.11, 151
anātman 10, 11, 13, 32
anekānta-vāda 86
anitya (impermanence) 4, 10–11
arhat (worthy one) 5, 49
Aristotelian tradition 34n.7
art 3n.2, 32n.3, 40, 114
Asian philosophy 148–50
Aṣṭadaśasāhasrikā Prajñāpāramitā Sūtra 52–3
Aṣṭasāhasrikā Prajñāpāramitā Sūtra 53, 65
Asuras 52
ātman 4
atomism 34–5, 37–43, 55, 72–3, 121
attachment 4, 8, 10, 15, 18
auditory sensations 14
aufgehoben 99
Avataṃsaka Sūtra 113
avidyā (ignorance) 9–10
avyākṛta 26–7
awakened 5n.8
  awareness 132
  being 125
  state 130
awakened one 4
awakening 16, 49, 53, 55, 125, 132, 140, *see also* enlightenment
Awakening of Faith in Mahāyāna 111, 127, 130
Axiom of Extensionality 41
Axiom of Foundation 119n.31, *see also* foundation
being 5n.8, 10, 18, 37, 42, 49, 54, 56–7, 77, 84–5, 96–8, 102, 114, 117, 120, 125, 130, 140, 148, *see also* non-being
beings 36–7, 42, 59, 77, 95, 112, 125, 135, 137
Big Bang 10
birth 98n.10, 111, 130, 134–5, 135n.25, *see also* rebirth
Bodhicāryāvatāra 6
Bodhisattva of Wisdom 82
Bodhisattva Path (Way) 5, 125
bodhisattvas 49, 51, 82–3, 141
Bön 6
Brahman 4
brain 11–12, 14
Bṛhadāraṇyaka Upaniṣad 18
Buddha 4, 16–17, 19–20, 27, 33n.6, 35, 52–4, 57–8, 61, 64–5, 81, 97, 103, 112, 125, 128n.6, 130n.9, 136–7, 139–40
Buddha-Dharma 135
Buddhahood 110
Buddha nature 7, 110, 113–14, 126–7, 135, 142n.37
Buddha's silence 26, 29, 60
Buddhism 3–8, 13, 16, 32–3, 39, 41–2, 44, 49, 58, 61–2, 83, 85, 88, 95–6, 103, 105, 108, 110–11, 112n.13, 113, 116n.25, 117, 125–7, 130, 133n.15, 135, 142n.37, 147–8
  doctrine 103, 125
  heresy 51
  ideal 49
  ideas 6–7
  institutions 3
  logicians 84
  metaphysics 52, 95, 133, 147
  nominalists 72
  philosophers 25, 41, 52, 76
  philosophy 3–6, 13, 17n.3, 32n.3, 69, 142, 148
  practice 127
  reality 6
  reflection 132
  religion 148
  schools 96
  teachings 62, 130n.9
  texts 6, 16, 19n.8, 62–3, 81, 96, 147
  thinkers 12–13, 84–5, 96
  thought 4–5, 10, 29, 79, 84, 96, 124–5
  traditions 33, 42n.28

university 5
view of rebirth 62–3
view of the self 12
Buddhists 4n.5, 7, 10–11, 21n.13, 72, 80, 83, 86, 87n.25, 96, 103, 113, 133, 148

Caodong 133, 151
catuṣkoṭi 15–19, 22, 25–6, 28–9, 32, 49, 55, 60–1, 63–6, 68, 70–1, 73, 75–6, 79–80, 84–5, 87n.25, 89, 95, 98–9, 104–5, 108, 114, 124–5, 131, 142, 147
5-valued 68, 73, 79–80, 89, 99, 108, 114, 124–5, 131
causal
connections 33, 43, 55
explanation 14
flux 10, 44
impact 73
relations 14, 43–4
causality 13
causation 13, 43–4, 54–5
causes 9, 33, 44n.33, 135
and conditions 10, 50n.6, 56, 97
Central Asia 6, 113
Central Meaner 12
Chan 7–8, 64, 95, 113, 125–8, 130n.9, 131, 133n.16, 133, 134, 151
China 3, 6–7, 83, 95–6, 111, 113, 126, 133, 150
Chinese
Buddhism 6–7, 58, 83, 103, 105, 108, 111, 112n.113, 113, 116n.25, 117, 133n.15
conception of enlightenment 126
ideas 8
language 23, 114, 127
philosophies 6
philosophy 95
pronunciations 151
schools 95, 103
sūtra 64
texts 50n.4, 114n.17, 133
thought 96
traditions 42n.28, 54, 125
version of Madhyamaka 97
Christ 4
Christian
concept of heaven 16
miracle 148
philosophers 11, 77
Christianity 3
Cittamātra 5, 109
classical
Buddhist texts 81
Chinese thought 96
Daoist texts 95
cognition 34
cognitive
apparatus 40
awareness 51
overlay 132
science 12
compassion 5, 49, 57, 126
complex
formula 66
objects 33
panjiaos 103
sentences 23–4
states of affairs 72
complexes 67, 86
composite
objects 37, 39
substances 36
composition 36
compositional factors 50
conceptual
constructions 34, 39–40, 42, 44n.33, 65, 129
dependence 41, 43
difference 114
discriminations 52
idealism 42
impositions 59
imputations 50n.6
interdependence 43–4
proliferations 76
superposition 132
thought 127–8, 133
Confucianism 6, 96, 113
consciousness 5, 10, 12, 50–1, 58, 82, 109–10
contradictions 21n.13, 22, 25, 55n.14, 61, 70n.14, 73, 75–7, 83–5, 87, 135
conventional reality 4–5, 33–5, 51n.6, 52–3, 58–9, 96, 111–12, 120, 122, 128, *see also* phenomenal reality, two realities, ultimate reality
cosmos 10, 18–19, 42, 61
Cūḷamūllunkya Sutta 26–7
cyclical existence/cycle of life and death (saṃsāra) 4, 62, 98
cyclical reversal 95

Dao 6–7, 95, 97, 111–13, 126, 130, 139, 151
Daode jing 6, 151
Daoism 6, 95–6, 126, 130
Daoist
influence 108
sage 6–7, 130
terms 96
texts 95
Dasheng qixinlun 111, 151
Dasheng xuanlun 101, 151
De Morgan's laws 19
death 4, 7n.11, 16–17, 19, 26–8, 40, 51, 60, 65, 98, 111, 128, 130, 134–5

Dharmadhātu 121, 123
Dharmakāya 61
dharmas 32–5, 38–9, 43–4, 50, 52, 55, 58, 97, 117, 121, 122n.37, 135
dhyāna (meditation) 7, 127
Discourse to Kātyāyana 54
Disjunctive Syllogism 24–5
double negation 19–21, 99, *see also* negation, Principle of Double Negation
Dōyō 151
dualism 81–2
duality 5, 52, 81–3, 95, 98–9, 104–5, 108–10, 121, 124–5, 128, 131, 136, 141–2
duḥkha 8–9, 15, 28, 125
Dvādaśanikāya Śāstra 97

East Asia 3, 85
effability 67, 81, 83, 101, 142
Eightfold Noble Path 9
empiricism 13, 43
emptiness (śūnyatā) 5, 7, 49–52, 58, 62, 65–6, 73, 96, 102, 113–14, 116–17, 132–3, 139
empty 5, 20–1, 51–2, 56–8, 60, 61n.28, 62, 72–3, 97, 112, 115n.21, 117–18, 119n.31, 120, 122
  of essence 50
  of inherent existence 132
  of matter and events 56
  of nature 97
  of self-nature 56
  space/time 10
  states of affairs 71
English
  language 23, 78, 79n.6
  translations 15, 33, 34n.7, 68, 113–14
enlightened
  person 7, 16, 26–9, 60, 126
  state 4n.5, 28, 134, 135
enlightened one 4
enlightenment 5n.8, 7, 16, 27, 49, 60n.25, 62, 81, 110, 124–31, 136, 139, 141, 144, *see also* awakening
Ensō 144
epistemologists 84
essence 34n.7, 37, 50, 60, 130, 139
ethical
  developments 50n.2
  innovations 49
  path 5
ethics 9, 50, 86, 147n.1
Europe/European 150
  countries 149
  powers 149
evaluation 8, 24, 30, 131, 150
events 6, 8, 10–11, 13–14, 44n.33, 55–6, 109, 132n.13
existence 4, 10, 12–13, 18, 29, 33, 37–40, 43–4, 50n.6, 52, 57, 62, 86, 97, 115, 121, 128, 132–3, 148
experience 4–5, 8, 13–15, 32, 33n.5, 44, 61, 109, 128–32, 140, 148
extinction 28, 42, 44n.33, 125, 135

fifth corner (koṭi) 64–5
First Noble Truth 8
Flower Sūtra 64
foundation 32n.3, 58, 102, 119n.31, *see also* Axiom of Foundation
four corners 16, 19–21, 26, 63, 70, 75
Four Noble Truths 3–4, 8, 51, 62
Foxing 110, 151

Gandharvas 59n.25
Gautama (Gotama), Siddhārtha 4, 16–17, 28, 57, 127n.6
Gelugpa Students' Welfare Committee 85n.15
God 38, 77, 115n.21
godhead 4
gods/goddesses 52, 81–2, 114, 141, 147n.1
golden lion 108, 121, 123
gong'an (kōan) 127, 151
Great Death 128
Greece 150
Greek
  philosophy 6
  tetralemma 16, 60

Hasse diagram 26, 66
Heart Sūtra (*Prajñāpāramitāhṛdaya*) 5, 49–50, 114n.17
Hindu
  Advaita Vedānta 61
  Ājīvika sect 18
  literature 17
  Nyāya epistemologists 84
  orthodoxy 11
  philosophy 4, 18, 85
  religion 4
  Vaiśeṣika philosophers 37n.14
Hindus 4n.5, 83, 86
Huayan 42n.28, 95, 108, 113, 117, 122, 125, 131, 133, 140, 151
  metaphysics 121
  notion of interpenetration 120
  Patriarch 112
  philosophers 114
  philosophy 113n.15
  school 7, 130
  teaching 115
  thinkers 112
  thought 141
  tradition 42n.28, 105
  version of Mahāyāna 50

Huayan Sūtra 113–14
human 34n.7
  concepts 77
  condition 4–5
  language 77
  species 42
Hwaom 7

idealism/idealist 42–3, 59, 71, 109
identity 12, 41, 50n.6, 57n.20, 58, 65, 72n.20, 115–17, 123
ignorance 9–10, 51, 132, 150
illusion 11, 59n.25
  of self 15, 49, 128, *see also* self
  of the substantial world 128
impermanence 4, 10–11, 51
India 3–6, 75, 83, 103, 108, 128, 150
  Buddhism 6, 83, 111, 117, 125, 135
  doctrine 103, 130n.9
  heritage 6
  ideas 108
  Mahāyāna 7, 44, 80, 83, 109, 125–6
  notion of emptiness 7
  perspective 128
  philosophy 85
  texts 4, 6–7, 80, 83
  thinker 4
  thought 84, 109
  traditions 54
Indians 33n.5, 111, 130n.9
ineffability 60, 64, 66–8, 73, 75, 81–3, 99, 101, 131, 142
inference 10, 23–6, 66, 80
interconnectedness 22, 44, 114
interdependence (pratītyasamutpāda) 4, 10, 44
interpenetration 7, 108, 114, 116–17, 120–2, 124, 131, 133, 140, 141
interpretation 17n.3, 19n.8, 20, 22, 24–5, 30, 54, 68, 70n.15, 71n.18, 75, 79–80, 87n.25, 89–90, 95, 105–7, 108n.1, 113n.15, 115–16, 127n.5, 131, 134n.21, 139, 148n.2
Islam 3

Jaina
  logicians 86
  metaphysics 86
  method of syād-vāda 87
  theory of sevenfold division 87
Jainism 4, 85–6, 88
Jains 4n.5, 83, 85–6, 89
Japan 3, 125, 127n.4, 133
Japanese
  Buddhism 7–8
  philosophers 125
  pronunciations 151
  thinkers 128n.7, 133

ji 113–15, 121–4
Jingtu (Jōdo) 7, 151
Jizang hierarchy 101, 104–5, 128, 141
Jōdo (Jingtu) 7, 151
Jōshū 128, 153

Kantian
  scruples 36
  thought 13
Kantianism 54
karuṇā (compassion) 5, 49
Kegon 7, 95, 130, 133, 151
kenshō 127, 152
kliṣṭa-manas 109
kōan (gong'an) 127, 133, 151
Kong/kū 152
König's paradox 78–9
Korea 7
koṭis 18–22, 28–9, 55, 65, 79, 84, 104–5, 142

Laozi 6, 95, 152
laws
  of change 38
  of nature 39n.20
  of physics 38, 42
li 113–14, 120–2, 124, 137, 152
Liar Paradox 69, 78
liberation 4n.5, 58, 81, 135
Linji 133n.16, 152
lishi wuai 121, 152
logic 16, 18–23, 25–6, 29–31, 66–7, 69, 73–5, 78–80, 85–6, 88–91, 100, 147–9
  Bochvar 89, 91
  Buddhist 75, 88–9
  classical 20, 25, 31, 90
  classical propositional 22–3
  FDEe 80, 90
  First Degree Entailment (FDE) 16, 22, 25–6, 29–31, 66, 73–4, 79–80, 90–1, 105–6
  Indian 22
  Jaina 75, 85, 88–90
  many-valued 26, 30, 73, 80, 88–9
  non-classical 16, 21–2, 147
  paraconsistent 25n.22, 31, 89–90
  plurivalent 80, 85, 88–90, 100
  propositional 22, 30
  strong Kleene 31, 89
logical
  consequence 72n.2071
  interconnection 22
  notation 19n.9
  truth 30
logicians 23–4, 70n.15, 72, 84, 86
Lotus Sūtra 103
Lunyu 6

ma 114, 152
Madhyamaka 5, 7, 44, 50n.6, 71–3, 80, 97, 108–10, 112, 117
Mahābhārata 4n.4
Mahākāśyapa 139
Mahāparinirvāṇa Sūtra 142n.37
Mahāyāna 5–7, 39, 44, 49–50, 52–3, 62, 64–5, 76, 80–1, 83, 85, 101–3, 109, 111, 125, 133
Mālunkyāputta 27
manifestations 110–14, 134, 137, 140
meaning of *i* 88
meditation 6–7, 13, 127, 133, 137–8, 147–8
meditative
  experience 148
  practices 59, 128, 132
  techniques 135
mental
  attitudes 8, 9
  events 11, 13
  experience 14
  fabrication 61
  formations 10
  imposition 59
  life 11
  object 51
  parts 4, 10, 34n.7
  removal 34
  states 9, 13
mereological
  analysis 34n.7
  compound 41
  considerations 73
  explanation 38
  nihilists 35
  simples 36
  universalists 35
mereology 32, 35, 36n.11
metaphysical
  atomism 73
  atoms 33–4
  consequences 54
  developments 50n.2
  ideas 53
  nature 49
  presuppositions 86
  term of art 32n.3
metaphysics 5, 9, 29, 32, 42n.28, 49–50, 52, 63, 78, 86, 87n.25, 95, 121, 125, 133, 147
  of ignorance 9
  of the catuṣkoṭi 25
methodological
  coda 147
  principle 13
monastic living 4
monism 112
Moslem invasion 6
Mūlamadhyamakakārikā (MMK) 5, 49, 53–5, 57–8, 59n.23, 60–2, 65, 75, 84, 97, 132
Myanmar 6
myriad things 95–6, 111, 135n.25

Nālandā 5–6
natural deduction 31
negation 22–3, 66, 68, 70, 84, 97, 100–1, *see also* double negation, Principle of Double Negation
Neo-Confucianism 113
Neo-Daoism 95–6
neti, neti (not, not) 18
Net of Indra 114–15, 117, 122–4
nihilism/nihilists 35, 38, 54
nirvāṇa 4, 28, 51, 55, 60, 62, 64, 84–5, 98, 125–6, 132, 134, 142
nominalism 72
non-being 18, 84–5, 95–6, 98, 102, 112–13, 139, *see also* being
non-duality 52, 82–3, 98–9, 105, 109
noneist 28
non-emptiness 102
non-existence 15, 18, 29, 52, 54, 58, 60, 109, 117, 122, 213
nothingness 95–6
Nyāya epistemologists 84

Ockham's Razor (Principle of Lightness) 13
ontological
  catuṣkoṭi 68, 73
  dependence 58
  footing 39
  free lunch 39
  status 58
  structure 119–20
ordinals 78, 79n.6, 104n.18
Orientalism 149
Ox-Herding Pictures 128, 132

Pacific Ocean 40–1
Padmakara Translation Group 58n.24
Pāli Canon 4n.7
pañcakoṭi (five corners) 68
panjiao 103, 152
paradox 53, 69, 75, 77, 79, 135
  of ineffability 75, 101, 142
  of self-reference 69, 78
paramārtha satya 4, 33
parinirvāṇa 49, 126
partite objects 32, 34, 38–9, 41, 72
perception 8, 10, 12, 14n.23, 43, 50–1, 58–9, 110, 113, 130
phenomena 11, 50, 70, 76, 102, 114, 123, 130, 132, 134

phenomenal
objects 7
reality 111–12, 114, 130, 132n.13, *see also* conventional reality, two realities, ultimate reality
world 95–7, 109–10
Phi Phenomenon 11
physical parts 4, 34n.7, 38
post-enlightenment 62
state 129–30, 141
Postmodernism 54
Prajñāpāramitā Sūtras (Perfection of Wisdom) 5, 49–50, 52–3, 56, 58, 61–2, 73, 75, 81, 141
pratītyasamutpāda (interdependence) 4, 10, 44
pre-enlightenment
meditative practices 132
state 62
view of the world 60n.25
presupposition 22, 86
failure 28
Principle
of Double Negation 19, *see also* double negation, negation
of Excluded Middle (PEM) 19–20, 31, 74, 78, 79n.6, 84, 90, *see also* Weak Excluded Middle
of Explosion 25, 31, 91
of Lightness (Ockham's Razor) 13
of Non-Contradiction (PNC) 19, 21n.13, 55n.14, 77–9, 84–5
of Sufficient Reason 38
of the Excluded Fifth 17, 29
propositional parameters 23–4, 30, 74, 89–90, 105
propositions 67, 77, 142
Pseudo Jizang 101–5
Pure Land Buddhism 7n.11

quantum mechanics 38, 42
quintum non-datur 26

realism 42–3, 56n.17, 71
reality, *see* conventional reality, phenomenal reality, two realities, ultimate reality
rebirth 3–4, 62, 125, 130n.9, 134, *see also* birth
regress 37–8, 55–6, 85
reification 54
religion 4, 6, 77, 147–8, 150
religious
documents 75
experience 148n.2
practices 3n.2
return to the ordinary 132, 136
Ṛg Veda 4, 18
Rinzai 133n.16, 152
Russell's theory of descriptions 29n.28

Samavayāṇga-Sūtra 18
Sāṃkhya 85
saṃsāra 62, 111, 132
Sanlun 7, 95–7, 101, 152
Sanron 95, 152
Sanskrit 7–8, 20, 32n.3, 33–4, 51, 53, 59, 68, 109, 113, 127
Sarvāstivāda 37n.14
Śata Śāstra 97
satōri 127, 136, 152
Second Noble Truth 8–9
self 9–15, 18, 49, *see also* illusion of self
self-being 34
self-certifying 148n.2
self-existent void 51n.6
selfhood 122
self-nature 5, 34, 54, 56, 60n.25, 62, 97, 112, 117, 130, 135
self-reference 69, 78
self-subsistent beings 36
semantic
bearers 79, 80, 114, 124
catuṣkoṭi 68, 71, 73
disambiguation 86n.21
notion of truth 69
paradoxes 78
status 87
values 67–8, 74, 79, 89n.27, 108
semantics 23, 26, 31
sentient
beings 42, 125, 135n.25
creatures 5
life 42
sevenfold predication 87
shi 113–14, 120–2, 124, 138, 152
shikantaza 136, 152
Shintō 8, 152
shishi wuai 121–2, 152
Silk Route 6
skandhas 4, 10, 32, 51, 139
sociology 3n.2
soteriological
consequences 54
importance 27
matters 62
soteriology 147n.1
Sōtō 133, 151
soul 11, 18, 27, 86–7
as birth-and-death 111
as suchness 111
South East Asia 3
speech 9, 81, 140
speech act 22n.17
Sri Lanka 6
state of affairs 38, 67–8, 71–2, 77, 79–80, 83, 99, 122, 124, 131
subatomic particles 10, 39, 42

subject/object duality 5, 109–10, 136, 141
suchness 52–3, 111
Suddharma Puṇḍarika Sūtra 103n.16
sūtras (suttas) 4–5, 7, 16–18, 21n.13, 26–7, 49–50, 52–4, 56, 58, 61–2, 64–5, 73, 75, 80–1, 83, 96, 103, 110–11, 113–14, 127n.3, 141, 142n.37, 142
svabhāva 5, 29, 34–5, 41, 50–1, 53–5, 57, 71–3, 97, 112, 117, 121–3, 135

tantric practices 6
tathāgata 16–17, 20, 27, 60
Tathāgata-Garbha Sūtras 110–11
tathātā 53, 112
taxonomy 4, 10, 51
Tendai 7, 133, 152
Thailand 6
Theravāda 4, 6
Third Noble Truth 9
thusness 53, 61, 130
Tiantai 152
Tiantong 138
Tibet 3, 6
Tibetan
  Buddhism 85
  Buddhist thinkers 85
  Buddhist thought 84
  philosopher 76
  religion 6
  traditions 54, 58
Tientai 7, 133n.15, 142
Tower of Maitreya 115n.19
Trairāṣikas 18
transcending dualities 83, 105, 125, 141–2
Tripiṭaka (Three Baskets) 4
Trisvabhāvanirdeśa 109
tṛṣṇa 8–9, 15, 125
truth
  conditions 24
  values 30, 70n.15, 79, 87, 132
two realities 33, 51, 57–8, 62, 95, 105, 108, 111–12, 114, 124, 131, *see also* conventional reality, phenomenal reality, ultimate reality
two truths 33, 57–8, 68, 95, 97–8, 102–3

ultimate reality 4, 6–7, 33–5, 51–3, 57–8, 60–1, 64–5, 66n.4, 69n.9, 81–3, 96, 98n.10, 105, 108, 111–14, 128, 132, 137, 138, 148, *see also* conventional reality, phenomenal reality, two realities
universalists 35
universals 33, 72–3
Upaniṣads 4, 18

Vaccha 16–17, 28–9
Vajracchedikā Sūtra 61
Vedas 4
Vimalakīrti 82, 83, 141
Vimalakīrti Nirdeśa Sūtra 75, 80–1, 83, 96, 127n.3, 141, 142
visual sensations 14

Weak Excluded Middle 74, *see also* Principle of Excluded Middle (PEM)
Weixin 7, 152
Western
  connections 76
  countries 3
  ethical terms 9
  formal logic 18
  ideas 150
  notion of being 33
  philosophers 10n.15, 77, 115n.21, 148, 150
  philosophy 44, 56, 69–70, 76, 150
  thought 109
wisdom 5, 9, 49–50, 58, 61, 65, 82, 122n.37
worthy one 5, 49
wu 5n.8, 95, 112, 127, 152
Wumenguan 127, 152

Xi'an 96
xin 111, 153
Xuanxue 96, 153

yang 95, 153
Yijing 95, 153
yin 95, 153
Yogācāra 5, 7, 42, 103, 109–10
You 153
Yuwang 137

zazen 133, 135–6, 138, 141, 153
Zen 7–8, 95, 125, 126n.1, 130–4, 136, 138, 144, 148n.3, 151
Zhuangzi 6, 153
zi 153
Zongzhi 139, 153